Mourning Glory

CRITICAL AUTHORS & ISSUES
Josué Harari, Series Editor

A complete list of books in the series
is available from the publisher.

Mourning Glory

The Will of the French Revolution

Marie-Hélène Huet

PENN

University of Pennsylvania Press

Philadelphia

10 9 8 7 6 5 4 3 2 1

Published by
University of Pennsylvania Press
Philadelphia, Pennsylvania 19104-4011

Library of Congress Cataloging-in-Publication Data

Huet, Marie Hélène.
Mourning glory : the will of the French Revolution /
Marie-Hélène Huet.
p.   cm. — (Critical authors & issues)
Includes bibliographical references and index.
ISBN 0-8122-3414-6 (cloth : alk. paper). —
ISBN 0-8122-1617-2 (pbk. : alk. paper)
1. France—History—Revolution, 1789–1799.   2. Enlightenment—
France—Influence.   3. Robespierre, Maximilien, 1758–1794—
Philosophy.   4. Political science—Philosophy—History—18th
century.   5. France—History—Reign of Terror, 1793–1794—Influence.
I. Title.   II. Series.
DC148.H84   1997   97-2936
944.04—dc21   CIP

Contents

Illustrations

Acknowledgments

WHEN SOME PARISIAN MUSEUMS were still poorly-lit repositories for sacred and dusty relics, the Musée Carnavalet had a room designated with the words "The Terror." This room offered two antithetical images of the French Revolution. In the back of the room, one could see a life-size replica of the Temple cell where the royal family had spent their last days. The reconstruction of the dismal jail, a powerful evocation of the Monarchy's downfall and martyrdom, was meant to appeal to the visitor's emotions. In sharp contrast to this staging of royal adversity, an old glass case displayed an odd assortment of objects and papers. Among them, unidentified, was one of the most extraordinary documents of the Revolution: the call to arms that, according to some historians, could have saved Robespierre's life had he agreed to sign it on the night of 9 Thermidor.

There was no visible identification and no legend to explain the document. Only visitors who had read historical accounts of the fall of Robespierre would have recognized, at the bottom of the yellowed piece of paper, his unfinished signature.

These two exhibits appealed to entirely different sensibilities; they also presented the public with different approaches to the past. The Temple cell was a rather crude reproduction, not unlike some of Madame Tussaud's exhibits, but its impact on the spectator was immediate. In its own way, it was as powerful as the 1935 Hollywood conclusion to *A Tale of Two Cities*, when the guillotine consummates Sidney Carton's sacrifice and the audience shudders at the sound of the falling knife. By contrast, the document dated 9 Thermidor, a fragment of revolutionary history, left most visitors indifferent, unaware that in 1794 this scrap of paper had carried so much weight and generated so much controversy.

The Musée Carnavalet has recently undergone a major renovation.

Gone are the dubious artifacts unworthy of a museum. The royal cell has been dismantled and Robespierre's last unfinished signature now hangs, framed and under glass, with a dry identification. Somehow, this old sheet of paper has also lost some of the power it held when I first saw it, quite by chance, in the spring of 1983. That is when this book started taking shape.

A Fellowship at the University of Virginia Center for Advanced Studies gave me released time and support for this project. Research in France was also funded by a Faculty Fellowship from Amherst College and research funds from the University of Michigan. Versions or parts of certain chapters appeared in the following: an early version of chapter 1 was published in *The French Revolution, 1789–1989: Two Hundred Years of Rethinking*, edited by Sandy Petrey (Lubbock: Texas Tech University Press, 1989); parts of chapters 2 and 5 were incorporated in essays that appeared in *Modern Language Notes* (1985 and 1988) and *Representing the French Revolution: Literature, Historiography, and Art*, edited by James A. W. Heffernan (Hanover, N.H.: University Press of New England, 1992); an early version of chapter 3 was published in *Eighteenth-Century Studies* (1994); and parts of chapter 5 were published in *Rhétoriques fin de siècle*, edited by François Cornilliat and Mary Shaw (Paris: Bourgois, 1992.)

Introduction: Revolutionary Will

Intents and Purposes

IN A NOTE TO HIMSELF Saint-Just once wrote that "the revolution must culminate in the perfection of happiness."[1] We all know that the French Revolution's pursuit of happiness degenerated into violence and death, the glorious ideals of the Declaration of Rights and the conquest of liberty compromised forever by war, civil strife, mob violence, and the specter of the guillotine. History has explored at great length the reasons the dreams of 1789 became the nightmare of 1793. Multiple causes, of a social, economic, and political nature, have been cited to explain the dramatic downfall of the Republic. Strikingly, the undoing of the revolutionary ideal has never been explicitly related to the ideal itself.[2] Philosophically and ideologically, 1789 and 1793 stand as two unrelated events, two revolutions: one a celebration of happiness and freedom inherited from the Enlightenment ("a perfectly *pious* vision of the Revolution," as Jean Baudrillard puts it);[3] the other a largely unfathomable nightmare of blood and violence that historians prefer to erase or else dramatize to emphasize the illegitimacy of the revolutionary project.

Yet the philosophical ideals so brilliantly at work in the events of 1789 also inspired the darker days leading to the end of the Revolution.[4] On 10 May 1793, during the period known as the Terror, Robespierre began his speech on the Constitution with these words:

Man is born for happiness and liberty, and everywhere he is a slave and unhappy. The goal of society is the conservation of his rights and the perfection of his being; and everywhere society degrades and oppresses him. The time has come to recall him to his true destinies; the progress of human reason has prepared the way for this great revolution, and to you especially falls the duty of pressing it forward.[5]

Better than any others perhaps, these few lines offer a privileged example of revolutionary rhetoric, the expression of an uncompromised ideal confronted with the demands of an increasingly tragic reality. A declaration of rights and principles is followed by a call for immediate action. These words spell out the revolutionaries' primary duty in these troubled times: to give new impetus to the revolutionary movement.

As for the program Robespierre is about to delineate in great detail, he introduces it in lapidary fashion: "To fulfill your mission," he continues, "you must do exactly the contrary of what existed before you" (p. 495). With this sentence, Robespierre declares in his forceful manner that the Revolution is more than a radical break with the past: it is a complete reversal of everything the past has represented. The present does more than erase the past, it revokes it. This is a Revolution.

In this eloquent opening, however, Robespierre himself does not entirely repudiate his own debts to the years before the Revolution. They are acknowledged by his reference to "the progress of human reason,"[6] which made possible the Great Revolution. Moreover, Robespierre's opening lines ("man is born for happiness and liberty, and everywhere he is a slave and unhappy") are a direct echo of the words that begin the first book of Rousseau's *On the Social Contract*, "Man is born free, and everywhere he is in chains."[7] Thus, even in times of political urgency, when an absolute reversal of the past is called for, the past is recalled and reappropriated as a guide and model for future political pursuits.

A few paragraphs later, Robespierre addresses another pressing matter, what he calls the "disease of political bodies": the anarchy that seemed to have wrecked Paris and the country since 10 August 1792, when the Tuileries palace was stormed and the king put under arrest. But true anarchy, Robespierre argues, is not the social disorder that followed the August Revolution, it is despotism itself: "What is anarchy, if not tyranny that makes nature and law step down from the throne to put men in their place!" (p. 496). Anarchy is not a social state but the reign of a conceptual fraud. To insist that all events be understood in terms of their intellectual and philosophical foundations is also characteristic of revolutionary rhetoric.

The relationship between events and ideas, nature and the law, the throne and the people, or between the present and the complex legacy of the past, shapes what I have called revolutionary will. The word "will" has to be taken not just as resolve, but as a reasoned declaration of intent and purpose. Revolutionary will means premeditation. Revolutionary will—the will to the perfection of happiness and liberty—strove, to the very end and in the most desperate circumstances, to reconcile intellectual rigor and inexorable actions. What is lacking in the numerous and complacent accounts of the Revolution's failure, or in the critical examinations of its violence, is an assessment of the active philosophical scrutiny that aimed to secure the Revolution's ultimate goal against all odds. More specifically, revolutionary will tried to relate the need for political action to a continuing inquiry, a task that confronted the most radical scrutiny with the demands of everyday survival.

In these essays I have examined political and theoretical issues that involved, or created, new and conflicting discourses. More specifically, the continuing debates about the nature of laws—whether they are founded on a natural model or whether all civil laws violate the nature of civil rights—were of particular importance to Robespierre when he defended Benjamin Franklin's invention of the lightning rod a few years before the Revolution, or to Saint-Just when he contrasted the gentleness of institutions with the violence of corrupted laws.

Terror aroused political passion and outrage. It also precipitated a form of philosophical and linguistic collapse; terror reached an almost unthinkable limit where all words failed, unable to convey the daily horror of the guillotine or the sublime idea of revolutionary virtue. Representation itself in all its forms came under scrutiny. Not only was representation controlled through censorship of plays, images, and the press, but, at a more profound level, the possibility

—or impossibility—of representing the political will of the people yielded a surprising meditation on the limits of the political process itself.

This continuing inquiry, this absolute rethinking, is also the reverse of fanaticism, which never makes place for internal contradictions and sweeps away all divisions with ideological fervor. What I intend to explore here is a form of radical will that recognized simultaneously the urgency of its mission and, in the most lucid evaluation of its own limits, the very impossibility of its realization.

Last Will and Testament

Revolutionary will is also a testament, and the same paradoxes that tore apart the revolutionary ideal also divided its heirs apparent. The second part of this book deals with specific instances of confronting the revolutionary past and struggling with its legacy. As Dominick LaCapra has argued, history is an act of mourning: "It is not confined to neopositivistic protocols but rather engages, at least discursively, in its own variant of working-through problems represented by mourning."[8] Of the many histories of the French Revolution that shaped nineteenth-century political thinking, none equals Michelet's passionate and lyrical account of the tragic events that gave birth to the modern state.[9] It is ironic that the nascent discipline of history, the systematic evaluation of our past, assigned itself as one of its first tasks to account for the Revolution, an event that had hoped to erase the past, to do away with all legacies. I have focused on what it meant for Michelet to write the *end* of his *Histoire de la Révolution française*, to give it a conclusion and thus a meaning.

It is well known that the Revolution left no monuments to commemorate its achievements. In powerful contrast with the "Great Projects" that have changed the skyline of Paris in recent years, none of the architects' visions of revolutionary splendor were ever built. Baudrillard describes France's recent explosion of monumental architectural projects as "a veritable ritual of mourning and condolence." And he adds: "All our monuments are mausoleums: the Pyramid, the

Arch of la Défense, the Musée d'Orsay, that fine Pharaonic chamber, the new National Library, cenotaph of culture."[10] The Revolution, with its natural suspicion of the past, dealt with death in a paradoxical manner. I consider one of the most striking instances of revolutionary mourning: the powerful contrast between the rededication of the Panthéon as monument to the great (dead) men of the Fatherland and the wasteland of the cemeteries of the Terror. On the one hand are a few elaborate tombs, surrounded by architectural splendor and displays of patriotic fervor. The remains buried there were to stay forever, and the memory of the great men forever be honored. On the other hand, victims of the guillotine were thrown in mass graves, covered with quicklime in overflowing cemeteries. They disappeared but could not be forgotten. It is ironic that, in recent years, what Baudrillard calls our culture of "mourning and condolence" has fashioned an almost unnoticed but lasting mausoleum, not for the glorious insurrection of 1789 but for the sacrificed king of 1793.

Finally, the revolutionary will was torn open and read through the passionately partisan accounts of nineteenth-century historians. The last chapter examines how a durable legend was born, one that portrayed the fatal collapse of the Revolution as an epic battle between two monstrous figures: Danton and Robespierre. The creation of these monstrous images and the fact that they were never repudiated cannot be attributed to historiographical neglect alone. On the contrary, when myth pervades historical accounts, myth unveils what history still withholds.

PART I

INTENTS AND PURPOSES

I

Political Science

IN 1756, UNDER THE ARTICLE *Thunder*, Diderot's *Encyclopedia* provided the following information on how to protect oneself from thunderbolts:

The thunderbolt can be broken up or turned away by the sound of several large bells or by shooting a cannon; this stimulates in the air a great agitation that disperses the thunderbolt into separate parts; but it is essential to take care not to toll the bells when the cloud is directly overhead, for then the cloud may split and drop its thunderbolt. In 1718, lightning struck twenty-four churches in lower Brittany, in the coastal region extending from Landerneau to Saint-Pol de Léon; it struck precisely those churches where the bells were tolling to drive it away; neighboring churches where bells were not tolling were spared.[1]

This text points out the two principles that simultaneously mediate and limit the power conferred by human knowledge: the church, and the essentially whimsical character of nature. The bells that tolled in the hope of turning away the lightning, a modest scientific experiment, brought upon themselves the fire of the gods with uncanny precision and devastating magnitude. The exercise of knowledge—that the sound of bells drives lightning away—is here immediately punished, on an almost divine scale, destroying moreover the very churches humans had constructed for their worship of God. By contrast, the silent steeples remain unscathed, spared by the furious storm, a paradoxical metaphor for a religious and ignorant people, unconcerned with understanding the fire from Heaven, forever resigned and gloriously rewarded for their blind submission.

This article from the *Encyclopedia* obviously did not take account of the theories on lightning first published by Benjamin Franklin in London in 1751 under the title *Experiments and Observations on Electricity*.[2] Preliminary application of Franklin's theories would come a year later and take various forms, such as the kite or the "fulminating bars" of François Thomas Dalibard in France. The 1777 *Supplement* to the *Encyclopedia*, however, did full justice to Franklin's invention and ingenuity. A second *Thunder* article was written, and the text read as follows:

It is a truth now recognized by all physicists that the matter which flames up in clouds, which produces lightning and thunderbolts, is nothing other than electric fire; the famous Franklin assembled the proofs of this in his fifth letter on electricity. . . . M. Franklin proposed as early as 1750 to use these means [electric kites, fulminating bars, and other sorts of apparatus] to protect buildings and ships from lightning; observations have proven so successful that it is now of interest to explain, in a way everyone can understand, how to build these conductors or *lightning rods*.[3]

Dismissing the fallen steeples of the Brittany coast, the author gave as examples of enlightened technology an imposing list of individuals and institutions that had successfully installed lightning rods on their roofs. The article's author was none other than Louis-Bernard Guyton-Morveau, a distinguished chemist who was later to play an active role in the French Revolution.[4] However, it would be a long time before the *Encyclopedia*'s conclusive pronouncements on lightning and thunder would be accepted.

In 1780, Monsieur de Vissery de Bois-Valé, a lawyer from Saint-Omer, a town in northern France, installed a lightning rod on his roof. His frightened neighbors sought redress, convinced that the lightning rod, like the tolling bells of Saint-Pol de Léon, was more likely to attract bolts that would strike them dead than to protect them from the storm. On 14 June 1780, the magistrates of Saint-Omer, siding with the concerned population, ordered the lightning rod removed within twenty-four hours. On 16 June Monsieur de Vissery submitted to the court a petition "accompanied by a special report, the object of which was to furnish the judges with a complete demonstration of the electrical machine placed above his house."[5]

Figure 1. Benjamin Franklin's experiments with an electric kite, 1752. Engraving. Collection Viollet.

Arguments were heard on 21 June, and Monsieur de Vissery's petition to keep the lightning rod was denied. Two days later, he appealed to the Artois Council, after agreeing in the interval to dismantle the apparatus so distressing to the population. In fact, he did nothing more than remove the sword blade that was the most visible part and substitute a shorter blade. And, so that no one should see even this concession as a signifying abasement of the ruling class symbolized by the sword, Vissery confided to his lawyer, "This is how to deal with the ignorant masses."[6]

Monsieur de Vissery entrusted the affair to Antoine-Joseph Buissart,[7] then a member of the Arras and Dijon Academies, who regularly contributed to the *Journal de Physique*. Buissart took the affair to heart, and interminable consultations took place throughout France. The man slowest to answer Buissart's repeated requests for scientific data was Jean-Antoine-Nicolas Caritat, Marquis de Condorcet, who eventually let it be known that, speaking in his capacity as perpetual secretary of the Academy of Sciences, he considered the best defense to be a detailed and documented report containing all the scientific arguments in favor of the lightning rod. Buissart went to work and published his report in 1782. The Appeal reached the Council of Artois in May of 1783, when Buissart gave Maximilien Robespierre, then a very young lawyer, the task of representing to the Court the combined interest of science and Monsieur de Vissery.

The trial, which aroused passing but intense interest, is revealing not only because it brought together, some years before the Revolution, the names of Marat, Condorcet, Franklin, and Robespierre, but also because it sparked a debate on Enlightenment and religion, science and human progress, that was to continue until Robespierre's death, near the close of the Revolution, in July 1794.[8]

The party fiercely opposed to the lightning rod invoked the authority of two learned men, one of whom was none other than Jean-Paul Marat, the future "Ami du peuple." The Abbé Bertholon, himself an eminent physicist, wrote Buissart that Marat was "a crazy man who thought he could become famous by attacking great men and producing paradoxes that seduced no one." But, undeterred by critics, Marat in his *Recherches physiques sur l'électricité* had noted: "It is obvious that the fluid accumulated in clouds is beyond the sphere of attraction of the highest conductor." He also enumerated eleven cases of conductors "blasted by lightning."[9]

In response, Robespierre made two speeches that took their scientific content, their examples, and a part of their logic from the work to which Buissart had devoted two years. Yet the final formulation is that of the young lawyer who published his two discourses under the title *Arguments for the Sieur de Vissery de Bois-Valé, appealing a judgement of the magistrates of Saint-Omer, who had ordered that a lightning rod erected on his house be destroyed.*[10] Robespierre's argument was persuasive; the Council of Artois found in favor of his client, Monsieur de Vissery. Emboldened by this success, Robespierre sent a copy of his argument to Franklin himself, along with a letter that, although often quoted, deserves another hearing. It is dated 1 October 1783, four months after its author's striking success. Robespierre wrote:

Sir,
A writ of condemnation by the magistrates of Saint-Omer against electrical conductors furnished me the opportunity to appear before the Council of Artois and plead the cause of a sublime discovery for which the human race owes you its thanks. The desire to help root out the prejudices that opposed its extension in our province led me to publish the speeches I made during this affair. I dare hope, Sir, that you will deign to have the goodness to accept a copy of this work, the object of which was to induce my fellow citizens to accept one of your gifts: happy to have been useful to my country by persuading its first magistrates to welcome this important discovery; happier still if I can add to this advantage that of being honored by the good graces of a man whose least merit is to be the most illustrious scientist of the universe. I have the honor of being with respect, Sir, your most humble and obedient servant.[11]

In the France of the 1780s, Franklin's glory was at its apogee. He was the man of the lightning rod and of the American Revolution, a double achievement Turgot[12] captured in a Latin epigram that spread among the Paris salons: "Eripuit coelo fulmen, sceptrumque tyrannis."[13] This epigram became tremendously popular. It appeared in 1778 beneath the bust of Franklin sculpted by Jean-Baptiste Houdon, and it was the beginning of countless poetic essays—of unequal

Figure 2. Portrait of Benjamin Franklin. Engraving by Labadye. Collection Viollet.

merit—dedicated to the glory of the American scientist and politi-
cian. In an exchange of letters between d'Alembert and Jean-Baptiste
Suard, the encyclopedist undertook to translate Turgot's epigram
and hesitated between two possible versions. D'Alembert first wrote:

Tu vois le sage courageux / Dont l'heureux et mâle génie / Arracha le tonnerre aux dieux / Et le sceptre à la tyrannie. (See the brave and wise man /
Whose happy and male genius / Wrested thunder from the gods / And the
scepter from tyranny.)

D'Alembert reflected that one might say that Franklin wrestled
lightning either from the skies or from the gods, *aux cieux* or *au dieux*
(p. 128). This literary and philosophical hesitation, as to whether
the conquest of lightning is a victory over nature or a more Promethean triumph over a sacred principle, echoes in fact the two
Thunder articles in the *Encyclopedia*. They both emphasize the fact
that all knowledge is a seizure of power, a challenge, a deed of the
same stamp as a political revolution. Turgot's epigram, d'Alembert's
double translation, and the Saint-Omer trial form an ideological
nexus structured by the Enlightenment's connection to science as
well as the Enlightenment's contribution to the Revolution. In these
heated and often contradictory debates, a recurrent series of metaphors put lightning and enlightenment into serious play.

Scientific Laws

In a work entitled *Clartés et ombres au siècle des Lumières*,[14] Roland
Mortier traces the history of the philosophical meaning of the word
lumières from Genesis to Kant's celebrated *Was ist Aufklärung?* He
notes, in particular, that the use of *lumières* was secularized in the
seventeenth century.[15] The metaphor of Enlightenment as reasoned
knowledge would become general in the eighteenth century. The *Encyclopedia* provided the metaphor's richest field of expression. Here,
far from being associated with knowledge of a religious nature, Enlightenment was directly opposed to all knowledge transmitted, or
authorized, in the strict sense of the term, by the church. Diderot

contrasted an "enlightened century" to "times of darkness and ignorance" (p. 30). Voltaire complained that "a Gothic government had
snuffed out all enlightenment for almost 1200 years" and D'Alembert
congratulated himself that "enlightenment has prevailed in France"
(p. 31).[16]

His legal arguments on the lightning rod gave Robespierre the
opportunity to develop his own version of the familiar metaphor
of Enlightenment. Ridiculing his opponents, he proclaimed, "How
dangerous to want to *enlighten* one's fellow citizens! Ignorance, prejudices and passions have formed an awesome front against men of
genius, in order to punish them for the good they do their fellows."
Elsewhere, Robespierre celebrated "the progress of enlightenment,"
"enlightened nations," "the torch of the arts," and "the torch of true
principles."[17]

More important, the physical description of lightning and
thunderbolts served as a privileged illustration of the complex relationship between Enlightenment and nature. Indeed, lightning is the
prime example of a power *without reason* that strikes *blindly*, by pure
chance.[18] Lightning is disorder in nature, prompting Robespierre to
describe Franklin's discovery as a step toward correcting both anar-
chical violence and unreason. Thanks to the lightning rod, "Lightning accepted its laws and thereby immediately lost this *blind* and
irresistible impulse to strike, smash, overturn, crash all that stands
in its way; it has *learned* to recognize the objects it is to spare."[19] In
other terms, and this may be the most interesting part of this description, Franklin has not so much discovered a scientific law as imposed
on nature a law made possible by scientific knowledge. Nature—
a blind force that destroys indiscriminately—is *arraisonnée*, that is,
conquered, put to reason. It is for the true Enlightenment to tame
this energy and submit nature to its laws. Robespierre sets out to
demonstrate simultaneously—here he is in no way Rousseau's disciple[20]—the savage, crude, and noxious character of untamed nature,
and in contrast the purely beneficent powers of science and reason.
To illustrate the lightning rod's virtues, Robespierre compares it to
inoculation, itself far from unanimously accepted by scientists. "We
must calculate," he said, "the victims art has saved, and those nature
has sacrificed; but, because this calculation generally proved that men

gain more from confiding themselves to art than from giving themselves to nature, inoculation has triumphed over all obstacles."[21]

In the opposition he was powerfully drawing between Enlightenment and nature, Robespierre demystified the idea of an inspired nature, the manifestation of a benevolent and hidden God whose secrets were forever closed to humanity. Did this mean that science took the place of a deposed God? Not in the least; and this is perhaps the most curious point in Robespierre's arguments: humans must no more let themselves be dazzled by science than by the lightning that threatens to strike them dead. This is in fact the lawyer's most extensively developed theme. Conflating at one point the power of Enlightenment and the conquest of the Americas, Robespierre exclaimed:

The Enlightened European had become a God for the savage inhabitants of America; I call those peoples as witness, for they gave no other name to their conquerors. Were they so very wrong? Was not lightning in the hands of these terrible warriors? Was not their arrival in those unknown regions a prodigious deed accomplished to justify such an idea? And, whether they descended from Heaven, as in the opinion of the inhabitants of that savage country, or opened a road across the immensity of the seas, braving the fury of the waves, commanding the tempest, subjugating a fearsome element, is not either *miracle* far beyond the strength of human beings?" (p. 35, emphasis added)

Only the ignorant see in the enlightened European a divine force, only they see in the conquest of nature—as of the Americas—the manifestation of divine or godlike knowledge. In his second speech, Robespierre dwelt at length on the idea that science properly understood is no more extraordinary, no more frightening, no more divine than nature itself, or, for that matter, no more striking than the lightning explained by Franklin:

The effects of lightning rods, so you have heard, are so miraculous that men are right to be wary of them. Man commanding the thunderbolt! Tracing the route it must follow! Is this phenomenon plausible? Is it not natural to see it at first as a shimmering illusion brought to life by the pride of the human mind? The effects of lightning rods are too prestigious to earn our confidence! . . . Is man so unfamiliar with miracles that another prodigy leaves him stupefied? Have the Sciences produced for his benefit few miracles that he must consider this new boon beyond their power? . . . But what am I saying? *There is no miracle here.* That man has dared wrest the lightning from heaven; that he controls all its movements however he chooses; that he says to it: be careful not to touch these buildings; come follow the route I have set for you, and hasten to bury yourself in the abyss I have made for you; *there is a prodigy: but it is also nothing more than a product of the imagination.* The Poet or the Orator, animated by a fitting enthusiasm, has the right to deploy such brilliant figures. (p. 69, emphasis added)

For Robespierre there is neither an avenging God nor a Promethean scientist; those, he tells us, are poetic figures. Perhaps a basic difference between poetry and science is to be found, rhetorically, in the poet's legitimate license to transform a simple mechanical process into a prodigy and to use fear aroused by a destructive nature to frame the rhetoric of blindness and lightning. But not that of Enlightenment.[22]

Indeed, Robespierre insists, "When we examine this phenomenon as a physicist, *the miracle vanishes.* In the place of lightning, which escapes from eternal hands to pass into those of men, *I see nothing* except a quantity of electrical matter . . . which betakes itself . . . towards a metal bar. Is that a prodigy? No, it is a law of nature, it is an ordinary phenomenon" (p. 69, emphasis added). Now, in the Age of Enlightenment, there is no miracle in understanding or dominating nature. Heaven is emptied of an avenging God. "Neither let us be afraid that Heaven will see this step as an audacious effort to defy its anger, to take from it the power to punish our crimes. Do we believe that the Omnipotent needs this meteor that terrifies us, that without it His weaponless arm could no longer strike us?" (p. 70).

If there is a crucial opposition between the blind force of nature and the rational laws of science, there is no incompatibility between a reasonable God and Enlightenment. On the contrary, the first speech for the defense begins with this declaration: "The Arts and Sciences are the richest gift that Heaven has made to men"—another belief quite alien to Rousseau's philosophy, and which Robespierre nonetheless never abandoned. Just as Providence has given us medicinal plants to cure us, Robespierre argues, "Today she presents us with electrical conductors to protect us from the ravages of lightning" (p. 70). This is precisely why Franklin's discovery is called *sublime.*

The sciences perform no miracles; they are the fruit of a reason that itself emanates from a sublime God.

The Revolutionary Storm

Mary Wollstonecraft described the Revolution of 1789 as similar in its convulsions to "hurricanes, whirling over the face of nature."[23] The revolutionary storm broke over France some years after the lightning rod trial. Richard Price, even more explicit in his metaphors than Mary Wollstonecraft, exclaimed: "Behold, the light you have struck out, after setting America free, reflected in France, and there kindled into a blaze that lays despotism in ashes, and warms and illuminates all Europe" (p. 58).[24] The French Revolution becomes like the thunderbolt that Franklin, far from mastering, unleashed to spread from America to Europe. As foreign observers saw it,[25] the torch of Reason set the powder afire, and if nature was for an instant tamed by Reason, human nature in turn was unleashed in such a dramatic way that no reason could stop it. Indeed, two questions were repeatedly put to revolutionary thinkers. (1) Was Enlightenment responsible for the revolutionary storm? (2) Can there be a political revolution without a philosophical revolution? From these two questions proceeded two lines of thought on what every revolution should be. And here again Franklin was to act as a catalyst in a debate with consequences that would weigh heavily on the fate of the Revolution itself.

Franklin's death was dramatically announced to the National Assembly on 11 June 1790.[26] In a brief but eloquent speech, Mirabeau asked the Assembly to wear mourning for three days in honor of the American patriot. Several eulogies were printed in the following months. The most interesting one, for our purpose, was written by Félix Vicq d'Azir, a member of the Academy of Sciences and perpetual secretary of the Royal Society of Medicine. On 14 March 1791 he spoke in front of the Academy of Medicine in these terms:

Franklin's last wish was that no inscription decorate his tomb; but his illustrious name, which nothing could take from him, will always be his tomb's most beautiful ornament. Let a pyramid be raised there, with one of the sides

showing the initials of the United States intertwined with those of the French
Republic, and topped by the attributes of liberty and equality; on the other
face, let there be an electrical conductor stretching into the clouds.[27]

Condorcet's more ideological eulogy, "Eloge de Franklin," emphasized what he saw as the indispensable link between Enlightenment
and political progress:

When, through the progress of enlightenment, a real science replaced systems, and a philosophy founded on nature and observation succeeded scho-
lastic prejudices, enlightened men of all nations began to form a single body,
guided by the same principles and marching toward a common goal. Then
reason and liberty had everywhere peaceful apostles, independent in their
opinions but united in the cult they maintained for these benevolent divini-
ties.[28]

Furthermore, added Condorcet, there can be no successful revolution without enlightenment. Any revolution showing contempt for
the sciences would be like a destructive storm without benefit for
humanity. This passionate call for an enlightened regime also shows
the magnitude of the gap, opened as early as 1790, between the Revolution and the last *philosophes*:

Is there anyone who has yet to see that the people need not choose between cultivating the sciences and struggling under the yoke of prejudices?
For, *in the natural order political enlightenment walks in the path of the sciences,
depends on their progress, or else, as in antiquity, it produces only an uncertain,
ephemeral flame, flickering in the storm.* (423, emphasis added)

The reconciliation between knowledge and political freedom echoes
perfectly Franklin's successful taming of thunder, itself a natural in-
duction to his patriotic achievements. But Condorcet added these
words of warning:

Let us beware of those envious detractors who dare accuse the sciences of
thriving under despotism: without doubt, they sense confusedly that nations
deprived of enlightenment are easier to deceive and lead astray; that the
more a people is enlightened, the more its support is difficult to retain un-
worthily. They fear the patriotism of reason and virtue, that which hypocrisy
can neither counterfeit nor mislead; and, concealing the desire to dominate
under the mask of enthusiasm for liberty, they seem to have guessed that,

even under the freest constitution, an ignorant people is always composed of slaves. (p. 423)

Although Franklin had been on excellent terms with the court during his stay in Paris, his role in the American Revolution endowed him with unparalleled prestige. Franklin's reputation grew throughout the Revolution; engravings and prints represented him as a trustworthy guide. His bust was honored along with those of Voltaire and Rousseau during the great festivals.[29] If ever a scientist could make a link in the popular imagination between revolutionary integrity and the progress of Enlightenment, it was Franklin.

The Scientific Revolution

Franklin's prestige was of no help, however, when, less than two years after his nationally mourned demise, Condorcet, now a firm ally of Brissot,[30] voted in favor of the declaration of war that would ultimately destroy both the monarchy and the Revolution.

Robespierre, a lone dissenter, had resigned just a few days earlier from his position of public prosecutor, and the appointment of a successor provoked endless debates between Brissot, Guadet, and Condorcet on one side, and Robespierre on the other. Interestingly, these debates provided a few key concepts about the necessary relationship between the sciences and revolutionary thought.

Brissot, defending Condorcet at the Club des Jacobins, exclaimed: "Do you not see that it is only because the burning geniuses of these men [Condorcet, Voltaire, d'Alembert] *set fire to soul after soul* . . . that today's tribune can ring with your speeches on liberty?"[31] But Robespierre's views on Enlightenment and revolution were now more complex. Having himself once pleaded the cause of the sciences, he remembered quite well that the first beneficiaries of great discoveries were usually those with great power and fortunes. He had noted it himself: "All Princes seem to have taken it as their duty to show the value [of lightning rods] by example, by using them to protect their palaces."[32] All the examples Buissart had furnished Robespierre were in fact cathedrals, powder magazines, and the dwellings of monarchs. If Franklin stood above criticism because of his glorious role in the American Revolution, such was not the case for the Encyclopedists and their friends. They had too often enjoyed the support of Catherine the Great, Frederick II, or, in the case of Condorcet, Louis XVI himself not to compromise their political reputation.[33] Condorcet, far from reneging on his past, had mentioned the productive relationship between the philosophers and the kings in his eulogy of Franklin: "At times, enlightenment came down from the throne to the people; most often it went up from the people to the throne."[34]

For Robespierre, however, Enlightenment, far from having led the people to democracy, was suspect for having too long consorted with tyrants. On 27 April 1792, defending himself against Brissot's charge that he was sowing dissension among the members of the Society of Friends of the Constitution (later the Jacobin Club), Robespierre counterattacked, with a pointed allusion to Condorcet:

The Revolution has shrunken many great men. If the Academicians and Geometers Brissot is offering as models fought and ridiculed priests, they nonetheless courted Nobility and adored Kings, from whom they received considerable benefit; and who can ignore their relentless persecution of virtue and Liberty in the person of Jean-Jacques, whose sacred image I see here. He was the one and only Philosopher who, in my opinion, deserved the public homages that have been since prostituted by intrigues to glorify political charlatans and despicable heroes.[35]

It is worth noting that, despite their opposing political views, Robespierre and Condorcet, in different ways, both contested the idea that the Enlightenment influenced the Revolution. For Condorcet, who, like Diderot, conceived history within the natural order, political enlightenment follows philosophical enlightenment, not in a relation of cause to effect, but in an inescapable sequence inscribed in nature and in the nature of history. For Robespierre, philosophical enlightenment, however desirable it may be, had made common cause with despotism and could in no way be considered the forerunner of the Revolution.

The real question setting Robespierre and Condorcet at odds was this: can there be a political revolution without a philosophical revolution? With his usual passion, Condorcet would always maintain that an enlightened revolution alone was capable of succeeding and effecting the people's happiness. His *Esquisse d'un tableau historique des progrès de l'esprit humain* said so repeatedly. Not only do the arts and sciences enrich one another, but the political progress marching in their path is irreversible: "We will point out that the principles of philosophy, the maxims of freedom, the knowledge of man's true rights and real interests, are spread through too great a number of nations, and direct in each the opinions of too great a number of enlightened men, for there to be any prospect that they will ever fall back into oblivion."[36]

Robespierre—in this he agreed with Condorcet and distanced himself from Rousseau's views—never questioned the idea that the human mind continued to progress. One of his last speeches (18 Floréal, year II; 7 May 1794) again took up the theme of the Saint-Omer trial:

The world has changed; yet it must change more. What is there in common between what is now and what was then? Civilized nations succeeded savages wandering in deserted lands. A world has appeared beyond the boundaries of the world; the inhabitants of the earth have added the seas to their vast domain; man has conquered lightning and exorcised it from heaven.

After this direct homage to Franklin, Robespierre continued:

Compare the imperfect language of hieroglyphs to the miracle of printing; set the voyage of the argonauts next to that of La Peyrouse; calculate the distance between the astronomical observations of the magi of Asia and Newton's discoveries, or between the sketch from the hand of Dibutade and the paintings of David.

Then he concluded:

Everything has changed in the physical order; everything must change in the moral and political order. Half the Revolution of the world has been done; the other half must be accomplished. Man's reason resembles the earth he inhabits; one half is plunged in darkness, when the other one is enlightened.[37]

It is certainly remarkable that Condorcet, condemned by name in Robespierre's speech, himself would make a strikingly similar assessment in his posthumous *Esquisse des progrès de l'esprit humain*:

If everything tells us that the human species will not return to its old barbarism; if everything must reassure us against the pusillanimous and corrupt
system that condemns men to eternal oscillations between truth and error,
liberty and slavery, nevertheless we still see that enlightenment only occupies
a restricted space on the earth. . . . We observe that the discoveries of recent
ages had done much for the progress of the human mind, but little for the
improvement of the human species. (p. 249)

The difference between Robespierre and Condorcet is that, for
Robespierre, the scientific revolution allows the political one, *but it
does not necessarily produce it*. For Robespierre, the only historical necessity is moral. As an act of will, as the mastery of passion parallel
with the mastery of nature, Robespierre's revolution owes everything to the *philosophes*, but it does not *result* from their work. On the
contrary, the unequal development of enlightenment and political
progress opened a dangerous gap, a dangerous imbalance between
scientific discoveries and moral ideas. On the same day, he added:

The peoples of Europe have made astonishing progress in what are named
the arts and sciences, and they seem to ignore the first principles of public
morality. They know everything, except their rights and their duties. What
causes this mixture of genius and stupidity? The answer is that, in order to
make ourselves adept in the arts, we need only follow our own passions,
while we must conquer them in order to defend and respect the rights of
others. (p. 444)

Not only do the general principles of historical progress separate
Enlightenment and revolution, but, Robespierre pointed out, the
enlightened men of the Revolution had compromised themselves
heavily with all the symbols of oppression. "The kings who make the
destiny of the earth fear neither great geometers, nor great painters,
nor great poets, and they dread stern philosophers, and the defenders
of humanity" (p. 444).

In the same speech, Robespierre bitterly attacked the Encyclopedists, although it was not clear if their worst crime had been to perse-
cute Jean-Jacques Rousseau or to betray the Republic: "They fought
the Revolution the moment they feared it would raise the people
above all their individual vanities. . . . In general, men of letters dis-

honored themselves in this Revolution, and, to the eternal shame of
the intellect, the reason of the people had to pay for it" (p. 455).

One project, however, was underlying Robespierre's precise attack
against the philosophers, the Cult of the Supreme Being, a response
to their declared materialism. Robespierre thus fought two enemies
simultaneously: the old religion—the priests—who had praised the
kings by stating that they were *"the image of God on earth"* (p. 458,
Robespierre's emphasis), and the Encyclopedists, who had made reason their only God. Atheism and Catholicism are equally dangerous,
and Robespierre took up, once more and with the same determination, the successful argument of the lightning rod trial: science does
not perform miracles. Man's conquests of nature are a victory of reason that in no way calls the idea of the Supreme Being into question:

How different is the God of nature from the God of priests! He knows nothing so close to atheism as the religion they have made. By disfiguring the
Supreme Being, they destroyed Him to the best of their abilities; they sometimes made Him into a globe of fire, sometimes an ox, sometimes a tree,
sometimes a man, sometimes a king. The priests created God in their own
image. (p. 457)

The Nature of the Law

The relationship between science and revolution is made still more
complicated by the conflicting uses of the word *law* among the philosophers, on the one hand, and Robespierre, on the other. Does the
scientific project uncover the laws of a reasonable nature or does it
impose on an unreasonable nature the rigor of its own laws? Rousseau had long meditated on the ambiguous use of the term *law* in
his preface to the *Discourse on the Origin of Inequality*.[38] But scientific discoveries were in fact described in terms of imposing rules
on an unruly nature, order on disorder, laws on anarchy. The many
epigrams greeting the invention of the lightning rod almost all contained this use of the word *law*. See Target, an attorney: "Le voilà
ce mortel, dont l'heureuse industrie / Au tonnerre imposa des *loix*."
("There is the mortal whose industry successfully imposed *laws* on

the thunderbolt.") Dupont de Nemours: "C'est Franklin, ce mortel dont l'heureuse industrie / Sut enchaîner la foudre et lui donner des *loix*." ("Here is Franklin, the mortal whose industry succeeded in chaining up lightning and giving it *laws*.") Hilliard d'Auberteuil: "Si Jupiter veut nous réduire en poudre, / Sage Franklin, tu lui précis tes *loix*." ("If Jupiter wants to blast us to bits, wise Franklin, you remind him of your *laws*.")[39]

But, in a more serious vein, Vicq d'Azir's 1791 *Eloge de Franklin* described the invention in these terms:

Torrents of light inundate space and, variously transformed, light produces fire, that soul of nature which vivifies, destroys, recomposes, and moves all. . . . Franklin perceives that these effects are due to electric matter; he analyzes it, understands it, dares attack it on the cloud that bears it. Along the conductor he presents to it, lightning will descend *submissive to the law governing it, and tame to the hand guiding it*; the anger of heaven will seem to be pacified; the atmosphere will again become calm and pure; from their refuge men and fearful flocks will again emerge, and the earth will bless the mortal who had this daring thought and offered it such a boon.[40]

This reads, of course, as the allegory of successful Revolution. For the Encyclopedists as for Condorcet, the political order is an ideal extension of the scientific order. Just as man has learned to subdue the storm, he will learn to subdue tyrants. Scientific law anticipates political law and serves as its model; it is founded on reason, it is enlightened by knowledge, and it strives for the good of humanity. For Robespierre, however, the laws scientists impose on nature give them a power that is a usurpation, for it does not come from the people. This is why scientists should eschew all forms of political compromise or, as Franklin did, put their fame and power at the service of the people. Any invention not put immediately at the service of the people, any law or power serving the privileged classes, is a form of political tyranny. The people are sovereign, and the principle of people's sovereignty transcends the principle of scientific authority.

Thus the speech of 24 April 1793, on the new Declaration of Rights contains these words: "The Law is the free and solemn expression of the people's will."[41] And its corollary: "any law that violates the imprescriptible rights of man, is essentially unjust and tyrannical: it is not a law" (p. 467). These last words help elucidate both the wider meaning of the word law for Robespierre and its strict limitations. Either the law emanates from the people or else it is not a law. The semiotic encounter of scientific laws and political laws discloses the patterns of power, the imposition of order concomitant with the establishment of any rule, be it over the physical world or the human species. In both cases it reveals an authority, an empowerment that can too easily be turned away from its only legitimate purpose to benefit tyranny. This is why all Robespierre's great speeches are so fascinated with, and haunted by, the glory and perils of Enlightenment. On 18 Floréal, Year II (7 May 1794), in proposing the Cult of the Supreme Being, he added forcefully: "You are fortunate to live in an age and in a nation where enlightenment has so progressed that your only task is to recall men to nature and to truth" (p. 453).

Condorcet died under mysterious circumstances—assassination, death from exhaustion, or suicide—in the spring of 1794.[42] Robespierre was executed without trial in July of the same year. In much the same way as Robespierre had engaged in an implicit dialogue with Franklin during his entire career, first as a lawyer, then as a revolutionary leader, in 1794 Donatien-Alphonse-François de Sade began a dialogue with Robespierre that marks an ironic conclusion to the debate, begun fifteen years earlier, on the question of Revolution and Enlightenment. Sade had been secretary president of the Section des Piques (Robespierre's section), but had been arrested at the end of 1793. From jail, he wrote a text that is largely a response to Robespierre's Cult of the Supreme Being. In *Yet another effort, Frenchmen, if you would become republicans*, Sade promptly chose Enlightenment over both law and religion. In his preface to the text, Maurice Blanchot emphasizes the radical nature of Sade's rejection of law. He quotes the following lines from *L'Histoire de Juliette*: "Without laws and religions, human knowledge would today be at an unimaginable height of glory and greatness; to an unmeasurable degree, those unworthy brakes have held back progress. . . . It is only in the moment of the laws' silence that great actions burst forth."[43] But for Sade the fate and benefits of the Enlightenment were not to promote political progress or shape political laws on the model of scientific laws. En-

lightenment was an end in itself. Sade's thought appears more radical
and startling still if we consider Justine's repeated death as a strangely
anachronistic proclamation that knowledge has no law and could not
impose any laws. It is only pleasure.

In 1787 the virtuous heroine, who refused both pleasure and
knowledge, died, brutally struck by lightning:

> Madame de Lorsange, terribly afraid of lightning begs her sister to close
> everything as fast as she can; M. de Corville was returning at that mo-
> ment. Justine, rushing to calm her sister, flies to a window, she tries briefly
> to struggle against the wind pushing it back, just then a burst of lightning
> strikes her down in the middle of the salon and leaves her lifeless on the
> floor. . . . The thunderbolt had gone through the right breast, burned the
> chest, and gone back out through the mouth, so disfiguring the face that she
> was horrible to see.[44]

In the second version of *Justine*, M. de Corville, whom Sade identifies as the character who "truly knows the heart of man and the spirit
of the law," is just as powerless to save the unfortunate victim "struck
in such wise, hope itself can no longer subsist for her; the lightning
entered her right breast, found the heart, and after having consumed
her chest and face, burst out through her belly. The miserable thing
was hideous to look upon."[45]

These deaths might be seen as historically inscribed in the years immediately preceding the Revolution and in the very beginning of the
Revolution itself. Critics have explored at great length Sade's translation of revolutionary themes in the subsequent *La Nouvelle Justine*
and *L'Histoire de Juliette*. The scaffold and a machine resembling the
guillotine appear at the end of *La Nouvelle Justine*. "Plots, betrayals,
denunciations, beheadings: these fictional motifs and Sadean phan-
tasies are linked with the reality and the imaginary of the Revolution," notes Lucienne Frappier-Mazur.[46] But the early versions of
Justine refer more visibly to the already declining influence of Enlightenment thought. As Nancy Miller notes regarding the 1791
Justine ou les malheurs de la vertu, "the novel opens with the all-
purpose eighteenth-century celebration of the truth as guiding light."
Although Justine's "disfiguring death blow dealt by a divine hand"
is a "narrative cliché perfectly consistent with the plausibility of the

eighteenth-century novel," she adds, "mimesis is subverted by conversion: Justine is given the punishment the ideology of the period
would have visited on Juliette, and Juliette is given the privilege of
a retreat from the world that would have suited Justine."[47] Madame
de Lorsange draws a double conclusion that also serves as the novel's
epigraph. After exclaiming that the "caprices of Heaven's hand are
enigmas it is not for us to sound," she adds: "The prosperity of
crime . . . is like unto the lightning, whose traitorous brilliancies but
for an instant embellish the atmosphere, in order to hurl into death's
very deeps the luckless one they have dazzled" (p. 742).

The enigma of an unpredictable Heaven is the only object of
knowledge. But, at the same time, knowledge is the recognition that
Heaven is beyond all forms of knowing and thus beyond all laws. In
1794, Sade wrote:

Let a simple philosopher instruct these new pupils in the *incomprehensible sub-
limities* of nature. Let him prove to them that the knowledge of a god, often
very dangerous to men, never served their happiness, and that they will be
happier admitting as a cause of what they don't understand, something they
understand even less; it is less important to understand nature than to draw
pleasure from it and to respect its laws; let him tell them that these laws are
as wise as they are simple; that they are written in men's hearts, and that it is
enough to question one's heart to explain its movements.[48]

Not unexpectedly, the lightning metaphor in Sade illustrates a
thought that expresses itself in terms of veils and blindness. "If it is
true," he writes, "that passions *blind*, that their effect is to raise before
our eyes a *cloud* that disguises from us the dangers with which passions are surrounded, how can we suppose that distant dangers, like
the punishments announced by our God, could ever manage to dissi-
pate this *cloud* impervious even to the sword of the laws always hang-
ing over passions?" (p. 72, emphasis added). A disturbing paradox:
lightning becomes like the passion it spares, it is *blind*, and for that
reason it acts like the passion of an incomprehensible Providence,
it becomes the cruel parody of a law that strikes down virtue—like
the steeples of Saint-Pol de Léon—with terrifying magnitude. What
lightning illuminates for an instant is immediately so disfigured that
it is no longer recognizable. Lightning destroys the possibility of

knowing. It suggests an absolute limit, far beyond reason that lights our way and passion that blinds us.

But, above all, Sade suggests another sort of opposition. Enlightenment is not opposed to ignorance or religion as the lightning rod to superstition. Enlightenment is opposed to shadows and fear: "Man is afraid in the dark, physically and morally as well," he states simply (p. 77). We might say that with this sentence Sade distances himself from the thought of the eighteenth century, whose Encyclopedic obsession he represented elsewhere, and that he was already announcing a Romantic interpretation of the question of Enlightenment. Man is not afraid *of* the dark, but *in* the dark. The primordial fear of the night surrounding him is still present and remains determinant even under the ephemeral brightness of reason.

One might add that this evocation was already implicitly inscribed in the first *Thunder* article of the *Encyclopedia*. That the monuments consecrated to God, raised toward the heavens, ringing with supplicating bells, be the very ones pitilessly struck by lightning is not entirely explained by theories about the mass of the clouds. The fallen steeples, like Justine, illustrate a Sadean logic of the blindness of Providence and the limits of Promethean defiance. The refusal Sade opposes to the laws may come less from their being, in Blanchot's words, "abased by precepts,"[49] or from their positing a criminal humanity ("As for me," wrote Saint-Just, "I will not submit to any law that assumes I am ungrateful and corrupt")[50] than from the fact they claim a natural model that does not exist.

"In six months," Sade wrote in the spring of 1794, "it will be all over."[51] These words allude to the predictable failure of the Cult of the Supreme Being ("your infamous God will be precipitated into nothingness," adds Sade);[52] they may also have prophesied the end of the revolutionary fervor that disappeared with Robespierre on 9 Thermidor. Yet this announcement may also signal that the passionate debate among *philosophes* and politicians on the relationship between scientific progress and Revolution would, too, soon be a thing of the past. Franklin had incarnated the ideal figure of the enlightened man, dedicated to both scientific knowledge and political progress; but this ideal would soon lose priority to darker and more pressing concerns. In the spring of 1794, Sade's vigorous opposition to Robespierre's religious program, his eloquent refusal of the republican definition of law, and his repeated evocations of nature as the blind force that strikes down virtue and spares vice offered a violent rebuttal to the scientific discourse which had successfully imposed its laws on thunder and lightning and to the revolutionary discourse which had placed such an emphasis on virtue. It suggested, among other things, the end of Enlightenment.

2

The End of Representation

The Theatrical Revolution

"CAST A GLANCE AT THE THEATER of the State," wrote Marat on 7 July 1792: "[The] props have changed, but the same actors remain, the same masks, the same intrigues, the same tricks. . . . Today, the principal actors are behind the curtain; it is there that they plot at their ease with those who play the parts before our eyes. Most of the latter have already disappeared, new actors have come forth to play the same roles." In a text entitled, "La Révolution française en pantalonnades," Marat asked: "How could liberty ever have established itself among us? At several nearly tragic scenes, the revolution has only been a web of *pantalonnades* [farcical representations]."[1]

With these words, Marat shrewdly underlined both the strength and the weakness of the new revolutionary regime. In its desire to separate itself from the secrecy that characterized the former Monarchy, as Joseph Butwin puts it:

strictly theatrical conventions of audience and performance provided a model for the daily conduct of government that could not be derived from a repudiated and often irrelevant political tradition. . . . Their natural meeting places were the centers of entertainment of the old regime, the *Salle du Manège*, and after 10 May 1793, the old *Salle de Spectacle*, the theater at the Tuileries. David had a hand in the redecoration and conversion of the old building which never lost its theatrical character. . . . The official events of the Revolution—celebration, legislation, execution—all claimed an audience. (pp. 143–44)[2]

More than any other regime, the Revolution encouraged spectacles and promoted theatricality. Three months after the decree allowing the freedom of theaters (13 January 1791), one counted no fewer than forty-five theaters and three puppet shows in Paris. It is estimated that more than 750 plays were produced there between 1792 and 1794. Belying most popular images of a city devastated by political struggles and the Terror, Parisians, who frequently lacked bread, never lacked for a play to entertain them and went in unprecedented numbers to the theaters. Furthermore, the Convention voted that, for the education and benefit of all citizens, a selection of patriotic plays would be produced regularly and at no charge to the public. The freedom of theaters, followed by the freedom of festivals, did not preclude complex regulations, and theatrical matters constantly preoccupied the various assemblies of the Revolution.

The desire for a public revolution was reinforced by a series of decrees that reorganized public life and allowed the rehabilitation of all actors who, after centuries of legal discrimination, finally gained civil rights along with the executioners. Moreover, the Revolution deliberately staged the death penalty (to quote the judicial debates of 1792) as "a tragedy . . . meant to fill the spectator with terror."[3]

In the legislative process which demanded a spectator or a witness at every stage of its operations, the solicitation of an ever-expanding public was a way of repudiating the secret character of the old Monarchy. Robespierre dreamed of a Convention Hall that would accommodate 12,000 spectators. The prisons themselves became theaters, the improbable stages of elaborate representations. According to Michelet: "Grave men, serious women, abandoned themselves to frenzied displays, to mockeries of death. Their favorite recreation was the preliminary rehearsal of the supreme drama, to try on their last outfit and the graces of the guillotine. These lugubrious parodies included daring exhibitions of beauty."[4] But if the guillotine could become the dubious object of these representations this is also because it was, itself, a spectacle. André Chénier decried the families who spent their days watching executions: "The [father] comes home from the show. He goes back with his wife and the children who have been good."[5]

Hébert's death on 24 March 1794 reached a sort of paroxysm of theatricality. Three days earlier, the Committee of Public Safety had decreed that the Théâtre-Français, now renamed Theater of the People, would give patriotic plays with no admission charge every ten days. Hébert's execution seemed to have been the first of these spectacles. As Michelet described it: "Odious audience! His death was a sort of festival. People were curious to see what figure the *Père Duchesne* would cut when he would appear himself, in person, in front of the guillotine he had talked so much about: it was another spectacle. Speculation started early in the morning; carts, benches, scaffolding, everything was done to facilitate this pleasant spectacle. The place became a theater" (2: 782). The stage of execution was the other stage of the Revolution; the commonplace of erasure and repetition: tragic on the day the Girondins were led to their deaths, grotesque on the day of Hébert's execution, pitiless for Robespierre's demise. Spectacle was everywhere.

The use of Paris as a stage for the revolutionary project was extraordinarily successful, and observers could not help seeing the events of 1789 and 1792 as a powerful, if mixed, theatrical genre. "A monstrous tragi-comic scene" for Burke, a farce or a tragedy for others, a spectacle for all. As early as 9 August 1789, Burke had exclaimed: "What Spectators, and what actors!"[6] But when he attempted to describe the state of France on 11 April 1794, he reflected: "The condition of France at this moment is so frightful and horrible that, if a painter wished to portray a description of hell, he could not find so terrible a model, or a subject so pregnant with horror and fit for his purpose. Milton, with all his genius which enabled him to excel in his description of this nature, would have been ashamed to present to his readers such a hell as France." Ronald Paulson comments on these lines as follows:

This passage, with its reference to the "terrible" and to painting, recalls Burke's own *Philosophical Enquiry into the Sublime and the Beautiful*, in terms of which he is now saying that the true sublime in government is a mixture of fear and awe or admiration, whereas the false sublime, a perversion of this (like the false *light* versus the true) generates only fear and a grotesque energy. . . . While regarding the Revolution as a false sublime, Burke sees the terrors of something like the sublime experience as a warning to Englishmen who might see the Revolution as beautiful. (pp. 66, 71)

One could add that, particularly from 1793 to 1794, the Revolution had been at times the perfect example of the false sublime that is both grotesque and terrifying, tragically theatrical. But in the last months of the Revolution, Robespierre attempted to rescue the revolutionary project from the grotesque theatricality which had disfigured its ideal. If the theatrical model underlined the desire for a public regime, a regime devoted to the people and free of plotting behind a closed curtain, it also suggested a dramatic fusion between actors and politicians on the one hand, spectators and the revolutionary crowds on the other.

The desire for a public stage where the Revolution would act out its glorious destiny before an increasingly large audience was not, as Marat pointed out, without pitfalls. If politicians were to be the actors of this heroic drama, who could tell the masks from the faces, who would separate the stage from the truth? What would become of the Revolution once the spectacle was over?

The effectiveness of the theater as pedagogical instrument came to be questioned as well. The right to produce the classical repertory that had been denied them for so long was first seen as a victory for small theaters; and the success of plays representing the major events of the Revolution—the Fall of the Bastille, the death of Marat, for example—gave the small theaters an undeniable patriotic aura, but the theatricality of the Revolution could not be contained in the narrow confines of the stage or the playhouses. The changing values of the new regime, the constant suspicion that the most revolutionary proclamations only served to hide or mask aristocratic plots, all these elements contributed to a chaotic image of the political drama that was taking place just outside the theaters.

In the spring of 1794, Plancher-Valcour, director of the *Délassements-Comiques*, renounced the classical repertory entirely with these words: "Plays recalling the Old Regime should no longer be produced, even if they attack it, recall its vices, its follies, its monstrous abuses. It is not enough to decree that counterrevolutionary plays must not be given. We should dispense with all classics for at least half a year."[7] Censorship was officially reinstated on 2 Floréal, Year II (21 April 1794), and Claude-François Payan, a member of the Commission on Public Instruction, declared: "The theaters are still encumbered with the rubbish of the Old Regime, feeble copies of the masters. . . . We must sweep this chaotic mass out of our theaters. . . . *We must clear the stage.*"[8]

This last appeal, "we must clear the stage," signals a break in the Revolution's attitude toward the theater and, more generally, toward all spectacles, be they inspired by faith, royalist nostalgia, or revolutionary virtue. Just a few weeks before, Payan, on 24 Ventôse, Year II (14 March 1794) had requested that it be made illegal to bring benches for the audience to the executions. After having encouraged the creation of a multiplicity of public stages, it seems that the Convention (inasmuch as it followed Robespierre and his friend Payan) was attempting to check the uncontrolled proliferation of spectators and to tear revolutionary ideology away from its profane staging. In the spring of 1794, the determination to "clear the stage" announced a renunciation to the dramatic closure of the Revolution.

The Fear of Images

On 17 Germinal, Year II (6 April 1794), the day after Danton's execution, Couthon announced to the Convention "a project for a *fête décadaire* dedicated to the Eternal, whose consoling image the Hébertists have not succeeded in erasing."[9] The principles outlining the Cult of the Supreme Being were offered at some length just a few weeks later by Robespierre, in his speech of 18 Floréal (7 May) entitled "Report on religious and moral ideas and on décadaires festivals." The last sentence of the speech decreed that "On 20 Prairial a national festival be celebrated in honor of the Supreme Being."[10]

Accordingly, on 20 Prairial, Year II (8 June 1794) there took place in Paris one of the most brilliant and famous festivals of the Revolution. Inspired by Rousseau, the Festival of the Supreme Being inaugurated a return to religion that would owe nothing to Old-Regime Christianity. Like most revolutionary acts, the festival expressed first a doing away with a repudiated past and, second, a glorious celebration of the new spiritual order. The first stage of the

Figure 3. Festival of the Supreme Being, 20 Prairial, Year II (8 June 1794). Engraving by Bure. Collection Viollet.

festival, which had been planned by David in all its surprising detail, featured a ritual burning of several colossal effigies representing Egoism, Atheism, and Nothingness (*le Néant*). Much could be said of this ceremonial gesture: burning the idols of the past illustrated the Revolution's anxiety over new beginnings, its constant desire to start anew, to let nothing of past history interfere with the new world it was creating.[11] By burning idols, as we shall see, Robespierre also had in mind a form of religion that would forfeit all representations. One cannot but wonder at the selection of "monsters" to be thus publicly sacrificed, particularly that of Nothingness. The conception of Nothingness as a colossal and grotesque representation to be publicly destroyed offers a glimpse at the sometimes extraordinary strategies to which the Revolution resorted in its educational concerns. On the one hand, Nothingness could be interpreted as the ghost of Atheism, both its double and its consequence. Robespierre had once declared to the Jacobins: "Atheism is *aristocratic*."[12] Nothingness was also the fate of atheism: "[Atheism], this monster vomited on France by the genius of Kings, has entered Nothingness," proclaimed Robespierre after the sacrifice (p. 314). But Nothingness is also a more generalized form of destiny, that which awaits all false virtues. Following the revolutionary rhetoric of bringing to light what was hidden, and making manifest all invisible agents of political abuse, nothing could be more legitimate, in its irony, than a visible image of Nothingness, as a monster made explicit, not for all to see but for all to see destroyed.

Not everything went according to plan. As Michelet described it: "The statue of wisdom emerged, unveiled, from the charred group. As could be expected, she appeared smoky and black, to the great satisfaction of Robespierre's enemies."[13] Undeterred by this apparent setback, the long procession, led by Robespierre, proceeded from the Tuileries to the Champ de Mars (then called Champ de la Réunion). Gathered around a symbolic mountain, the people sang a Hymn to the Supreme Being, the text of which had been composed by Marie-Joseph Chénier.[14] The last of fourteen stanzas proclaimed:

The slave and the tyrant pay no homage to Thee.
Thy worship is virtue, thy law equality;
In the free and good man, Thy work and Thy deed,
Thou instillest immortality.[15]

"No festival ever aroused such sweet expectation, none was celebrated with such a joy," wrote Michelet.[16]

Soon afterward, on 11 Messidor (29 June), the Commission of Public Instruction denied an author permission to stage a play inspired by the Festival of the Supreme Being. Its decision makes a striking statement on the status of spectacle and religion in the last spring of the Revolution. The Committee argued:

What stage, with its cardboard rocks and tree, its sky in rags and tatters, can rival the magnificence of 20 Prairial or erase its image? The drums, the music, the roaring bronze, the cries of joy rising to heaven . . . the humid veils, these clouds blown around above our heads, and parted by playful winds to let the rays of the sun shine through, as if they had meant it to be witness to the most beautiful moments of the festival; finally the victory hymn, the union of the people and its representants, all with their arms raised toward the sky, swearing under the sun the virtues and the Republic; . . . Only in memory can one bring back those deep feelings that so moved our hearts: to look elsewhere is to diminish them; to put this sublime spectacle on stage is to make a parody of it. He who first conceived the idea of staging such festivals has degraded their majesty and damaged their effect. . . . The writer who, instead of lessons offers only needless repetitions, and instead of a grand tableau, offers caricatures, such a man is useless to Letters, to morals, to the State, and Plato would have driven him out of his Republic.[17]

A few days later, the Committee of Public Safety approved the decision in these terms:

In accordance with these reflections, the Commission on Public Instruction, considering that plays devoted to representing the Festival of the Supreme Being, whatever the intent of their authors, present only a limited framework rather than an immense tableau;
That they are beneath nature and truth;
That they tend to spoil the effect and destroy the interest of the national festivals by breaking their unity into artless copies, lifeless images, by substituting groups for the mass of the people, and by insulating its majesty;
That they hinder the progress of art, stifle talent, and corrupt taste without instructing the nation;
Decrees:
That the Festival of the Supreme Being may not be represented on any stage of the Republic.[18]

As F. A. Aulard pointed out, this decree consecrated the Festival of the Supreme Being as a religious ceremonial. It might be added that, by opposing the sacred character of the festival to the profane quality of theatrical performances, the decree also articulated a series of aesthetic assumptions that defined the nature and functions of revolutionary spectacle.

All historians of the Revolution, from Aulard to Mona Ozouf,[19] have stressed that, although the festival is itself a representation and a spectacle, it differs from the theater in several important ways, all more or less derived from Jean-Jacques Rousseau's iconoclastic suspicion of the stage. One remembers that in his 1756 *Lettre à d'Alembert sur les Spectacles*, Rousseau had formally denounced the bad influence of theater which stimulated vices, endorsed inequality by its unequal pricing and distribution of seats, and encouraged the poor to live beyond their means in paying for an amusement they could not afford. Rousseau suggested replacing the elitist and ruinous stage with open-air festivals where all would be invited and nothing would be shown, for the spectators would themselves be the spectacle. Accordingly, in opposition to the enclosed and restricted space of theaters, the revolutionary open-air festivals took place on a large esplanade; nature (trees and foliage) replaced the "cardboard rocks and trees" of the stage; the majesty of the united people succeeded the small number of privileged spectators. The theater reduces everything: "limited framework rather than an immense tableau," "groups" rather than the "mass of the people." Moreover, the structural organization of the theater separates the stage from the audience; conversely, according to a schema brilliantly illustrated by Lévi-Strauss in his analysis of rituals, the festival invites not spectators but participants.[20]

Finally, and consequently, the theater threatens the sacred character of the religious festival: it parodies a "sublime spectacle"; it offers nothing but repetitions and "pantomime." In response perhaps to this indictment, an anonymous work was published in Paris exactly a year after the Festival of the Supreme Being, with the title: "Model for a drama festival where the rules of the art will not be respected, and which cannot suit any of our public theaters."[21] Interestingly, the dramatic aspect of the festival was not the source of concern. Rather, the title makes explicit the anxiety that, precisely *because it is already a spectacle*, the festival might be desecrated on the stage of the theaters.

The decree of the Committee of Public Safety also throws light on the complex relationship between the sacred and representation in the last months of the Revolution.[22] Indeed, unlike the festivals before it, the spectacle of 20 Prairial was organized in celebration of a God who could not be shown. "When it comes to defining the Supreme Being," wrote Claude-François Payan, "we shall have an idea of him that is so *sublime* that we shall not degrade him by giving him a face or a body similar to ours."[23] In a deliberate attempt to resist the idolatry of images which had such a corrupting effect on

Figure 4. Reception of the Decree of 18 Floréal, announcing the Festival of the Supreme Being. Collection Viollet. Engraving by Legrand after Debucourt. The first sentence of the legend is an excerpt from Robespierre's speech at the Convention, 28 Floréal, Year II (7 May 1794).

the Old Regime, the National Convention emphasized the idea that the sublime is not representable. In this way, it briefly translated into public policy one of the aesthetic elements discussed by Kant in his 1790 *Critique of Judgement*: "The sublime, in the strict sense of the word, cannot be contained in any sensuous form, but rather concerns ideas of reason which, although no adequate representation of them is possible, may be excited and called into the mind by that very inadequacy itself which does admit of sensuous presentation."[24]

The Festival of the Supreme Being tended to fulfill two desires.

First, as Mona Ozouf put it, "everyone dreamed of the Revolutionary festival as a village festival without spectacle, enlarged to the dimensions of the entire nation. This was to believe in the need for a divorce between theater and festival, in the possibility of a completely detheatricalized festival" (p. 206). More radically, however, the Revolution aspired to a form of religion free of all appeals to the senses. The historian Edgar Quinet later wrote that, the day after the Festival of the Supreme Being, Revolutionary France would have converted to Protestantism.[25]

But, although the Festival of the Supreme Being was organized around a subject sublimely beyond representation, it was nonetheless planned and experienced as a theatrical spectacle. David's careful planning with its unfolding "acts" (1. Robespierre burns the effigies, 2. the procession walks towards the Champ de la Réunion, 3. the participants, wearing costumes, sing a hymn after having been separated and regrouped according to sexes around the mountain, etc.)[26] suggested a sumptuous staging and an inspired direction. In his speech of 18 Floréal (7 May 1794), Robespierre had already acknowledged that "the most magnificent of all spectacles is that of a great people assembled."[27]

Because the festival of 20 Prairial was itself a spectacular representation, it also had the power intrinsic to all representation (so clearly emphasized by the Committee on Public Instruction), that of "erasing the memory" of the scene that inspired it. (We shall see later what image and what memory the festival so successfully erased.) For there is no repetition, no representation, that does not entail a form of substitution, and thus, of erasure; all spectacles paradoxically contribute to the obliteration of the very subject they aim to represent. Stendhal, whose aesthetic was in many ways inherited from the Revolution, later commented on the power of images to erase that which they claim to represent: "I have clearly in my mind the descent [from the Mont Saint-Bernard]. But I cannot hide the fact that, four or five years later, I saw an engraving that I found very resembling, and my memory is now nothing but the engraving. Soon, the engraving shapes the entire memory and erases the actual memory. This is what happened to me with the San Sistro Madonna of Dresden. The beautiful Muller engraving destroyed it for me."[28]

Similarly, the spectacle, as representation, also has the power to erase the memory. It was a dangerous and fascinating tool for the Revolution. Indeed, there was no revolutionary spectacle that did not work as a palimpsest, seizing all the possibility of theatrical representations, both to signify and to erase. Much has been said about revolutionary theater as an instrument of propaganda, but the Committee's decision underlines the equally important political strategy of erasure. It proceeded with successive erasures, substituting a new concept for an old idea, a living image for a fixed tableau, a revolutionary cult for a traditional religion.

Palimpsest

Indeed, the Cult of the Supreme Being had a double goal: to found a new religion and to erase the Cult of Reason, instituted a few months before during the de-Christianization campaign. Festivals and performances thus followed one another like so many gestures of propaganda and erasure. On Chaumette's suggestion, the Festival of Reason, hurriedly celebrated on 20 Brumaire (10 November 1793), took place at Notre-Dame in order better to emphasize its role as a substitute cult. Until 7 November, the plan had been to have a statue representing Reason. But, for fear of creating a new form of idolatry, a living image was substituted. As Michelet wrote,

It was objected that a fixed simulacrum might remind the people of the Virgin *and create another idolatry*. So a mobile, live, animated image was preferred. This image, changing with every festival, could not become an object of superstitious adoration. The founders of the new cult, who in no way intended to trivialize it, expressly recommended in their newspapers, that those who would like to have a festival in other cities, *chose, to fill this august part, persons whose characters made their beauty respectable, whose heartfelt behavior and modest gaze discouraged licentiousness and filled the heart with pure and honest feelings*. (2: 645–66, emphasis in original)

A magistrate's wife incarnated Reason at Saint-Sulpice, and a well-known actress at Notre-Dame. The singing of Marie-Joseph Chénier's "*Hymne à la Liberté*" marked the occasion. Later these living goddesses were perceived as representing Liberty or Reason, and,

Figure 5. Revolutionary festival. Watercolor. Collection Viollet.

a few days later, Marie-Joseph Chénier composed another patriotic song entitled *Hymne à la Raison*.[29]

As a revolutionary strategy aimed at replacing an old cult with a new one, however, the Cult of Reason, in Paris or the provinces, was not a complete success. Besides the obvious difficulty involved in the repudiation of a long-established religion, some of the reasons for the partial failure of the Cult of Reason, at least in terms of general opinion, were eloquently summarized in a letter published in the *Annales Patriotiques et Littéraires* and quoted by Aulard:

> What shocks the philosopher's senses and imagination is as much the idea of a *woman* representing *Reason*, as the woman's youth. In women, this purest of faculties is identified with *weakness, prejudice*, and the very *attractiveness* of her enchanting sex. In men, the empire of Reason is free of all errors: *strength, energy, severity* follow in her wake. Reason is *mature*, she is *grave*, she is *austere*, qualities that would be unbecoming in a young woman. (pp. 88–89, emphasis in original)

As Aulard points out, not everyone objected to Reason being represented by a woman. The *Père Hébert* expressed a somewhat profane exultation at the sight of this new goddess incarnated "by a masterpiece of nature. . . . A charming woman, as beautiful as the goddess she represented . . . she was surrounded by the all the damned beauties of the Opera, who in turn excommunicated the priests, singing patriotic hymns better than angels."[30] An older David would remember "superb women, Monsieur. The Greek line in all its purity."[31]

But the Cult of Reason did not entirely avoid the temptation of idolatry. An ardent follower exclaimed: "You present to us an image of Reason which is so natural that we might be tempted to take the copy for the original."[32] Aulard rightly dedicates several pages to what may have been the most thoughtful criticism of the Cult of Reason. Jean-Baptiste Salaville, a man of letters who may have been one of Mirabeau's aides, published in the *Annales Patriotiques* a series of articles in which Aulard detects the influence of Diderot's philosophy. On 23 Brumaire (13 November), Salaville wrote:

> If we wish to bring the people to the pure worship of Reason, we must counter its propensity to materialize abstractions and personify moral beings. We must cure it of this mania; Locke's and Condillac's metaphysical

principles must become popular; the people must get used to seeing nothing but stone in a statue, and nothing but canvas and colors in an image.[33]

This iconoclastic appeal was heeded by the partisans of the Cult of the Supreme Being who discredited the Cult of Reason for both its atheism and its idolatry. On 25 Floréal, Year II (14 April 1794), Payan severely criticized the role women had played in this profane worship: "So did the word *reason* in their mouths tell on any and all meanings that could serve their interests. Sometimes it was insurrection against liberty, sometimes a conspirator's wife carried in triumph among the people. One day it was an actress, who on the previous day had played the role of Venus or Juno."[34] This last allusion to the theater emphasizes the palimpsest character of the cult. Moreover, the incarnation of Reason by women is unstable, impure, polymorphic. It is primarily, as on the stage, a role, and a feminine one at that. As Mona Ozouf notes: "There are . . . features that gave the Festival of Reason an additional theatricality. . . . As in the theater, there was the presence of living actors, in this case women. Was it not, perhaps, in some obscure way, this triumph of the feminine that was found so shocking in the Festival of Reason?" (p. 101).

In his analysis of iconoclastic traditions, Jean-Joseph Goux comments on Freud's idea that "the prohibition against making an image of God implies that sensory perception takes a back seat to the abstract idea. It consecrates the triumph of the spirit over the senses, or more specifically, a renunciation of instincts."[35] And he adds:

Freud explicitly links this religious innovation to a passage from matriarchy to patriarchy, but his lack of insistence on this point is noteworthy. It is odd that he does not explicitly establish what we find to be the particularly illuminating relationship *between the Judaic prohibition against image adoration and the incest taboo with the mother*. By carving images of Gods, one is making a material image of the mother, and adoring the maternal figure through the senses. By tearing oneself away from the seduction of the senses and elevating one's thoughts towards an unrepresentable god one turns away from desire for the mother, ascends to the sublime father and respects the law. (p. 13, emphasis in original)

The image and the maternal are inextricably linked. They were linked as well for the backers of the Cult of the Supreme Being who sought, in their determination to create a "sublime" religion, the double repudiation of idols and the feminine.

The Cult of the Supreme Being thus sought to erase the Cult of Reason—this was made explicit in Robespierre's burning of the statue representing Atheism—as well as to erase the feminine, which had temporarily triumphed in these sensuous representations of Reason and Liberty. The Committee of Public Safety ordered one more palimpsest on 23 Floréal (12 April 1794) when it decreed: "On the facade of buildings formerly devoted to worship, in place of the inscription *Temple of Reason*, those words from the first article of the decree of the National Convention of 18 Floréal will be inscribed: 'The French People recognizes the existence of the Supreme Being and the immortality of the soul.'"[36] The Cult of Reason had been too feminine; the Cult of the Supreme Being would be resolutely virile. Inspired by what Robespierre described as "Rousseau's male eloquence," its program was unequivocal. David's script segregated women, young children, and the elderly from fathers and sons old enough to bear arms:

> The chaste bride braids her dear daughter's hair with flowers; while the suckling child—a mother's most beautiful ornament—presses her breast; the son seizes his weapons with a vigorous arm; he wants to receive his baldric from his father alone. . . . The mothers leave their spouses and sons . . . the fathers lead their sons armed with swords; both carry an oak branch in their hands.[37]

At the Champ de la Réunion, the men placed themselves to the right of the mountain, the women to the left. Some stanzas from Marie-Joseph Chénier's hymn were sung by men alone, others by women. According to some accounts, however, the artists of the Opera then performed a hymn by Desforges entitled "Father of the Universe." But while the pageantry offered indeed a somewhat majestic spectacle, the Supreme Being remained an abstract, unrepresentable, sublime object of worship.

The cult of images and the cult of women were thus replaced by a new religion and a new spectacle: a stage without actors, a theater without an audience, a God without representation. In fact, the iconoclastic strategy that presided over the creation of the Cult of the Supreme Being echoes a certain revolutionary ideology which coexisted paradoxically with a passion for the spectacle: the suspicion of all images. Stanley J. Idzerda has explored at great length the iconoclastic campaign that, during the Revolution, saw to it that all effigies of the past were destroyed, not only because they reminded the spectator of a repudiated history but, more profoundly, because the creation and possession of images had been a royal prerogative.[38] (Louis Marin spoke eloquently of such a privilege in *Portrait of the King*.)[39] In this perspective the 1793 creation of the Louvre Museum offered the perfect resolution to this ideological conflict. A seizure of the pictorial domain by the state, the museum is both a temple and a prison. It separates images from their historical context and production and removes them from public scrutiny, controlling their partial exposure to a small group of viewers.

Terror and the Sublime

The Festival of the Supreme Being was like a brief pause in the last spring of the Revolution. The guillotine disappeared from the Place de la Révolution (today's Place de la Concorde) and was moved to the Faubourg Saint-Antoine, where it would remain briefly before being removed even farther from the center of Paris to the Barrière du Trône.[40] One observer reported to the "surveillance de l'esprit public" department: "After the ceremony [the people] went to their homes with the tranquillity and the propriety of a nation truly free. To-day they have rejoiced at the change of place of the guillotine. I have heard a great number of citizens say: 'With this change the sword of the law will lose none of its effect, and we can enjoy a promenade which will become the finest in Europe.'"[41] According to Michelet, other people believed that the new cult also signaled an end to the executions.

But far from signifying a decline in the number of executions, this move preceded, by just a few hours, the onset of what has been called the Great Terror. Indeed, two days after the Festival of the Supreme Being, the Convention voted the Law of 22 Prairial, submitted by

Couthon (and generally thought to have been inspired by Robespierre). The Law of 22 Prairial eliminated the right to legal counsel and left the Tribunal with but two options: acquittal or death. Georges Lefebvre estimated that 1,376 victims died in Paris between 22 Prairial and 9 Thermidor (10 June and 27 July).[42] The contrast between the peaceful glory of the Festival of the Supreme Being and the onset, two days later, of the Great Terror has not failed to puzzle witnesses, critics, and historians.[43] Just as the Festival of the Supreme Being experimented with the possibility of a theater whose subject would remain beyond representation, the Law of 22 Prairial precipitated a series of deaths moved away from their usual audience; the Sublime and the Terror were thus joined in a gesture that removed them from the spectator's gaze. Sacred and dreadful, "the scaffold would no longer be pressed by the crowd," Michelet wrote, "it was the emancipation of the guillotine. She was to take a deep exterminating breath, outside the civilized world, having nothing more to be ashamed of" (2: 882).

It is worth noting here that the theoretical Terror proposed by Robespierre was meant to be a principle of justice and government unrelated to the excesses that later gave the Revolutionary Tribunal its terrifying reputation. The word *terror* had acquired a second meaning for the *sans-culottes*—the simple elimination of the "enemies" of the Republic. "Terror alone can secure our Liberty, no more leniency. Let the blade of the law graze upon all the guilty heads," wrote the *Journal Universel* on 24 Brumaire, Year II (14 November 1793). To this day, historians are deeply divided in their estimation of Robespierre's responsibility in regard to the Terror. Some have even accepted the dubious vision proposed by the Thermidorians (some, like Billaud-Varenne, well-documented terrorists) that Robespierre alone had been responsible for all the executions of the Revolution. Although few will question Robespierre's opposition to Carrier's infamous drownings in Nantes—to which Robespierre successfully put an end—so powerful is the need to assign responsibility that, as we shall see, Robespierre for many remains the "Dictator" who alone instituted the "*reign* of terror," a strange expression indeed. An unresolved question remains whether Robespierre could have successfully put an end to the Terror itself by using his prestige and authority. This debate and the partisan passions associated with it have somewhat obscured an examination of Robespierre's last attempt to rescue the Revolution from its grotesque and horrifying theatricality. Robespierre's negative terror, as we shall see, is precisely the reverse side of the monstrous theatricality that would endow death with a parodic ceremonial in the last two months of the Revolution.

In his discourse of 17 Pluviôse, Year II (5 February 1794), on "The Principles of political morality that must guide the Convention in its administration of the Republic," Robespierre stated: "If the mainspring of popular government in peacetime is virtue, the mainspring of popular government in time of war is both *virtue and terror*; virtue without which terror is fateful; terror without which virtue is helpless. Terror is nothing but prompt, severe and inflexible justice; it is thus an emanation of virtue" (10: 357). What this discourse conveyed more forcefully still is that if the Revolution is to realize the sublimity and virtue that makes up its very definition, it must transcend not only the sensible presentation of ideas but also the *representation that is part and parcel of language itself*; it must transcend "the abuses of language" (p. 352), which are always capable of betraying the meaning and truth of the sublime. The Law of 22 Prairial eliminated all those who would speak *in the name of* the suspects, testify for them, in short, *represent* them. This reduction of the rhetorical system of the defense aided and abetted a tragic simplification of the trial's outcome; there were no more degrees of innocence and guilt. "Liberty or Death," which had been one of the great slogans of the year 1792, took on its most literal meaning.

This absolute reduction of the *sentence*—which should be understood here as both a judgment and a unit of discourse—should also be seen in the context of what Robespierre sought to define as purity. Not, he specified, the austerity of Sparta or that of the corrupted cloisters. "We have just presented, in all its purity," he said, "the moral and political principle of popular government" (p. 355). "How easily we are misled by words!" he exclaimed. The judicial system that allows for the representation of suspects also allows for the representation of crime, for one speaks *in the name of crime*.

Describing the old system of justice, and arguing that aristocrats and traitors had dominated political rhetoric by "murderous maxims," Robespierre noted: "Some want to govern revolution through legal cavil. Some treat conspiracies against the Republic as one would an individual trial. Tyranny kills, and Liberty pleads; and the code made by conspirators themselves is the law by which they are sentenced" (p. 359). Liberty, this sublime idea, should not have to defend its own cause. Language cannot be trusted.

Robespierre lashed out at the false rumors masterfully spread by his enemies:

Would you believe that, in the provinces where superstition has been most influential, not satisfied with adding to religious ceremonies all the forms that could render them odious, they have also spread terror among the people by spreading the rumor that we were going to kill all children less than ten years old and all the elderly more than seventy years old? These rumors were spread more specifically in the former Brittany and in the department of Rhin and Moselle. This is one of the crimes imputed to the public prosecutor of the criminal tribunal in Strasbourg. The tyrannic madness of this man, makes everything attributed to Caligula and Heliogobale believable. (10: 362)

Euloge Schneider, the target of Robespierre's anger, was neither an aristocrat nor a moderate, but one of the bloodiest terrorists and—like Carrier—had done much to discredit revolutionary justice. Saint-Just himself had played a crucial role in putting an end to what Gérard Walter calls Schneider's "mission of extermination."[44] For Robespierre, the Revolution was thus betrayed from without by monarchist powers united against France and, more dangerously, from within, by those who spoke like patriots "abusing the sacred name of Liberty" (p. 359), while committing terrorist crimes against the people. "Woe unto him who would direct against the people the terror that should only threaten its enemies!" (p. 359).

For Robespierre, the suspicion that taints all sensible representation spreads in turn to the intangible and thus more powerful representation of language and words. Language is suspect, and the Law of 22 Prairial is also a law against words. Just as the old religion worshipped images, the previous system of justice, in its wordiness, spoke for tyrants and treason: "Let's not judge by the difference in language, but by the nature of the results" (p. 360), Robespierre warned. "It is so much more convenient to put on the mask of patriotism to *disfigure the sublime drama* of the Revolution with insolent parodies, to compromise the cause of Liberty with hypocritical moderation and studied extravagance. How many traitors interfere with us to ruin our efforts! Do you want to try them, to ask them true services instead of oaths and declamation! Is action needed? *They make speeches instead*" (p. 361, emphasis added).

In the last months of his life, Robespierre tried to define the Revolution as sublime, as an ideal that would transcend all representation and thus escape all misrepresentations, as a rhetorical purity that could only be expressed in its negative form. Immanuel Kant, perhaps more than Jean-Jacques Rousseau, might have offered the best assessment of Robespierre's sublime. In his *Critique of Judgement*, he noted: "The safeguard is the purely negative character of representation. For the inscrutability of the idea of freedom precludes all positive representation."[45] The concept of law, like the concept of liberty that law expresses and protects, also transcends all representation, even linguistic representation. "The laws of eternal justice have not been etched in marble or stone, but in the hearts of all men" (p. 352). The Mosaic prohibition of images is carried to its absolute negation, that is, to the denial of its engraving of the tables of the Law. Robespierre's views on the Revolution and the Law also find an echo in Kant's description of the experience of the sublime: "This astonishment amounting almost to a terror, the awe and thrill of devout feeling that takes hold of one when gazing upon the prospects of mountains ascending to heavens, deep ravines and torrents raging there . . . all this when we are assured of our own safety" (p. 121).

Robespierre's terror meant to pose no threat to the virtuous citizen. Virtue was, quite precisely, the safeguard of terror. In Robespierre's conception of a political morality rescued from writing and representation, virtue protects the honest citizen. "It is the terror of crime that guarantees the security of innocence" (10: 570), he added in his last discourse, after having denounced violently the "odious system of terror and calumny" (p. 546). For Robespierre, the false terror, the bloody terror, is always associated with words: "Who are those who confined the patriots to jails and spread terror everywhere? They are the very monsters who are accusing us. . . . The monsters whom we have accused" (p. 547). By contrast, Robespierre's virtuous terror, like the sublime, transcended material representation and allowed for no spectacle. In one of his last public acts, Robespierre proposed that the Place de la Révolution, where the guillotine had long stood, now be reserved for the exclusive use of revolutionary festivals. The stage was cleared. Terror and justice, like the sublime, disclaimed any form of representation.

Robespierre's explicit desire to create a sublime revolution, his attempts to denounce what he saw as a parody of liberty, a parody of justice, or a parody of religion, thus sustain a more radical decision to denounce treason and words, words that speak for treason, that are themselves always susceptible of betraying the ideal. Decrying what he called "the abuses of language" and the disguises of virtue, Robespierre's last discourses are entirely fraught with the paradox that consists of disclaiming all material and sensible representation of the Revolution, all suspicious verbal rhetoric, while using nothing but words to unmask words, a last performance to denounce all performances, a final testimony to unveil all testimonies. "This great purity which founds the French Republic, the very sublimity of its project, is both our strength and our weakness" (p. 356). Such is also the dilemma of a language, a rhetoric that would no longer be the "dupe of words" but would be driven by "the ascendancy of truth over imposture."

Robespierre, as is well known, was an avid reader of Rousseau. Given his expressed desire for a language of transparency, it would be tempting to see in his last discourse yet another symptom of the Rousseauist aspiration to tear away the veil and remove all masks, to achieve a purity that stems from a language spoken directly by the soul. The contrast between a law that is fallacious and etched in stone and the pure, incorruptible law written in the hearts of all men seems to repeat Rousseau's suspicion of *écriture*, of writing considered as a threat to the authenticity of an interior, and finally unattainable, language.[46] But Robespierre makes the immanent perversion of language more absolute still. "Everything you say," he warned his colleagues, "will be turned against you, even the truth you have just put forward" (p. 363). False terrors are misleading and paralyzing the Convention, he repeated. In this general betrayal of language, in the dramatic failure of language and representation to make truth prevail, what will be the last recourse of words? What will be their ultimate referent? "In their perfidious hands, all the remedies to these evils [*maux*] become poison" (p. 363). But he insisted: "Quel est le remède de tous ces maux?" The written form *maux* means "evils," but to the ear it can both mean "words" and "evils" so that a more accurate transcript of Robespierre's speech might read: "What then is the remedy to all these evil words," the words that turn into poison? "We know of no other than the development of the main force of the Republic: Virtue" (p. 364). Virtue comes to mean not only what drives and motivates revolutionary discourse but also, in its sublimity, what would elevate such discourse beyond all misrepresentation.

Death Toll

Robespierre delivered his last speech before an increasingly hostile assembly just a few hours before his arrest. It has been said that his discourse also caused his arrest, because he denounced a conspiracy without actually naming anyone, thus implicating the entire Convention. But what he attacked was no different from the abuses of language he had already denounced on 17 Pluviôse (5 February): "the odious system of terror and calumny" that had weakened the Republic (p. 546). He denounced with particular energy one of the accusations which, to this day, has successfully damaged Robespierre's reputation: that from his position on the Committee of Public Safety, he ordered all the death penalties.

Is it true they have circulated odious lists, where certain members of the Convention were designated as victims, and which they attributed first to the Committee of Public Safety, then to me? Is it true that they have dared assume shadow meetings of the Committee, rigorous decisions, chimeric accusations? Is it true that irreproachable representatives have been persuaded that their fate had been sealed? Is it true that these false rumors have been spread so effectively and so audaciously that a great number of members do not dare sleep home at night? Yes, the facts are known, and the proofs are at the Committee of Public Safety. (p. 548)

Faced with these uncontrollable rumors, Robespierre denounced once more—it is one of the leitmotifs of his discourse—the "systems of terror and calumny" that become inseparable, for terror is a also the terror of a deceitful language.

More simply and urgently, however, Robespierre claimed that the right to speak, the pure necessity of telling the truth at the risk of one's life, *is the sublime*. The right to speak, the duty to speak when death will follow, the conviction that death will result when truth is spoken: such is the last but absolute guarantee that words, on the edge of ruin and silence, on the shores of negation, have finally reached the sublimity that defies all representation, hence all misrepresentation. "What objection can be made," he asked, "to him who wishes to speak the truth and agrees to die for it?" (pp. 575–76). Death then becomes the referent of truth; and the one and only truth, guaranteed by the knowledge of his imminent death, is that he who is about to die *may* speak, is *entitled* to speak. "I shall conclude," continued Robespierre, "that principles are outlawed and that tyranny reigns among us, but not that I should remain silent, for what objection can be made to a man who is right and is willing to die for his country?" (p. 576).

In the proximity of a death that is both anticipated and accepted, language can no longer betray its purpose. Truth (which is nothing other than the right to speak the truth on the threshold of death) reveals its final purpose, its value as testament. Robespierre exclaimed: "I promised some time ago to leave a fearsome testament to the enemies of the people. I shall publish it now with the independence which suits the situation in which I have placed myself. I bequeath them the terrible truth, and death!" ("Je leur lègue la vérité terrible, et la mort!") (p. 567). The dreadful and terrible truth is the truth that brings terror without which virtue is helpless, and death in which truth alone mirrors itself.

Again as Farce

It could be said that Robespierre's desire to define and to further a sublime revolution failed twice. Robespierre tried to impose a cult devoid of all sensible representations, a religion worthy of its sublime project, but in that regard, the Festival of the Supreme Being was a spectacular failure. The theatrical nature of the procession staged by David, of the symbolic scenery built on the Champ de Mars, and even the sacrifice of idols burned publicly at the onset of the ceremony, all framed a stage where Robespierre became an unwilling actor and for some a high priest. Several historians have seen Robespierre's physical isolation at the head of the procession as an obscure prefiguration of his downfall. Thus Madame de Staël, who had not witnessed the event, wrote in her *Considérations sur la Révolution française*: "At the procession of this impious festival, Robespierre dared go first, claiming preeminence over his colleagues, and from then on, he was lost."[47] Not only did the festival fail to avoid the theatricality of all the great revolutionary events, it survived the death of Robespierre in a parodic form that was often associated with the feminine and idolatrous Cult of Reason it had sought to erase. The two forms of worship mixed, and Charles Nodier later decried "the scandalous orgies of the atheists . . . the stupid emblems of this absurd idolatry."[48] Jean Starobinski and Michel Vovelle, among others, acknowledge that, in Vovelle's words, the Revolution failed "to realize the Rousseauist dream of the abolition of spectacles."[49] Not only did terror fail to purify the language or the justice of the Revolution, but it was to be drowned in an excess of morbid spectacles that culminated with Robespierre's own death. His execution was organized as an impromptu festival, with hired actors performing along the route and crowds of inebriated spectators. "The crowd was vast," said the *Journal de Perlet*, "The sounds of rejoicing, the applause, the cries of: 'Down with the tyrant! Long live the Republic!' The curses resounded all along the way."

The *Annales de la République française* of 11 Thermidor added: "Never had there been so large a crowd as for this execution. Women, children, old people, all of Paris was there."[50] These testimonies may be suspect, of course, and may well have been written at the suggestion of the Convention, anxious to show that its condemnation of Robespierre had been received with popular acclaim. Indeed, other witnesses claimed not to have noticed any commotion on this fateful day and to have learned of Robespierre's death by the newspaper reports. Nevertheless, the descriptions, true or fabricated, played on the theatrical qualities of these frightful scenes. "This false tragedy around the true one, this concert of calculated cries, of premeditated furor, was the first scene of the royalist Terror," noted Michelet (2: 988).

The day after Robespierre's death, the guillotine was returned to the center stage of Paris, Place de la Révolution, for the largest number of executions ever ordered on a single day. Theaters reopened. The Law of 22 Prairial was voided. "After 9 Thermidor," wrote Paul Thureau-Dangin, "everything was diminished, events and men. The stage was given to walk-ons, things fell so low that creatures like Tallien and Barras became characters."[51] The sublime revolution died along with Robespierre in the parodic displays of democratic merriment that followed 9 Thermidor.

We are all familiar with Marx's comment that history always repeats itself twice in its own theatricality, "once as tragedy, and again as farce." In his presentation of the collective volume *Du Sublime*, Jean-Luc Nancy writes: "It may appear that our era is once again rediscovering the notion of the *sublime*, its name, its concept and the questions it entails; such is not the case of course, as one never returns to anything in History."[52] That the sublime should be precisely that which, in history, eludes repetition seems particularly appropriate here. If history should repeat itself, it can do so only insofar as it is, like theater, a performance. The symptomatic character of such a performance, its parodic repetitions, the betrayal of its own project, was further illustrated in the spectacles that slowly replaced the stage of the executions. On 18 Fructador, Year II (4 September 1794), the Cité-Variétés of Paris gave a play entitled *The Fall of the Last Tyrant, or the 9th Thermidor*. An anonymous letter to the *Abréviateur Universel* complained (25 Fructador, 11 September): "Citizens, shall we ever refrain from turning everything into an opera, a fantasy, a drama, a scenic play?" But Robespierre's own person, his *image*, was reappropriated by a legend that started to weave its fiction just a few months after his death.[53] Romantic historiography interpreted history as a scenic drama.

"Western historiography," wrote Michel de Certeau, "battles with fiction. . . . Not that it tells the truth. No historian has ever claimed to do so. Rather with the critical apparatus of discourse, the scholar removes error from 'fables.' The historian gains ground by diagnosing falsehood. He cuts through accepted language, to make room for his discipline . . . as if he devoted himself to hunting down lies rather than establishing the truth, or as if he could only determine truth by determining error."[54] As presented by Michel de Certeau, the historian's work briefly overlaps Robespierre's expressed desire to rid language of all false representations. But the search for truth through the negative sublime that contrasts so sharply with the symbolic output of the Revolution also meets its 9 Thermidor. If the fall of Robespierre has supplied the material for so many narratives, it is also because history testifies repeatedly to the failure of the sublime and the staying power of representations.

Between the multiplicity of false reports hastily written after Robespierre's fall to justify his execution and the still unresolved enigma of his last days,[55] between a surplus of tainted documents and the absence of reliable testimony, readers themselves are sometimes faced with the impossible task of "removing error from 'fables.'" If we take seriously Robespierre's efforts to propose a sublime revolution, will we not in turn view with some suspicion the multiplicity of images that flowered after 9 Thermidor? Caricatures, parodies, farcical representations, inebriated actors, the curtain was raised on a new stage more cluttered than ever with the shambles of a failed Revolution.

By contrast, the most appropriate epitaph to Robespierre's sublime dream may be found in this footnote to Michelet's *Histoire de la Révolution française*. Signed by Gérard Walter, it reads in very fine print: "Robespierre and his companions were buried in a plot adjacent to the Parc Monceau. During the Restoration, a public Ball was set up on the spot. After the Revolution of 1830, a group of admirers undertook excavations there in order to find his remains. These efforts yielded no results."[56]

3

The Revolutionary Sublime

In *The Ideology of the Aesthetic*, Terry Eagleton suggests that the extraordinary precedence of the aesthetic in European philosophy illustrates the fact that, when speaking of art, one is also speaking of the "struggle for political hegemony."[1] When studying aesthetic judgment, one examines a privileged mode of cognition that is also related to the political. I will argue that the same philosophical and ideological concerns that produced the *Critique of Judgement* also framed revolutionary thought, more particularly Robespierre's, on the nature and role of the sublime in the creation of the new state. From this perspective, Kant's analytic of the sublime provides an essential key to the understanding of political thought during the French Revolution. More specifically, it helps us understand several recurring revolutionary concerns: the injunction, repeated daily at the Assembly and in the newspapers, to tear away the veil of conspiracy, to unmask the traitors; the desire to create a sublime State; and finally, at a deeper level, the revolutionaries' obsession with the sublime reveals an anxiety about the nature of representation, a concept that had been radically challenged in Kant's *Critique of Judgement*. I will argue that the representation at stake in the case of the Revolution is, in fact, the very principle of political representation in its complex relationship to the (sublime) idea of the general will.[2]

The Truth of Unveiling

One of the most frequent injunctions issued from the tribunes of the Assembly was that treason was to be unmasked, its veil torn away.

After the arrest of the Girondins, Saint-Just exclaimed: "The conspiracy that I mean to speak to you about is finally unmasked" (8 July 1793).[3] He added on another occasion: "We have unveiled the factions. They are no longer. . . . All Frenchmen are warned to unveil the partisans of tyranny" (26 Germinal, Year II, 15 April 1794, 806, 819). When Robespierre made a tragic appeal to establish the Republic of Virtue, he warned: "A king, a proud senate, a Caesar, a Cromwell, must above all cover their plan with a religious veil,"[4] and he added: "It is so much more convenient to put on the mask of patriotism to disfigure the sublime drama of the Revolution with insolent parodies, to compromise the cause of Liberty with hypocritical moderation and studied extravagance. . . . If all hearts have not been changed, how many faces are masked!" (17 Pluviôse, Year II, 5 February 1794, 361). The Committee on Public Safety repeatedly spoke of its efforts to "unveil the foreign factions."[5] The trope of tearing away the veil and pulling off the masks is repeated in all revolutionary endeavors, from daily preoccupations with the weakening of patriotism to Marat's exposure in *L'Ami du peuple* of "a plan that has been unveiled to put the people to sleep and impede the constitution."[6]

The familiar idea that treason, in all its manifestations, must be exposed by tearing away the veil of falsehood can be seen as the patriotic denunciation of an anti-sublime counterrevolutionary project. Treason not only threatens national safety, it also, as Robespierre makes explicit, "disfigures" the sublime drama of the Revolution.

But the trope of unveiling, so familiar in political discourse, is further elucidated by one of the only two examples Kant gives of sublime utterances. In a footnote to the "Analytic of the Sublime," he writes: "Perhaps there has never been a more sublime utterance, or a thought more sublimely expressed than the well-known inscription upon the Temple of *Isis* (Mother *Nature*): 'I am all that is, and that was, and that shall be, and no mortal hath raised the veil from before my face'."[7] In "Sublime Truth," Philippe Lacoue-Labarthe comments on this example as follows: "We are confronted then, in Kantian terms (but also in pre-Kantian terms, for this has been said in any number of ways since Longinus), with the canonical definition of the sublime: the sublime is the presentation of the nonpresentable or,

Ainsi que l'Eglise dans les jours de pénitence voile l'image du Christ et des Saints; de même dans ces jours de calamité, nous voilons tout ce qui pourrait rappeller à nos sens l'éclat de la Majesté Royale

Figure 6. The people veiling all symbols of Monarchy following the flight and arrest of the royal family, June 1791. Engraving. Collection Viollet. "Just as the Church veils the images of Christ and the Saints on penitence days, so we veil everything that can remind our senses of the Royal Majesty's splendor."

more rigorously, to take up the formula of Lyotard, the presentation (of this:) that there is the nonpresentable."[8]

The sentence of Isis, moreover, also discloses an essential quality of truth, and Lacoue-Labarthe adds:

[T]he nonpresentable is conceived here as non-unveilable, and this makes a big difference because the prosopopoeia of nature in its totality, or of the totality of beings (it is the totality itself which is non-unveilable, that is, the unity of all that is: its Being), is also a prosopopoeia of truth. The sentence of Isis is not simply an utterance of truth but an utterance of the truth of the truth, that is, of the play of veiling and unveiling, of presentation and of the non-unveilable. . . . What does it mean, in effect, "to tell the truth"? By an immemorial constraint—at least as far back as philosophical memory can reach—which does not arise out of any metaphorical decision, telling the truth is unveiling the truth. . . . It renders manifest or patent, it unveils. . . . But what is produced in Isis's sentence—and this is probably the reason why it has been so fascinating—is that telling the truth about itself, telling the truth of the truth and unveiling itself as the truth, truth (unveiling) unveils itself as the impossibility of unveiling or the necessity, for finite (mortal) Being, of its veiling. (pp. 90–91)

Revolutionary rhetoric illustrated the literal quality of truth as disclosed in the Temple of Isis's inscription, that is, that *it is the quality of truth that it cannot be unveiled*. In this light, the revolutionary injunction to tear away the mask and to unveil conspiracies and factions takes on yet another, and more powerful, signification.

This signification might be illustrated by another dramatic veil torn away in the wake of the fall of the Bastille. Prior to the Revolution, as mentioned earlier, many of the small theaters thriving at the Foire Saint-Germain and the Foire Saint-Laurent had endured a series of oppressive measures imposed on them by the Comédie Française, anxious to protect its exclusive rights to the classical repertory. First, the small theaters were prohibited from reciting texts, and so sang them instead. When prohibited from singing texts, they carried placards displaying their lines. When prohibited from displaying the text under any form, they took to mime. In a desperate gesture to protect its privilege, the Comédie Française obtained an order that a veil be suspended between their rival actors and spectators during the entire performance. After the fall of the Bastille, Plancher-Valcour, director of the *Délassements-Comiques*, was reported to have ripped down the interfering veil, exclaiming "Vive la Liberté!"[9] Other reports claimed that the spectators had themselves intervened and pulled down the curtain. Such a patriotic and theatrical gesture perfectly suited the emerging rhetoric of public disclosure which, for a while, seemed to go hand in hand with freedom of expression, a new revolutionary conquest.

Yet what is revealed in 1789 when Plancher-Valcour tears away the veil separating actors from spectators is not truth but theater. When he gets rid of the curtain that masks the stage, what is uncovered is but a stage, not truth but a set, not persons but actors. This incident may serve as a privileged example of all instances of unveiling. In his attack against the Dantonists, Saint-Just remarked: "This party, devoid of courage, like all the others, conducted the Revolution like a theatrical plot" (p. 765). What is disclosed when masks are removed and veils are torn, is acting, duplicity, lies, untruth. Revolutionary rhetoric does not speak of unveiling the truth but of unveiling treason, bringing to light treachery and falsehood. Saint-Just again made explicit the function of the mask in his definition of the ideal revolutionary: "He thinks that coarseness is a mask of duplicity and remorse, and that it covers deceitfulness with enthusiasm" (p. 809). Remove the mask of the uncouth, for it is woven of remorse and treacherousness, and falsehood will stand exposed.

In his discourse of 8 Thermidor, Robespierre used the metaphor of unveiling several times: "Here, I must let truth emerge and unveil the veritable wounds of the Republic,"[10] he first exclaimed, alluding to counterrevolutionary efforts. But, a few minutes later, he cried: "I can't resolve myself to tear entirely the veil that covers this deep mystery of iniquities" (p. 560). For nothing is hidden under the veil but the most frightening deception: "How can one possibly bear to see this horrible succession of traitors more or less skilled in the art of hiding their hideous soul under the veil of virtue, even friendship?" (p. 567). And finally, Robespierre reiterated: "I dare not resolve myself to raise the veil that covers so many iniquities; but let it be known that among them are most of all men who opposed the decree that struck down atheism" (p. 578). Here, Robespierre's thoughts are elucidated. Those who opposed the Cult of the Supreme Being, this sublime religion that repudiated all forms of representation, are the same ones who dissimulate their dark designs under the veil of virtue. Whether in this case truth can be exposed by tearing the veil remains undecided. In his last discourse, as we shall see, Robespierre attempted to solve a more dramatic dilemma: the relationship between death and truth.

Indeed, truth participates in a different visual metaphor that consists in saying that truth enlightens, while conspiracies are linked to what Robespierre called "tenebrous plots" ("trames ténébreuses") (p. 41). But truth is never subject to unveiling, and the light it throws on the Revolution is unlike any other. Saint-Just expressed it better than any other orator when he exclaimed at the time of the king's trial: "Truth burns silently in every heart, like a blazing light in a tomb" (p. 401). Truth shines in silence and what it illuminates is already dead, purified, one might add, by the flame of truth and by death itself. It is indeed one of the recurrent themes of revolutionary discourse that the ultimate, perhaps the only, referent of truth is death itself.

In his last discourse, as we have seen, Robespierre, fighting rumors and calumny, argued for the necessity of telling the truth at the risk of one's life. Or rather, he argued that the knowledge of his imminent death was the only guarantee that his words spoke the truth. The extraordinary legacy of his testament ("I bequeath them the dreadful, the terrible truth and death") forever links truth and the tomb. Truth shines in death, the veil remains, if not figuratively draped over the face of Isis, then over the closed, unseeing eyes that alone, in the tomb, are allowed in the presence of truth. The veil of truth has been extended to cover the dead, like a funeral shroud.

The Sublime State

If the rhetoric of unveiling refers to an extreme that could be described as the negation of the sublime, or, more precisely—to echo Robespierre—as the "disfiguration of the sublime," at the other ex-

treme, the French Revolution strove to establish a sublime Republic. The word appears repeatedly in Robespierre's and Saint-Just's
discourses as the pure ideal to which one must aspire. "To consoli-
date his country a sublime man is needed," noted Saint-Just (p. 818).
Robespierre described the love of one's Fatherland as "a sublime
feeling" that "supposes a preference for the public interest over particular interests" (p. 215). He spoke of the "sublime enthusiasm, the
moral instinct of the people which is the principle of all great actions"
(p. 282). At many levels—aesthetic and political—this goal implied a
questioning of the very principle of representation.

In the "General Remarks on the Exposition of Aesthetic Reflective
Judgment," Kant stresses that the sublime "must in every case have
reference to our *way of thinking*, i.e., to maxims directed to giving
the intellectual side of our nature and the ideas of reason supremacy
over sensibility" (p. 127). Kant adds:

We have no reason to fear that the feeling of the sublime will suffer from
an abstract mode of presentation like this, which is altogether negative as to
what is sensuous. For though the imagination, no doubt, finds nothing beyond the sensible world to which it can lay hold, still this thrusting aside of
the sensible barriers gives it a feeling of being unbounded; and that removal
is thus a presentation of the infinite. As such it can never be anything more
than a negative presentation—but still it expands the soul. Perhaps there is
no more sublime passage in the Jewish Law than the commandment: Thou
shalt not make unto thee any graven image, or any likeness of any thing that
is in heaven or on earth. . . . The very same holds good of our representation
of the moral law and of our native capacity for morality. (p. 127)

As Lacoue-Labarthe has pointed out, this example of a sublime
utterance is radically different from the inscription on the Temple of
Isis. While in the inscription "presentation is thought as unveiling,"
in this case "the question . . . is indeed that of presentation and of the
limit of presentation" (p. 74).

First of all, for Kant, this principle is linked to our negative presentation of the moral law. This was indeed Robespierre's concern
when he repudiated the idolatrous Cult of Reason in favor of the
Cult of the Supreme Being. For Robespierre, the sublime project of
the Revolution would find its moral foundation in the Cult of the

Supreme Being alone. When he decided to substitute the Cult of the Supreme Being for the Cult of Reason, Robespierre gave his most articulate argument for a religion that would transcend all representations.

Indeed, the Revolution had a paradoxical relationship to images. It created the Louvre museum, but it also made a deliberate effort to destroy all images of the past, more specifically of the political past, that of Monarchy.[11] In this instance, the most interesting destruction was probably that of the Gallery of Kings that decorated the western portal of Notre-Dame.[12]

It would be naive to imagine this deliberate destruction merely as the senseless gesture of a brutal regime, too uncultured to recognize artistic beauty and too sectarian to accept the value of a religious treasure. In the demolition of the kings who figured the ancestry of Jesus, the Tree of Jesse, several important principles were at stake: (1) The principle of a privileged genealogy, the idea that a line of descent, similar to that of the king himself, and indeed, of royal quality, deserved to be valorized and admired in any way. (2) The religious association between the Kings' Gallery and the Catholic Church, the too-powerful symbol of an alliance that had become suspect. The king's entitlement, "by the grace of God," so radically rejected by the revolutionaries, had found a powerful echo in the statuary of Notre-Dame. (3) Finally, in its iconoclastic intent, the Revolution expressed the conviction that it was particularly symptomatic of the Monarchy and the church to have produced this profusion of images that had been turned into idols. These images had misled the people as surely as the golden cow had misled the Hebrews before Moses' iconoclastic dictate, for, in this particular instance, these icons reflected, and betrayed, the nature of their models: the nature of two institutions, the church and the Monarchy, that resorted to, and established their authority by, producing a profusion of images. Conversely, the fact that these institutions had produced so many images of themselves also betrayed their inner nature, their lack of spirituality, their foundation in a exclusively material world.

When, in the spring of 1794, Robespierre proceeded to attack and dismiss the recent and more revolutionary Cult of Reason that had been meant to replace Catholic practice, his goal was twofold: he aimed to dismiss both the idolatry which accompanied the newly established religion, and to make the very idea of Reason itself the object of a Cult. As we have seen, in his discourse, "Of the relationships between religious and moral ideas with republican principles and of national festivals" (18 Floréal, Year II, 7 April 1794), Robespierre criticized all forms of religion that had violated the Mosaic taboo against representations of God: "How different is the God of nature from the God of priests! He knows nothing so resembling atheism as the religions they have made. By disfiguring the Supreme Being, they have destroyed Him to the best of their abilities; they have made Him into a ball of fire, an ox, a tree, sometimes a man, sometimes a king. The priests have created God in their own image" (p. 274). By contrast, Robespierre's friend, Claude Payan, argued that: "When it comes to defining the Supreme Being, our idea of Him will be so sublime that we shall not degrade Him by giving Him a face or body similar to ours."[13]

The Sublime Contract

But the effort to reach the sublime, or simply to understand the sublime character of the revolutionary undertaking, was itself felt as a double-edged sword. Robespierre noted: "This great purity of the foundations of the French Republic, *the very sublimity of its intent*, is precisely what makes for our strength and our weakness; our strength because it gives us the ascendancy of truth over imposture, and the rights of public interest over private interest; our weakness because it rallies all depraved men against us, all those who in their hearts planned to plunder the people" (pp. 220–21, emphasis added).

This quotation is of particular interest in that it links the sublime project of the Revolution with the conflict between the rights of public interests and the protection of private interests. More specifically, the sublime ideal of the Revolution cannot be attained without first eliminating the private, individual interests that threaten the establishment of a government truly representative of the common will.

This ongoing battle is that of the private versus the public good. At a deeper level, however, it also questions a more fundamental principle: whether the common will, Rousseau's sublime idea, could ever be successfully represented. In Robespierre's view, the sublime is expressly linked to the idea of truth and public interests, truth and the common will—one might add, to the truth of the common will—but the very sublime quality of truth, and (to an extent that was to become tragically clear to Robespierre) the sublime quality of the common will, also makes it unrepresentable. If the common will cannot be represented, what is to become of a political system that has staked its future and legitimacy on the very principle of political representation? As we shall see, in Robespierre's view, the principle of political representation would betray the sublime project of the Revolution as surely as aesthetic representation failed to embody the sublime character of truth and the moral law.

Rousseau's most famous political legacy, *On the Social Contract*, proceeds through a series of paradoxes, many of them avowedly beyond resolution. From the foreword to the difficult question of the general will, Rousseau posits a series of axioms all framed by the first part of chapter 1, where he declares: "It will be asked if I am a prince or a legislator to write about politics. I reply that *I am neither, and that is why I write about politics*. If I were a prince or a legislator, I would not waste my time saying what has to be done. I would do it, or keep silent." [14] Rousseau thus posits his standing outside the body politic as the point of departure of this text. The possibility of writing about politics is inextricably linked to his negative identity: neither prince nor legislator. More interestingly, Rousseau suggests that, were he in a position of presumptive authority, he would not write.

The options then open to him would be twofold: do what has to be done or remain silent. The act of writing is thus opposed not just to the idea of doing but to the dual option of doing/keeping silent. Silence is the option of those who can act but cannot succeed in doing what is right; it stands in direct opposition not to writing but to doing. As for Rousseau himself, from the beginning of this controversial text he stands ready to assume its consequences: governmental reprisals that will try to silence him and prevent him from doing what is right—writing. In *On the Social Contract*, Rousseau always maintains writing on the edge of this double abyss: his own incapacity to act and the threat of silence.

The aspect of *On the Social Contract* that was to haunt revolutionary thought, especially Robespierre's, was the concept of the general will.[15] Much has been written about Rousseau's idealized view of a common will that always wills what is right, but the most curious warning Rousseau gives us is in a footnote to chapter III of Book II. Rousseau has just emphasized the radical difference between "the will of all," that considers private interests, and the "general will," that considers only the common interest. He then notes: " 'Each interest,' says the Marquis d'Argenson, 'has different principles. The agreement of two private interests is formed in opposition to the interest of a third.' He could have added that the agreement of all interests is formed in opposition to the interest of each. If there were no different interests, the common interest, which would never encounter any obstacle, would scarcely be felt. Everything would run smoothly by itself and politics would cease to be an art" (p. 61). Rousseau's rejection of the triangular structure, where two parties resolve their differences by opposing a third, is essential to his definition of the common will. The opposition—between private and common will— must be resolutely expressed and resolved at the individual level, or not at all. In the same way that the sovereign is formed solely of "private individuals," each giving himself to all, and thus to no one (p. 53), the general will results from the sum of individual wills from which individual private interests have been deducted.

Rousseau's rejection of the triangular structure is consonant with a more general and devastating warning regarding the very nature of the common will, that as soon as the fragile balance between the resolutely individual pluses and minuses is threatened, so is "the remaining sum of the differences" that constitutes the common will. Associations, groups of private interests, what revolutionary rhetoric will call "factions," destroy the fragile mathematical equilibrium:

If, when an adequately informed people deliberates, the citizens were to have no communication among themselves, the general will would always result from the large number of small differences, and the deliberation would always be good. But when factions, partial associations at the expense of the whole, are formed, the will of each of these associations become general with reference to its members and particular with reference to the State. One can say, then, that there are no longer as many voters as there are men, but merely as many as there are associations. The differences become less numerous and produce a result that is less general. Finally, when one of these associations is so big that it prevails over all the others, the result is no longer a sum of small differences, but a single difference. Then there is no longer a general will, and the opinion that prevails is merely a private opinion. (p. 61)

And Rousseau concludes: "In order for the general will to be well expressed, it is therefore important that there be no partial society in the State, and that each citizen give only his own opinion" (p. 61).

Partial societies, factions, thus constitute the major threat to the emergence of a legitimate common will, and this challenge to the common will became the legitimate basis for incriminating the Girondins, the Dantonists or the Hébertists. Robespierre's discourse against Dumouriez and the Girondins starts with the words: "A powerful faction is conspiring" (10 April 1793; 9: 376). During the Revolution, the word "faction" itself constitutes an indictment. Conversely, in his discourse on the new Declaration of Rights, Robespierre declares: "No portion of the people may exert the power of the entire people, but the desire it expresses must be respected as the desire of a portion of the people that must work toward forming the general will" (24 April 1793; 9: 467).

For the common will to find a valid expression in the new revolutionary regime, one must fight a double threat, that of private interests organized in factions, and that of limiting the governmental process to too small a number of citizens. In his speech on the Constitution, Robespierre wishes for "a sumptuous and majestic edifice open to twelve thousand spectators . . . the place of the sessions of the legislative Body. Before the eyes of so great a number of witnesses, neither corruption, nor intrigue, nor perfidy would dare to show its face; only the general will would be consulted, only the voice of reason and public interest would be heard" (10 May 1793; 9: 502–3).

Such is the importance of governing with the largest possible number of witnesses that Robespierre spends considerable time pondering the need for a special political arena. But the mathematical reasoning involved in determining the number of spectators/witnesses/

participants necessary to guarantee the triumph of the common will is just as destructive as Rousseau's addition and subtraction of private interests. "[The Constitution] must forbid the representatives to have any influence whatsoever on the composition of the audience, or arbitrarily to redraw the size of the place that is meant to welcome the people. It must assure that the legislature resides amidst an immense population, and deliberates before the eyes of an infinite multitude of citizens" (p. 504). In this paragraph, Robespierre sets out to limit, not the number of citizens participating in government (by being present when the government deliberates) but the rights of the "mandataires," that is, the elected representatives of the people. What legitimates these restrictions is that, as soon as the people has designated its representatives, a de facto faction is constituted, no longer representing—as ideally it should—the will of the electorate, but its own interests. The only way to check the constitution of private interests is continuously to confront the elected representatives to the wills (in the plural) of the people, to their infinite multitude. The key word is "infinite." "The legislature resides amidst an *immense* population, and deliberates before the eyes of an *infinite multitude of citizens*" (p. 504, emphasis added). Kant, of course, analyzes at length the relationship between the sublime and the infinite in his reflection on the mathematically sublime.[16]

This is where the question of political representation confronts the rhetoric of the sublime, or, rather, this is where Rousseau's idea of the common will comes to be acknowledged as a sublime idea, that cannot be represented, not even politically.[17]

In *Le Nombre et la raison: La Révolution française et les élections*, Patrice Guénniffey has offered a comprehensive account of the politics of election practices during the French Revolution.[18] The qualifications required to vote—which in practice excluded many citizens from the political process—the distinction between active and passive citizens so violently denounced by the left, the struggles disclosed in the several constitutions that were voted, more specifically that of June 1793, which was passed but never put into place, all these elements, added to the questions of national and regional elections, the conflicts between the Assembly and the Committees, have been explored and discussed in the context of the general history of the Revolution. Guéniffey gives examples of the staggering effects of the change from a regime of personification, when the king embodied the state and the will of God, to a politics of representation, perceived both as a stunning revolutionary conquest and as a deeply limited expression of the people's common will. On the one hand, Guéniffey notes, "the advent of a selective order marked a break with the old world of privilege and symbolized the inversion of the principle of command: all citizens henceforth could some day, *at least virtually*, be entrusted with important responsibilities, just as the power of elevating a citizen belonged to the sovereign people alone" (119, emphasis added). On the other hand, the very process of elections created inequalities, as critics were quick to point out. Thus, in 1793, "The member of the Convention François Agnès Montgilbert affirmed that the system of election was incompatible with the principles of the Revolution, and that it would not be possible for long to maintain equality among citizens under a regime that required them to set certain individuals apart to fulfill the functions of government" (p. 119, emphasis added).[19]

Indeed, in his discourse on the Constitution, Robespierre struggled with the limitations imposed by the concept of political representation.[20] While political representation is a revolutionary conquest, as soon as representatives form a government, they also create the threat of another faction, a group of common interests that will alter, disfigure, the idealized expression of the common will. Thus Robespierre imagines numerous restrictions on what he calls the *mandataires*, the elected or designated representatives of the people. First, they must be accountable at all times, for all their actions: "A people, whose representatives are accountable to no one for their management, has no Constitution; a people, whose representatives are only accountable to other inviolable representatives, has no constitution, since the latter may betray the constitution with impunity, and allow the others to betray the people. If this is what is meant by representative government, I confess that I adopt all the anathemas pronounced against it by Jean-Jacques Rousseau" (9: p. 504).

Second, representatives can be recalled, and their faction dissolved, at any time, by the people who chose them: "I want the people to be able to recall all the public servants that it names, according to forms that will be established, with no other justification than the imprescriptible right, which is its own, of recalling its representatives" (p. 505).

The limitations and dangers of political representation can thus be kept in check, yet the very principle of political representation remains imperfect. Robespierre laments the fact that national elections will favor "famous charlatans" and overlook "the man of merit and virtue who is only known in the region where he lives" (p. 506). Such is Robespierre's suspicion of the government that he adds:

> I may be asked how, with such reliable precautions against magistrates, I can assure obedience to the laws and to government? I respond that I am all the more assured by these very precautions themselves. I give back to the laws and to government all the force that I take away from the vices of men who govern and make laws. . . . When the principle of the law is public interest, it is upheld by the people itself, and the force of the law is that of all the citizens who have made it and to whom it belongs. The general will and public force have a common origin. (pp. 507–8)

This is a direct echo of Rousseau's definition of a rightful law. He writes in *On the Social Contract*: "When the entire people enacts something concerning the entire people, it considers only itself, and if a relationship is formed then, it is between the whole object viewed in one way and the whole object viewed in another, *without any division of the whole*. Then the subject matter of the enactment is general like the will that enacts. It is this act that I call a law" (p. 66, emphasis added).

The Mosaic Law

Rousseau's legislator, the semidivine intervention that makes the social contract possible, is introduced with these words: "The discovery of the best rules of society suited to nations would require a superior intelligence, who saw all men's passions *yet experienced none of them; who had no relationship at all to our nature* yet knew it thoroughly; whose happiness was independent of us, yet who was nevertheless willing to attend to ours" (p. 67, emphasis added). This series of paradoxes closely echoes Rousseau's introductory note that it is precisely because he is neither a prince nor a legislator that he can write about both. Negative qualifications enable the legislator to find a special place in the texture of the social contract. But the paradoxes do not stop here: "One finds combined in the work of legislation two things that seem incompatible: an undertaking beyond human force and, to execute it, an authority that amounts to nothing" (p. 69).

How this impossible task might be resolved is suggested in the following lines:

Since the legislator is therefore unable to use either force or reasoning, he must necessarily have recourse to another order of authority, which can win over without violence and persuade without convincing. . . . It is this sublime reason, which rises above the grasp of common men, whose decisions the legislator places in the mouth of the immortals in order to convince by divine authority those who cannot be moved by human prudence. (pp. 69–70)

The appeal to a "sublime" reason is to be taken in the strictest sense of the term; it is the feeling that, since Longinus, has confounded reason and imagination, transcending and defying all forms of material representation.

Anticipating Kant's commentary on the sublime character of the Jewish Law, Rousseau writes:

It is not every man who can make the Gods speak or be believed when he declares himself their interpreter. The legislator's great soul is the true miracle that should prove his mission. Any man can engrave stone tablets, buy an oracle, pretend to have a secret relationship with some divinity, train a bird to talk in his ear, or find other crude ways to impress the people. One who knows only that much might even assemble, by chance, a crowd of madmen, but he will never found an empire, and his extravagant work will soon die along with him. . . . The Jewish law, which is still in existence, and the law of the son of Ishmael, which has ruled half the world for ten centuries, still bear witness today to the great men who formulated them. (p. 70)

Kant, after having exclaimed that there was "no more sublime passage in the Jewish Law" than God's iconoclastic mandate, adds: "This commandment can alone explain the enthusiasm which the Jewish people, in their moral period, felt for their religion when comparing themselves with others, or the pride inspired by Mohammedanism. The very same holds good of our representation of the moral law and of our native capacity for morality" (p. 127). Later, Robespierre himself would speak of laws that have been graven "not on marble or stone, but in the hearts of men" (17 Pluviôse, Year II, 5 February 1794; 10: 352).

Thus at the heart of the moral law that alone can save the social contract is an appeal to the strength of the sublime. Kant comments: "The safeguard is the purely negative character of the presentation. For *the inscrutability of the idea of freedom* precludes all positive presentation. The moral law, however, is a sufficient and original source of determination within us" (p. 128, author's emphasis).[21]

Robespierre will argue that, at the heart of the moral law which alone can sustain the Republic, is the love of one's country and the love of equality. He presents it in these terms:

As the essence of the Republic or democracy is equality, it follows that love of country necessarily includes love of equality. It is still true that this sublime feeling supposes a preference for public interest over all particular interests; from which it results that love of one's country again supposes or produces all the virtues; for what are they if not the strength of soul that makes one capable of these sacrifices? and how could the slave of avarice or ambition, for example, sacrifice his idol to the country? (p. 353)

Thus, on the side of those who wear masks, whose veils must be torn away to reveal hypocrisy and treason, are those who revere the idols of avarice and ambition. Against them, there is just one recourse, and repeatedly, for Robespierre, this recourse is called the sublime. On 18 Floréal, Year II (7 May 1794) he will invoke "a sublime people" (p. 445). Speaking to the women who gave their sons to the fatherland, he exclaims, "With sublime abandon you have devoted them to your country" (p. 461), and he warns: "Woe unto him who seeks to extinguish this sublime enthusiasm and, with distressing doctrines, to stifle the moral instinct of the people, which is the principle of all great actions!" (p. 461).

Politics and Aesthetics

If we consider more closely Kant's description of the feeling of the sublime and the emergence of the moral law, a familiar paradox recurs: like Rousseau's idea of the common will, the feeling of the sublime encompasses both a universal appeal and a resolutely individual experience, without any mediation between the two.

> The delight in the sublime, no less than in the beautiful, by reason of its universal *communicability* not alone is plainly distinguished from other aesthetic judgements, but also from this same property acquires an interest in society (in which it admits of such communication). Yet, despite this, we have to note that *isolation from all society* is looked upon as something sublime, provided it rests upon ideas which disregard all sensible interest. (pp. 128–29, emphasis in original)

The lack of mediation between these two poles, the universal appeal of the sublime and its communicability on the one hand, the private experience of the sublime, better felt in isolation on the other, also excludes representation. For representation is meant to establish a link between the individual citizen, the private experience of the moral law, and its governing other, the elected government meant to be the expression of the (sublime) common will and the inscrutable moral law. This is why political representation fails. By instituting a system meant to translate the untranslatable, to mediate between the individual and the universal, political representation can never fail to betray the sublime.

Terry Eagleton makes this observation on the dual quality of the sublime experience (its individual component and its universal appeal):

> To judge aesthetically is implicitly to declare that a wholly subjective response is of the kind that every individual must necessarily experience, one that must elicit spontaneous agreement from them all. The aesthetic, one might argue, is in this sense the very paradigm of the ideological. . . . The aesthetic in Kant short-circuits the conceptual to link concrete particulars in their very immediacy to a kind of universal law, but a law which can be in no sense formulated. In the aesthetic, in contrast to the domains of pure and practical reason, the individual is not abstracted to the universal but is

somehow raised to the universal in its very particularity, manifesting it spontaneously on its surface. "In the phenomenon of the beautiful the inconceivable thing happens, that in contemplating beauty every subject remains in itself and is purely immersed in its own state, while at the same time it is absolved of all contingent particularity and knows itself to be the bearer of a total feeling which no longer belongs to 'this' or 'that'." (pp. 93–95) [22]

There are two points of particular importance in these comments. (1) The aesthetic experience "raises" the individual subject to the universal. There is no mediation. This experience has all the qualities of pure immediacy. (2) This universal law cannot be formulated, or rather it "can never be known in abstraction from the loose contingencies of subjective experience" (p. 95). This is, I would argue, where the aesthetic of the sublime comes to express the deepest anxiety of revolutionary thought, and this is why the word "sublime" is never simply an hyperbole in the richly hyperbolic revolutionary language. It expresses a feeling that can always be experienced subjectively and raise the subject to a recognizable universal level, but it also warns that there is no mediation possible between the subject and the universal. Kant's "short-circuit," to use Eagleton's word, cancels the very possibility of a go-between, and the space of the go-between is also that of political representation.

In a revolutionary ideology that meant to channel the "sublime enthusiasm" of the people toward a sublime religion, that of the Supreme Being, and to make the people favor public over private interests, the "sublime project" suffered from a double threat: the moral law it proclaimed defied all representation, and the political structure it relied on, by virtue of its representative principle, could only betray the sublime principles it meant to translate. The democratic intent of political representation was bound to be betrayed by the very system upon which it depended. It is possible that Robespierre's own words "sublime people" contained the key to that anxiety: that, for a category of eighteenth-century thinkers, and certainly for Rousseau, the very notion of "people" itself defied representation.

In *Leçons sur l'analytique du sublime*, Jean-François Lyotard, pondering Kant's historical situation, notes: "The beautiful contributed to Enlightenment, which is an emergence from childhood, as Kant said. But the sublime is a sudden blaze of light with no future."[23] Certainly Robespierre was aware of its impending demise when he wrote in his last discourse that the failure of universal moral law to guide the Republic would prevent any form of revolutionary victory. If crime and ambition are let loose, he added, armed victory alone will not save the revolutionary ideal. "Victory only arms ambition, puts patriotism to sleep, and, with its bright hands, digs the tomb of the Republic" (p. 572). In this instance, certainly, Bonaparte proved him right.

4

Against the Law

MICHELET, WHO WOULD ESTABLISH once and for all the great myths of the Revolution, described Saint-Just's discourse on the judgment of Louis XVI as follows: "Saint-Just went to the podium, and, dispassionately making an atrocious speech, said that there was no need to engage in a lengthy judgment of the King, but that he simply had to be killed."[1] It was Michelet's words, rather than Saint-Just's, that came to symbolize revolutionary violence: "dispassionately" conveying the cold and detached manner of the future terrorist, the cruelty implied by the powerful adjective "atrocious" and most of all, "to kill the king," which Michelet substitutes for Saint-Just's famous "le roi doit régner ou mourir" ("the King must reign or die"). With these words Michelet turns Saint-Just's legal argument into a cold order of execution. Michelet speaks of "terrible, outrageously violent, masterfully bloody words" (2: 73), but illustrates his point by simply quoting Saint-Just's appeal to posterity: "One day, men removed from our prejudices will marvel at the barbarism of a century when judging a tyrant was a religious act" (2: 73).

Michelet adds: "One could see already that this young man, this very young man, would not just be Robespierre's disciple, that he would walk at the same pace, or would even precede him in calling for violence, that one day perhaps he would be Robespierre's dangerous rival. And all this would have happened without Thermidor" (2: 74).

Michelet continues with an astonishing portrait of Saint-Just that is worth quoting in its entirety:

In shocking contrast, these cold and pitiless words came from a mouth that looked feminine. Without his fixed, hard blue stare, and the thick line of his brow, Saint-Just could have passed for a woman. Was it the Virgin of Taurid? No, neither the eyes nor the skin, white and delicate though it was, brought to mind a sense of purity. This very aristocratic skin had a singular brilliance and transparency, yet looked too beautiful and suggested a lack of health. The enormous cravat that he alone wore made his enemies say, perhaps without cause, that it hid his cold humors. His neck disappeared behind the cravat and the high starched collar; it made for a bizarre sight, as his long bust did not fit with this shortened neck. He had a very low forehead, and the top of his head seemed flattened so that his hair, although not long, almost touched his eyes. But strangest of all was his gait, which was quite characteristic and had the stiffness of an automaton. Next to Saint-Just's, Robespierre's rigidity was nothing. Was it the result of physical singularity, excessive pride or calculated dignity? It does not matter. One felt that a character so inflexible in his movements could similarly be inflexible in his heart. So when, in his discourse, as he went from the King to the Gironde, he turned suddenly toward the right side of the Assembly, and aimed his speech, his entire being and his deadly gaze at his colleagues, every one felt the chill of cold steel. (2: 74–75) [2]

Each line in this remarkable portrait betrays Michelet's own strange awe of Saint-Just,[3] as well as his belief that physical features reveal moral characteristics. Blue eyes are cold and calculating; they disclose Saint-Just's lack of passion, his insensitivity. The forehead is low, a sign of ferocity, and Saint-Just's physical stiffness displays for all to see his moral inflexibility.

Much could be written about Romantic historians' obsession with the skin. Mirabeau's face marked by smallpox, Marat's skin, repulsive and purulent, Robespierre's white face under his powdered wig, or Saint-Just's translucent skin: his was an aristocrat's white skin, but, Michelet warns, this was not a sign of purity. The remarkable lack of neck, or rather the dissimulation of the neck under the extravagant "cravate" and the high collar is teleological as well: Michelet's reading of Saint-Just is haunted by the guillotine. When he describes the audience already feeling the chill of cold steel, he himself responds to his own image of Saint-Just's gaze. During the Revolution and the Thermidorian reaction, the neck was the topic of strange and macabre jokes. One of them consisted in drawing a line around the neck, called the guillotine's necklace.

Strangest of all, however, is Michelet's sense of Saint-Just's femininity, suggested by the mouth and the fine quality of the skin, yet de-

Figure 7. Saint-Just. Eighteenth-century school. Collection Viollet.

nied by the steeliness of the gaze.[4] Or the claim that, while Saint-Just might have been taken for a woman, in no circumstances could he have been thought to be a virgin. For Michelet, Saint-Just is a combination of feminine softness (the mouth) and aristocratic haughtiness (the skin), a mixture of superficial virtue and deeper depravity (Saint-Just had just published an erotic satire called *Organt*). Inflexibility is inscribed in the physical stiffness, all dominated by a cold, calculating stare: a messenger of death.

The Sin of the Father

In order to understand Saint-Just's revolutionary ideal or his later assessment of the Terror, we must dwell a little longer on the exact nature of his contribution to the king's trial.[5] In the fall of 1792, the Convention endlessly debated the question of whether the king, a prisoner in the Temple, could be legally tried. Divided in its support for Louis XVI but pressed by the Parisian sections and the left wing of the Assembly, the Convention was preparing itself to judge the only person in France who was, in principle, "inviolable," that is, above the law. Until early November, the debate had been limited to questions of a legal nature, and no one had explicitly discussed the possible outcome of the trial: the king's death on the scaffold, a regicide.

"Fewer than sixty members of the Montagne wanted the King's execution," writes Michelet. "Who would brandish the sword of justice? The leaders of the Montagne abstained, remained in their seats. The sword of justice was borne by Saint-Just" (2: 73). Saint-Just, then a twenty-five-year-old representative from l'Aisne, gave his first speech to the Convention on 13 November. Michelet called this event the "terrible initiative" to make explicit to the Convention the necessary outcome of the trial, the beheading of Louis XVI.

Saint-Just's discourse had a chilling and powerful effect. Michelet adds: "His slow and measured words fell with a singular weight, sending shockwaves through the hall, like the weighty blade of the guillotine" (2: 74). Saint-Just's argument can be summed up in these few sentences from his speech: "This Committee's unique goal was to persuade you that the King had to be judged as a simple citizen; as for me, I say that the King must be judged as an enemy, and that our duty is not so much to judge as it is to punish," and he added: "I see no middle-ground: this man must reign or die."[6]

For Saint-Just—and in this he differed markedly from the rest of the Convention—the king was guilty because he was a king, that is

a usurper. Oblivious to the details of the prosecution, carefully prepared since August 1792, Saint-Just, followed by Robespierre, argued
that an ordinary trial was both illegitimate and unnecessary. Illegitimate, because the king was by definition inviolable, above the Law,
and thus could not be found guilty of any violation of the law. "You
seem to be looking for a law that would allow us to punish the King;
but in the form of government we have just abandoned, if there ever
was an inviolable man, he was that man" (p. 378).

An ordinary trial was also unnecessary, because a king was, by
virtue of being king, a criminal. Louis did not need to be judged,
but condemned, as would befit an enemy of the nation. For Saint-
Just, the king's guilt or innocence emanated not from his actions but
from the very nature of his authority. The king's empowerment, "by
the Grace of God," *de par la Grâce de Dieu*, was a usurpation, a theft
from the people's sacred rights. If the king had placed himself above
the law—that is, also in the position of an outlaw—there could be
no legitimate assessment of his guilt. The people's duty was not to
judge him but to punish his illegitimacy.

Saint-Just then delivered the most powerful and best-known words
of his discourse: "*On ne peut régner innocemment: la folie en est trop
évidente. Tout roi est un rebelle et un usurpateur*" (p. 379). ("One cannot reign innocently: the madness of it is quite obvious. A king is a
rebel and a usurper.") These five words, "*On ne peut régner innocemment*," have been taken to mean that power corrupts the powerful.
But this interpretation does not take into account the negative form
of Saint-Just's statement or its radically antithetical notion of power.
Saint-Just's wording suggests that the king is guilty by virtue of being
a king. But his guilt, his lack of innocence, is expressed in terms
that also entail the limits of his power. "One cannot" is expressed in
French by "*on ne peut*," a negative form of the verb "*pouvoir*." As a
substantive, "*pouvoir*" of course means "power," the very essence of
kingship. Thus the contradiction between "*on ne peut*" (a negation of
power) and "*régner*" (which is to hold *absolute* power) suggests that
the lack of innocence implicit in the exercise of absolute power also
limits absolute power, since he who holds absolute power does not
have the power to reign innocently.

The status of the absolute Monarch is thus doubly called into question. Not only is a king as such guilty (of usurping the power that should rightly belong to the people), but the king's absolute power (which was seen as a sacred right with supernatural effects) is an illusion as well. The oxymoronic formulation, *"On ne peut régner,"* denounces the belief that anyone can hold absolute power. Far from being the simple equivalent to the common idea that power has a corruptive effect on the empowered, *"on ne peut régner innocemment"* comes to represent a supreme negation of royal empowerment.

The failure of the king, an unavoidable loss of innocence, is not only a moral stain, an unforgivable sin, it also discloses for all to see the imposture of absolute monarchy: that there is no such thing as absolute power. If the king himself, the self-appointed holder of absolute power, has his power so strongly limited that he cannot be king without being guilty, what is then the nature of his power? And if the king cannot reign innocently, what, then, is the exact nature of his crime?

Against the Law

Just eighteen months before his discourse on the judgment of Louis XVI, Saint-Just had published a long essay entitled *L'Esprit de la Révolution et de la Constitution en France.* Historians have been puzzled by a work that decries the death penalty and whose idealism so strongly differs from the discourse that was to bring Louis XVI to the scaffold. Mona Ozouf calls it a "school exercise,"[7] a text she cannot reconcile with her image of Saint-Just as an intractable terrorist. Albert Soboul notes: "No historian has been able to understand how Saint-Just moved from an unreserved admiration for the Constitution of 1791 to the most inflexible republicanism, how he became a regicide."[8] I would like to argue that, contrary to most historians' views, *L'Esprit de la Révolution* explains Saint-Just's discourse on Louis XVI's trial by elucidating the nature of the king's crimes and his relationship to the nature of laws.

Indeed, *L'Esprit de la Révolution* offers the first intimation of Saint-Just's most constant and powerful belief: his passionate rejection of the laws. After criticizing the contemporary laws that, for example, penalized the adulterous wife while protecting the adulterous husband, or humiliated the innocent bastard, Saint-Just addresses the question of capital punishment. "Whatever my veneration for the authority of Jean-Jacques Rousseau, I do not forgive you, O great man, for having justified the death penalty; if the people cannot grant the right of sovereignty, how can it confer rights over life and death?" (p. 325).

Corrupt laws lead to crime, Saint-Just argues. He speaks of a people "made wicked by the nature of its laws" (p. 325). Thus, one should not pursue the crime but the abusive laws that push men to commit crimes in the first place. "As for me I will not submit to any law that assumes I am ungrateful and corrupt. . . . Arm yourself against the corruption of laws! . . . Let us make this clear: laws that reign through the power of the executioner, die in bloody violence and infamy" (pp. 325, 328). The laws "reign," writes Saint-Just, that is, laws exert a power similar to that of the king and father, since they are enacted by the king, in the name of the king, for his own sake and eternal glory.

Saint-Just's violent assault on the tyranny of the law has been thought to have influenced Sade. Indeed, Sade repeatedly echoed Saint-Just's admirable injunction against corrupt laws. "Without laws and religions human knowledge would today be at an unimaginable height of glory and greatness. . . . It is only in the moment of the laws' silence that great actions burst forth."[9] Gilles Deleuze comments on Saint-Just's political rejection of the laws and Sade's repeated attacks on them with these words: "It is significant that Sade attacks the regime of laws as being the regime of the tyrannized and of the tyrants. Only the law can tyrannize." Conversely, Deleuze notes: "Tyrants are created by the law alone: they flourish by virtue of the law."[10]

Whereas Sade proposes transcending the law by an absolute conversion to evil, Saint-Just proposes transcending the law by a resolute conversion to innocence. Like Sade's, Saint-Just's opposition does not result from his sole rejection of laws enacted by an abusive power, but more generally from his deep conviction that no law can possibly

reflect the people's will. As Miguel Abensour puts it, "The law is detached from the people's needs." Abensour quotes Saint-Just: "I dare
predict that sooner or later, man will trample his idols. What people
did not, eventually, despise its laws or its Gods?"[11]

In the chapter entitled "Of the Nature of Crimes," Saint-Just analyzes further the relationship between government and crime. Crime,
he argues, is always proportionate to the criminality of the governing
process: "In despotism, police legislates slavery; punishment is terrible; in humane governments, police protects freedom; punishment
is moderate and compassionate." And he adds: "All crimes stem from
tyranny which is the first crime of all" (p. 326). From this original
sin derive all others. First come repressive laws; they provoke crimes
that lead in turn to the ultimate iniquity, the death penalty.

Innocence, in this context, is not just the fact of being free from
guilt. Nor does it have anything to do with a Rousseauist state of
nature uncontaminated by society. In his unfinished *De la Nature,
de l'Etat civil, de la Cité*, probably written in 1792, Saint-Just specifies: "Alas! One can no longer dream of inspiring in men a taste for
innocence; men would become weak and depraved. Virtue itself is
no longer innocent. . . . Social man is a simple being, friend to other
men, but savage or political man is a cruel animal. The violence of
the law denatures him, tears him away from himself" (p. 926).

Jacques Lacan has made explicit the symbolic function that "since
the beginning of time" identifies the person of the father and the
"figure of the law."[12] Not surprisingly, Saint-Just directly links the
paternal order with the current state of corruption: "For example, in
most of our countries, the noble man recognizes only the eldest of his
sons and cuts out all others as offspring undeserving of his lineage"
(p. 927). For, above all, Saint-Just's opposition to laws stemmed from
his violent opposition to what the law represents, the name of the
father and the violence of paternal authority.

Saint-Just, in fact, founded his entire political argument on the rejection of the paternal image,[13] rejection of the name of the father,
be it embodied by the king, by the laws enacted by the king, or by
the aristocratic tradition of primogeniture that cut all children but
the first out of the father's will. The force of the law makes men

act against nature. The aristocrat, emulating the king, recognizes his firstborn son and rejects, "cuts off," symbolically castrates the others. The only innocence to which men who live in a depraved political state can aspire is the freedom from corrupted laws that generate such corrupted crimes as infanticide. It is not freedom from crimes, but freedom from the "law that assumes I am ungrateful and corrupt."

From this perspective, *"On ne peut régner innocemment"* takes on yet another meaning: the precise breach of innocence that characterizes tyranny is first of all the paternal enactment of criminal laws. Laws are criminal because they are designed not to protect the innocent, but to punish a crime they have in fact encouraged in the first place by their repressive character. Arguing eloquently against torture and the death penalty, Saint-Just had written before Louis XVI's trial: "Torture is a political crime, and the death penalty is a parricide enacted by the laws" (p. 327). This formulation is of particular interest since the crimes of parricide and regicide—that were to be so dramatically enacted in the execution of Louis XVI—were considered the most violent and heinous crimes of all. But, in *L'Esprit de la Révolution*, Saint-Just reversed the legal reasoning that led to such horrendous executions as that of Damiens, a case analyzed at length by Michel Foucault in *Discipline and Punish*.[14] In Saint-Just's mind, the crime is not the responsibility of the criminal, but that of tyranny which exacts the laws: "All crimes stem from tyranny which is the first crime of all" (p. 326). Crime is the burden of the law. Far from being a reparation toward the king, the death penalty is a double murder committed by the king himself, first through the person pushed to crime by tyrannical laws, then on the person of the guiltless, but convicted, victim.

It follows that the ultimate crime perpetrated by a corrupt law is the death penalty accompanied by torture. We know what atrocities were then committed in the name of the king on the body of the condemned: flesh torn, limbs severed, bodies burned. Saint-Just wrote, "The guilty man dies, and dies uselessly in rage and the cold sweat of a poignant agony; what indignity!" (p. 328). Such laws, which emanate from absolute power, themselves commit a parricide each and every time they send a man to the scaffold. For the natural father to whom an uncorrupted judicial system should always refer to is not the king, but the people.

"When I said that crime offended only the law [that declared them as crimes]", writes Saint-Just, "I did not, in any way, mean to infringe upon the rights of the wounded fatherland . . . [but] crimes of opinion are illusions created by customs and caused by laws. . . . The law that dictates making amends to God is fanatical. . . . In all cases, the blasphemer offends only the law on this earth that prohibits blasphemy. . . . Laws have been elevated to the rank of God" (pp. 326–27). Thus laws stand at the origin of corruption and crimes. And at the origin of laws, that have usurped God's power just as he has usurped the people's rights, stands the king. This is precisely what Saint-Just would mean a year later when he exclaimed: "*On ne peut régner innocemment.*" A king's crime is above all this: in order to maintain royal order, the king has to be unjust in the most serious and deadly manner, by enacting laws that are a crime against the people. The king stands as the origin, the cruel father of all the corrupted laws enacted in his name. Reversing the concept that every crime committed is a crime committed against the king, Saint-Just argued that every punishment, every torture and death executed under the laws of the king, is a crime committed by the king, the unnatural father, the "père dénaturé," against his children, the people.

Thus the king's criminality—which cannot be judged by laws he is not bound to obey—is compounded by all the crimes perpetrated by the people during his rule. "His crimes are written everywhere with the blood of the people," exclaims Saint-Just (p. 378). Louis XV should bear forever the double guilt of Damiens' attempted regicide and that of his horrendous death, just as Louis XVI must be found guilty of the crimes so publicly punished on the stage of the execution. Torture and the death penalty are but visible signs of the king's invisible but deadly sin. How appropriate, then, that the executioner be seen as the king's hand, veiled but lethal, endowed with the same illegitimate hereditary power. Kantorowitz and Foucault's well-known thesis that the body of the condemned man "represents the symmetrical, inverted figure of the king,"[15] like a somber double, is made yet more explicit and radical in Saint-Just's reflections on crime and innocence, but with the difference that, for Saint-Just, each and every condemned man being led to the scaffold stands really *where* the body of the king himself should stand. Not because the criminal has offended the king, but because he embodies the king's crime, which is the origin of all corruption.

Saint-Just's discourse on Louis XVI's trial, far from being a convenient, if forceful, accusation motivated by the politics of the Montagne, reflected, at a deeper level, his own thoughts on crime, innocence, and, above all, the unjust imposition of laws. Saint-Just's indictment of Louis XVI is the unavoidable conclusion of the absolute rejection of the name of the father already at work in his previous writings.

Maternal Institutions

To the blind ferocity of the paternal law, the law that allows the depraved father to cut out his sons, Saint-Just contrasted the "douceur" of the "institutions."[16] In his posthumous work *Fragments d'institutions républicaines*, Saint-Just proposed the establishment of a republic that would substitute for the criminal oppression of laws that always mask the name of the father, the power of institutions that above all protect the mother and her child. As Deleuze puts it:

The institution . . . tends to render laws unnecessary, to replace the system of rights and duties by a dynamic model of action, authority and power. Saint-Just accordingly demanded that there should be many institutions and few laws, and proclaimed that the Republic could not be a republic so long as laws had the supremacy over institutions. . . . Saint-Just pointed out the following inverse relation: the fewer the institutions, the greater the number of laws (as in monarchy and despotism); the fewer laws, the greater the number of institutions (the republic). (p. 77)

But the role of institutions, in Saint-Just's thought, is not only to protect the people from the rule of the tyrant; it is, more explicitly still, to protect the mother and her child from the violence of the father. Indeed, institutions are best defined as the system that will allow the child's freedom and shield it from an unjust father. He

writes: "Long laws are a public calamity. Wisdom is in children. . . .
We suggest to you civil institutions that will allow a child to resist the
oppression of a powerful and iniquitous man" (p. 968). The opposition between the wisdom of the oppressed child and the power of an
unjust man frames Saint-Just's political and social theory.

"There are too many laws and too few civilian institutions," he
repeats, "a law contrary to institutions is a tyrannical law. . . . One
needs few laws. Where there are so many, the people is in slavery. . . .
Where man has to obey a rule that does not recognize his goodness,
there is neither liberty nor homeland. He who gives his country too
many laws is a tyrant. The name of law can only sanction despotism."
"The idea of obeying the law is not clear," he observed, "for the law
is often nothing but the will of he who enacts it. One has the right to
resist an oppressive will" (p. 976).

By contrast, institutions will establish the innocent and humane
influence of a new family order where—and this has never been
pointed out—the maternal principle will be equal, if not superior to,
the paternal order. The first institution outlined by Saint-Just is that
of the family, and his first injunction is against violence: "He who
strikes a child will be banished" (p. 980). For this is the unforgivable
sin of the father, his repeated violence against children. In a first draft,
he had noted, "Male children are raised until the age of five by father
and mother" (p. 981). But on the following page he wrote: "Children belong to their *mother* until the age of five if she suckled them,
and then they belong to the republic until their death. . . . Between
the age of five and sixteen, children will be raised by the fatherland"
(p. 982). Thus the nourishing mother, and her symbolic equivalent,
the "patrie" (and for Saint-Just this oxymoronic concept is not derived from the paternal system but from the maternal order, "la mère
patrie") take over the education of all male children.

"No one is allowed to interfere with his child's wishes, no matter his social status" (p. 984). Children must be protected at all costs
from paternal violence and from the father's decisions regarding their
personal life. Further measures are added to protect women and children from paternal abuse. Indeed, the first death penalty mentioned
in the "Institutions" is required against batterers. "He who strikes a
woman will be punished by death" (p. 986). Thus, institutions are

systems designed to protect maternal filiation. They must be substituted for laws, systems that always, necessarily, betray paternal violence and lead to crimes.[17] Institutions are the guarantee of freedom; they vindicate the battered woman and child. Above all, institutions are the child's protection from the law of the father, from the father's name and his inescapable violence.

Law and Terror

During the course of the twenty months that separated his discourse on the trial of Louis XVI from his own death on the scaffold, Saint-Just delivered but a few powerful reports; paradoxically, they combined a sense of inflexible justice with a consistent desire for moderation. This last aspect has been often erased from analyses of his writings. On 26 February 1794 Saint-Just again addressed the Convention, in the name of the Committee of Public Safety and Committee of General Security. His report, which asked for the immediate release of persons unjustly incarcerated and for the seizure of all property belonging to known enemies of the Republic, contained curiously contrasting formulations. On the one hand, this text supplied the best examples of Saint-Just's rigid sense of justice: "I don't know how to express myself in half tones; I am without indulgence for the enemies of my country. I know only justice. . . . Justice is not clemency, but severity" (pp. 699, 702). Finally, perhaps his most famous formulation: "The people's liberty is founded by the sword of justice" (p. 703).

But the conclusion of the discourse remains ambiguous. In it, he uses the word "terror," as was current during the Revolution, to describe and condemn not the trials and executions ordered by the Revolutionary Tribunal, but rather the unchecked massacres, the street violence, and the excesses that accompanied the rule of the sans-culottes.

Let no wrong be excused or left unpunished by the government; justice is more formidable to the enemies of the Republic than terror alone. So many traitors have escaped terror, *that speaks*, who would not escape justice, that weighs all crimes in its hand! Justice condemns the enemies of the people and the supporters of tyranny among us to eternal slavery. Terror lets them hope for an end to it. . . . Justice serves the happiness of the people and consolidates the new order of things; terror is a double-edged sword, used by some to avenge the people, and by others to serve tyranny; terror filled the prisons but left the guilty unpunished; terror swept through like a storm. Expect durable severity in the public character only from the strength of institutions. (p. 706, emphasis added) [18]

Terror is the response to the tyranny of the laws, the crime of the father. But justice is the institution that, in the end, will restore a legitimate order and protect the innocent. For Saint-Just, terror once again masks the terrible face of the tyrant and his tragic inheritance.

As Michelet pointed out, Saint-Just's own idea of justice was to condemn "the privileged, the nobles and the priests," not to the guillotine but to forced labor: "Rights, morality, revolution, three identical things. The counterrevolutionary and the immoral man, who are one and the same, must be equally humiliated, put in chains, breaking stones to make roads and forming a group of slaves. They subjected the people to the *corvées*. Now it is theirs! . . . The privileged, the nobles and the priests will be, by right, galley slaves." Michelet comments: "When the dreamer brought his idea to the Committee of Public Safety, with the assurance of a sleepwalker advancing with closed eyes, he found a locked door. Not a single voice supported him" (2: 851).

It is interesting to note that in this instance of moderation, on the occasion when Saint-Just, left to himself, describes the most desirable way to punish the enemies of the nation while avoiding the death penalty, Michelet imagines him with closed eyes, the steely gaze that evoked the guillotine blade suddenly veiled, as in a preview of death. For Michelet, Saint-Just the terrorist, a few weeks from his own death, was already redeemed by his upcoming execution, purified by his sacrifice rather than by his call for a more humane justice. But for Saint-Just—and this is crucial—the opposition between terror and inflexible justice duplicates the opposition between the rule of an abusive father and the institution that protects innocence.

In his fateful indictment of Danton, Saint-Just once again defined his position in the most dramatic terms:

Those who have conspired under the veil of patriotism for the last four years, now that justice threatens them, repeat the words of Vergniaud: "The Revolution is like Saturn, it will devour all its children." . . . No, the Revolution will devour not its children but its enemies no matter the impenetrable disguise! Were the conspirators who have perished the children of liberty just because they resembled her for a moment? The Revolution will devour every single friend of tyranny; not a single true patriot will perish through justice. . . . Therefore be inflexible: leniency is ferocious because it threatens the fatherland. (p. 777)[19]

What is terror for Saint-Just? In his famous discourse of 17 Pluviôse, Year II (5 February 1794) Robespierre had exclaimed: "If the mainspring of popular government in peacetime is virtue, the mainspring of popular government in time of war is both virtue and terror: virtue without which terror is fateful; terror without which virtue is helpless."[20] But for Saint-Just "terror is a double-edged sword. . . . A republican government has only one principle, which is virtue; or else terror. What do they want, those who want neither virtue nor terror?" (p. 978). For Saint-Just, virtue is the only principle of the republic; terror is the failure of virtue. "All the intermediary powers had taken hold of terror," Saint-Just wrote just before his death. "Liberty and government had more to fear than aristocracy" (p. 1009). Reflecting on the desolate state of France in the spring of 1794, he added: "A chill has fallen on the Revolution; all principles have been weakened; all that remain are conspiracies in red caps. The exercise of terror has left crime indifferent, just as strong liquors eventually tire the palate" (p. 979).

Not that terror is avoidable: terror is the unavoidable answer to the violence of the father. But like the violent father, terror is contrary to nature: "Terror served tyranny." Terror represents the unnatural response to the unnatural crime of the oppressive tyrant. "Doubtless, it is not yet time to do good," Saint-Just writes. "The specific good we do now is a palliative. One must wait for a general evil powerful enough to move general opinion towards measures conducive to the general good. . . . Revolution must stop at the perfection of happiness and public liberty through law" (p. 979).

The perfection of happiness, the ultimate goal of all revolutions, coincides with the supreme moment when legitimate laws and public freedom are finally reconciled. But, far from suggesting a return to the *imperium* of the father's law, Saint-Just imagines the law integrated with, and contained by, domestic institutions.

The Name of the Father

Saint-Just wrote the last *Fragments d'institutions républicaines* just a few days before his execution. The knowledge of his impending death made him reflect not only on the changing values that were once again stifling the Revolutionary movement but also on his own ideals and the obvious failure of his dreams. The last fragments reveal an acute awareness of his approaching execution and an extraordinary reevaluation of his own debt to the father's name. Reflecting on his past idealism, he noted:

I believed that truth and its rule were invincible. This is why, no matter my fate, I shall leave this legacy to memory. . . . Circumstances are difficult only for those who fear the grave. I beg for the grave, as a blessing of providence, so that I will no longer be a witness to the infamous deeds plotted against my country and humanity. One leaves very little behind, when one leaves an unhappy life in which one is condemned to die an accomplice or a witness to crime. . . . All I have now before my eyes is the path that leads me to my dead father and the steps of the Panthéon. (p. 1008)

Thus, the death he awaits will bring an ultimate reconciliation, and a glorious one between the rebellious son and the dead father. Saint-Just will be reunited with his father and will enter the Pantheon, the revolutionary monument dedicated to the Great Men who served the fatherland.

The dead father is present as well in this striking admission, written probably a few days earlier: "I do not like new words, I know only the just and the unjust; these words are understood by all consciences" (p. 969).

This ultimate repudiation of the new symbolic order, Saint-Just's remarkable meditation on his own name and on his father's name, "*je ne connais que le juste et l'injuste,*" offers a single and poignant recognition of a legitimate paternal order, where the name of the father finally echoes the truth of the maternal institution: justice. Saint-Just knows he will die as a "martyr." One might add, as a saint. In these final, beautiful, and desperate notes, Saint-Just reconciles himself to the terrible truth of the father's name. In his name, he also recognizes the most powerful of institutions, knowing at the same time that justice will not be served by his death. Repudiating all new words, Saint-Just accepts in his father's name the truth of a name that rejects all tyrannical laws but whose path leads straight to the scaffold.

PART II

LAST WILL AND
TESTAMENT

5

Around Midnight: Closing Time

C'est le rêve pur d'un Minuit, en soi
disparu
—Mallarmé, *Igitur* (1869)[1]

Michelet's History

THE END OF A CENTURY rarely coincides with a date on the calendar. Least of all the end of the eighteenth century, the only one in modern history to have completed its centennial cycle well before the appointed day. Indeed, on December 31, 1799, no one was mourning a dying century. Still operating under the revolutionary calendar instituted eight years earlier, Bonaparte had just proclaimed a new constitution for the dawning century, the Constitution de l'An VIII, in which he proclaimed: "Citizens, the Revolution is now engraved in its original principles. The Revolution is over."

Bonaparte's words emphasized the fact that the only ending that mattered at this close of the eighteenth century was that of the Revolution. It was an ending not described, only announced, declared, officially ratified. This ending, however, could be seen not only as the final dismissal of revolutionary principles, but as a powerful death knell. The Revolution was over and the consul took power, not as usurper but as legitimate heir. In this way, an absolute ending was also erased. The Revolution was over but would live on through the new Constitution. This announced ending, Bonaparte tells us, does not *put an end* to the Revolution; on the contrary, it immortalizes it.

The act of describing an ending, the enunciation of closure, simultaneously dissimulates the historical rupture and transforms the conclusion into a new beginning. Linearity is restored, continuity is saved, legitimacy assured. How could it be possible to write the absolute end? How can the historian transcribe the irrevocable character of a complete rupture, which nothing and no one survives, with, above all, no witnesses, no participants, no narrators? Indeed, if there is a proper *narrative* of endings, it is never linked to the end itself, which is nothing but a silence comparable to Blanchot's vision of disaster. In Blanchot's words, to think the disaster is "to have no longer any future in which to think it."[2] *L'écriture de la fin* is, among other things, absolute silence, and thus the impossibility of writing the end. In this perspective, history itself is no longer conceivable.

By contrast, *stories* of endings, as they are related to us in historiographical narratives,[3] are never similar to what I would call the *écriture de la fin*, where death is the agency and where all form of writing is forever disrupted. Rather, these stories are comparable to narrative conclusions—that is, anticipated endings—or to the acknowledgment of a decease, an imposed and unannounced death quickly surrounded by multiple texts: testaments, autopsies, obituaries, epitaphs. In this context, Michelet's struggle with the end of the Revolution, linked in his mind to the end of the eighteenth century and the conclusion of his formidable opus, *Histoire de la Révolution française*, discloses a troubled relationship between the need to remember and the desire for oblivion. In his text the narrative of the end of the Revolution is disrupted by the *écriture de la fin*, this unforeseeable disruptive power that makes death impossible to *re-tell*. Narrative is thus interrupted and moments of silence, blanks, failed descriptions, punctuate the text. In these silences, in these failures, we can also witness the unspeakable end of the Revolution and the limits of historiography.

"Et ce temps ne va pas comme jadis s'arrêter . . ."

In the 1847 Introduction to his *Histoire de la Révolution française*, Michelet describes the loss that framed his great project. The people, he writes, "has repudiated its friend. . . . Nay, its own *father*, the great eighteenth century! They have forgotten that the eighteenth century founded liberty on the enfranchisement of the mind, — til then bound down by the flesh, bound by the material principle of the double incarnation, theological and political, kingly and sacerdotal."[4] The current century, he argues, has betrayed its paternal legacy, the glorious achievement of the Revolution. "Our fathers, we must repeat, did all that it was necessary then to do, — began precisely as it was incumbent on them to begin" (p. 9). For Michelet this "beginning," the legitimate foundation of the law, is first of all an erasure, the obliteration of a double hereditary burden. Our fathers, Michelet argues, first did away with the doctrine of original sin, which posits that "injustice is transmitted with our blood from father to son" (p. 10), as well as that of aristocratic entitlement, the unjust transmission of wealth and privileges from father to son. "Thus does this false liability for the action of others disappear from the world. The *unjust transmission of good*, perpetuated by the rights of the nobility; the *unjust transmission of evil*, by original sin, or the civil brand of being descended from sinners, are erased by the Revolution" (p. 10, emphasis in original).[5]

For Michelet, writing the history of the French Revolution consists in retrieving the lost century, the accomplishments of our fathers. Yet this accomplishment is first of all an erasure; it is in itself an abolition of the past. Michelet's project is thus framed by a double, at times conflictual, anxiety: to reassert the legitimacy of dismissing the past, as our fathers did, and the need for the sons to reclaim the very past that repudiated the burden of history. Michelet's history of the Revolution is both erasure and remembrance, a devout memorial to a dramatic disowning of the past. The text is punctuated by his efforts to translate, and account for, what he calls "le vide" or "l'effacement" ("emptiness" and "erasure"), metaphors of the *tabula rasa* that would allow history to start anew, innocent of all sins. Echoing the paternal project, Michelet opens the text with these lines:

At the present period of the year, when my teaching is suspended, — when my work weighs heavy upon me, and the weather becomes oppressive, . . . Then I wander to the Champ de Mars. I sit down on the parched grass, and I breathe in the great wind that flows over the arid plain.
The Champ de Mars! This is the only monument left behind by the Revo-

lution. . . . The Empire has its column, and engrosses almost exclusively the Arch of Triumph; Monarchy has its Louvre, its Invalids; the feudal church of the twelfth century is still enthroned at Notre-Dame; even the Romans have the Thermae of Caesar.

And the Revolution has for its monument . . . this emptiness.

Its monument is this sandy plain, flat as Arabia. (pp. 3–4, translation modified)

The repeated use of ellipses, not a frequent occurrence in Michelet's *Histoire*, inscribes in the text an absolute emptiness that words inevitably fail to convey. Rising up against "a forgetful generation" that dares to use this vast expanse "as the theater of its vain amusements," Michelet proposes to capture the elusive wind, an inspiration, that blows over the barren plain. It becomes in turn the measure and the goal of the historian's project: to fill a wasteland deserted by language.

Over the emptiness of a large esplanade stripped of monuments, like a blank page, Michelet can start to build his own literary memorial and to reconstruct on the Champ de Mars the verbal architecture of a forgotten legacy. Thus framed, his narrative restores as necessary beginning the act of erasure accomplished by the founding fathers. The *Histoire de la Révolution française* proclaims itself as the narrative of a paternal deed whose own end was to abolish hereditary transmission. How can Michelet accomplish the filial duty to commemorate a paternal oblivion? How can one express the duty to remember those who made it their duty to repudiate the past?

The genealogical disruptions presiding over the revolutionary project, as erasure, and Michelet's own narrative endeavor, as retrieval, are themselves framed by a loss, the death of Michelet's father. In the last lines of his Introduction, Michelet notes: "I have lost him who so often narrated the scenes of the Revolution to me, him whom I revered as the image and venerable witness of the Great Age, that is, of the eighteenth century. I have lost my father" (pp. 13–14). The day after his father's funeral, Michelet wrote in his *Journal*:

My father was my father, my cause and reason of being, in a sense much more special than that suggested by the word [father]. . . . With him, many things perished, not only for his son, but for the historian himself. He had

seen the Old Regime, the Revolution, the Restoration and the July Monarchy, and the ruin of the July Monarchy. He was tradition itself. Particularly
for the eighteenth century and for the Revolution.[6]

Michelet further associates the possibility of writing, or continuing
to write, the *Histoire de la Révolution française* as the echo of a voice
from the past, with that of finishing the history of a century/a Revolution, which is also the history of his own father. He notes: "Before
1800, my father starts dying within himself, starts living through me,
with faith in my future. . . . I was born of the eighteenth century, I
left it at times but always came back to it. Always, I found my father
there" (*Journal*, 1: 657). Michelet, born in 1798, is claiming the Revolution as his own personal legacy.

For Michelet, the formidable project of writing history consisted
in recovering in the darkest episodes of the Revolution the lost paternal image. His project expresses as well his need to reclaim the past
as spoken by this privileged witness, his father. In *Michelet, Historian: Rebirth and Romanticism in Nineteenth-Century France*, Arthur
Mitzman offers a scrupulous evaluation of the relationship between
Michelet's biography and the writing of his works. He pays particular attention to the writing of the fall of the Bastille, written at the
time Michelet lost his father.[7] But the loss first resulted in a dramatic
interruption of Michelet's work. "The Present claims me again" (1:
655). The present is seen as the loss of these "irretrievable days" that
vanished too soon (p. 657). Michelet is experiencing an historical dis-
ruption, a rupture comparable to the one he set out to describe and
evaluate in his *Histoire*. From then on, his writing is subtly transformed. He sets out to explain and evaluate this "erasure," which is
also the condition of all beginnings; the same day, Michelet writes
in his *Journal*: "The new life is more demanding: it claims the sacrifice and the death of all that preceded it" (p. 656). But—and this
is also the paradox with which he was struggling—he has to break
the silence of the survivors. Gérard Walter notes "this role, new for
him, as undertaker of exhumations."[8] Michelet writes to the families
of members of the Convention, asking them to send to him writings
and letters, but he meets with indifference or hostility at almost every
turn. He complains bitterly: "Strange reaction: very few families

are willing to help me; they would prefer to forget entirely those horrible memories, burying the ghosts that frighten them and whose names they still bear with regret" (p. xxii).

At this point a number of personal and intellectual anxieties interrupt Michelet's writing of the French Revolution. Against the repudiation of the father's name by indifferent heirs, Michelet set the legitimation of his own historical project, a testimonial to his father's memories of the great century. Fascinated by the revolutionary repudiation of "false legacies," he struggles to recreate his father's words. Just before beginning the writing of the last months of the Revolution, exiled in Nantes, he notes: "I plunge into my subject in the night of winter. The howling winds and tempests that have been rattling my windows for the last two months offer a grave and harrowing accompaniment to my 93 *Dies Irae*. Legitimate harmonies!" (*HR*, 2: 696) Michelet's *Journal* echoes these images of death: "*From witra in wintra.*—From winter to winter. I plunge into both winters, that of '52 and that of '93. Twice, thrice dark: for I too, walk towards winter. . . . I finished yesterday *The Death of the Girondins*'" (*Journal*, 2: 208).

But just a few months earlier, before leaving Paris for Nantes where he would complete the last terrible days of the Revolution and the conclusion of his great work,[9] Michelet visited a cemetery. Not, as one might expect, his father's grave, this "dreadful burial place," this "hideous human sepulture" at the Père-Lachaise, but the anonymous public land where the remains of the great revolutionaries were buried. He wrote on 19 May 1852 that leaving Paris, his familiar routine, and above all "these papers, that are like an old child's entrails," was like dying. "Dying to them was also in part dying myself, since they had lived through me for the last thirty years. But on the way I had taken a vigorous tonic, an homeopathic remedy against death. I had visited the cemetery of the Terror" (p. 193).

His description of the Monceau Gardens, where Madame Roland, Vergniaud, Robespierre, and Saint-Just were buried, is strangely similar to that of the Champ de Mars, a barren and sandy plain, sterile and deserted. But, he notes, "This miserable little piece of earth holds these immense remains, the sacred alluvial deposits of a vanished world. And it hardly shows. Nothing but a few bones, some dry and empty skulls. . . . I started writing again" (pp. 193–94). In the long and extraordinary description of the *Journal*,[10] images of silence and sterility yield renewed energy. The miraculous "homeopathic remedy against death" retrieves from this abandoned land the buried passions of Robespierre, the courage of Madame Roland, the fatal words of Saint-Just. For Michelet, writing is not associated with the idea of breaking the silence, retrieving the Revolution from oblivion; writing results directly from these multiple deaths: his father's death, Robespierre's death. From their silence Michelet draws the strength to write. Between the inaccessible experience of those who lived the Revolution and what Blanchot calls "the inexperience of dying,"[11] Michelet found his reason for writing. His concluding chapters of the *Histoire* are an epitaph engraved on these forgotten tombstones. After this visit, Michelet tells us, he can proceed with writing the end.

Robespierre's Signature

". . . la parole qui absolut Minuit"

For many historians, the end of Robespierre coincided with the end of the Revolution itself. Albert Mathiez stated it clearly in the opening pages of his work on the aftermath of the Revolution: "The great era of the Republic is now *over*. The Convention became a free-for-all where shady, more or less clever dealers displayed their varying talents. . . . Most of the Romantic historians could not withstand this spectacle. Michelet ended his *Histoire de la Révolution* on 9 Thermidor, as if what came later was not worth retelling."[12] Gérard Walter, commenting on Michelet's dramatic writing of the last days, noted: "The end: Michelet and Robespierre face off alone, their eyes locked. There is no one else left. Just corpses lying at the foot of the scaffold. And when the time comes for the Master of the Revolution to take his place among them, Michelet understands that the Revolution is over. All that remains for him to do is to draw the final line after the date of 9 Thermidor" (Avant-Propos, *HR*, 1: xxv).

In February 1853, Michelet foresaw the end of his work. He notes in his *Journal*: "The cemetery of the Terror left me with a sad, powerful but arid impression that I took with me when I left Paris. It grew in me, in the concentration of my work. I travelled through the arid wasteland without seeing anything." Past "the terrible companion of '93", Michelet emerged "from the winter, and from that moral [spiritual] winter. . . . I have reached in my book April 6, the day of Danton's death. I still have to go through the death of the Terror itself" (*Journal*, 2: 213). Then, strikingly, the *Journal* falls silent. Michelet was writing the end. On 15 June he notes: "Two and a half months, filled, without taking a breath, with the great rush of events that concluded the *Revolution*" (215). Nine days later, his exile ended and his work completed, Michelet returned to Paris.

If the *Journal* remains silent on what it meant to write the death of Robespierre, which is also the death of the Revolution and, finally, that of the great century to which his father bore testimony, Michelet betrayed on several occasions, in the *Histoire* itself, the funereal rituals that presided over his closing remarks. The first chapter of the last book is entitled "Of the Cemeteries of the Terror." The reader recognizes in these pages the vivid impressions Michelet previously noted in his *Journal*: "Having reached the height of the Terror, I find, like on the summit of great mountains, an extreme aridity, a lifeless desert" (*HR*, 2: 923). The pun seems to be there by chance alone. The idea of aridity, of a desert swept by revolutionary winds, also echoes the premises of the 1847 Preface. The next sentences, however, immediately deny the emotion that we now know—but only since the publication of the *Journal*—Michelet was experiencing and remembering. He lies: "Everything I am about to describe is literally extracted from the dry administrative documents of the time. Pity was dead or mute" (2: 923). There is no mention of his visit to the cemetery, of his personal and moving notes on the barren piece of earth, *mute* also, that received the last remains of the great revolutionaries. ("How can the earth . . . remain so cold and so mute?") Like the unmarked graves of the abandoned cemetery, Michelet remains silent.

Another episode in the last book of the *Histoire* allows a glimpse into Michelet's struggle. Here again what we have called *l'écriture de la fin* undermines the very text that attempts to describe and circumscribe the ending. The episode described by Michelet took place a few hours before Robespierre's execution. The plot to overthrow Robespierre, led by Tallien and Billaud-Varenne, had been anticipated by Saint-Just, who discussed it explicitly in his last writings. Robespierre himself came to the Convention on the morning of 8 Thermidor ready to confront his enemies. In a long and dogmatic discourse, he denounced, without naming them, the "traitors" who were, as he was speaking, betraying the fatherland. This discourse may have precipitated his arrest; he read it again that same evening at the Société des Jacobins, adding simply, "My friends, you have just heard my death testament." [13]

On 9 Thermidor, when Robespierre returned to the Convention and tried to speak, he was interrupted and a decree of arrest was immediately voted against him and four of his friends, Lebas, Couthon, Saint-Just, and the young Robespierre. They were taken to various jails, only to be freed a few hours later by forces of the Commune that had remained loyal to them. When night fell, Robespierre found himself with his brother Robespierre the young, Saint-Just, Legrand, Payan, Lerebours, Louvet, and Couthon at the Commune House, where they deliberated at some length on what to do next. The situation was critical. Although the troops of the Paris Commune had been loyal to Robespierre, the Convention was still in command of the army. Indeed, when the Convention learned of the liberation of its latest victims, it voted them *hors-la-loi, proscrits*, that is, for all purposes, deserving of death in the name of the law.

During the long night, as Robespierre and his friends debated their next move, several messages may have been sent. One letter, addressed to the Section des Piques, Robespierre's and Saint-Just's own section, bore the following words:

Courage, Patriots of the Section des Piques. Liberty triumphs. Already, those whose resolve has made them formidable to traitors are free. Everywhere the people shows itself worthy of its character. The meeting place is at the Commune, whose orders will be carried out by the brave Henriot in order to save the Fatherland.

At the bottom of the page, one can still decipher the signatures of Legrand, Payan, Lerebours, and Louvet, all members of the Executive Committee of the Commune, and, further down, what looks like the unfinished, yet unmistakable, signature of Robespierre. In his very precise, small hand appear the first two letters of his name, *Ro*.

These two letters are the last to have been written by Robespierre's hand. At the very moment he was signing, or perhaps a few moments later—there are contradictory accounts—the Commune was invaded by troops that had remained loyal to the Convention. In the brief struggle that ensued, Robespierre was wounded in the jaw, either by himself or by others.[14] He was executed the next day with twenty of his friends, their bodies thrown into a common grave and covered with quicklime.

Here is Michelet's account of Robespierre's unfinished signature:

Saint-Just, Couthon, Coffinhal, almost all of them wanted to act. Robespierre wanted to wait. And, in spite of what has been said, he had good reasons. To change role, to start a war against the Law, was also to erase in a single instant the goal of his entire life, to ink out with his own hand the idea that had inspired his life, that had given him his strength. On the other hand, to have asked Couthon to come, to have imperiled so many friends! . . . "Then, all we have left to do is die?" said Couthon.

These words seemed to shake his resolve. He took a sheet of paper with the stamp of the Commune, a paper on which a call to insurrection had been already written, and writing slowly and with a calm hand, he wrote three letters which are still visible: Rob. . . . [sic] But at that point, his conscience cried out, and he threw away his pen.

"Go ahead, and write," they told him. —*But in whose name?*

He sealed his fate with these words. But he saved himself in history, and posterity. (*HR*, 2: 980, emphasis in original)

In his *Mémoires*, Barras, a member of the National Convention who had been actively engaged in the plot against Robespierre, wrote the following: "In a report which was made to me on the circumstances of Robespierre's agony, I found that on several occasions he had asked for a pen, as he could no longer speak, and that the members of the committee had refused to accede to his request. I was told of this fact and did not witness it, for I should not have refused the dying man a pen which, in the absence of speech, could have pro-

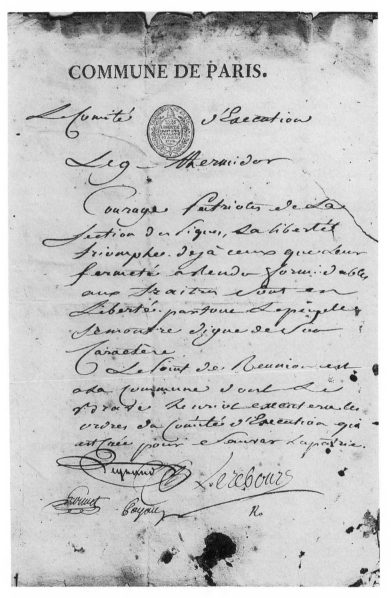

Figure 8. Robespierre's last unfinished signature, 9 Thermidor. Musée Carnavalet. Collection Viollet.

duced some revelations, that last cry of truth, which others might want to suppress."[15]

The letter to the Section des Piques, bearing Robespierre's incomplete signature, is thus also his last writing. It can be said to have expressed Robespierre's last will if his signature was interrupted by the arrival of the Convention troops, or simply his last scruple if he himself had ultimately refused to endorse what he saw as an illegitimate call to insurrection. This letter became immediately controversial. Barère, who presided over the Convention on 11 Thermidor, anxious to justify the hasty executions that had taken place the previous day, exclaimed: "Here is the letter, on which are written the two letters R. B. [sic], the first letters of the name of this cruel and deceitful conspirator. Here it is, this infamous letter which, at the time of danger to the Republic, sees nothing but the civil servants of a commune, and in revolutionary turmoil, can imagine no worthier meeting place than the commune house."[16]

Directly implicated by this letter, the Section des Piques later suggested, as proof of its loyalty to the Convention, that the letter had been sent and received but that, angered by Robespierre's duplicity, the Section had forwarded it to the Convention. There is of course no evidence of this and Barère never mentioned it. But certainly, from the 9th to the 11th of Thermidor, possession of this letter was dangerous. Until after Robespierre's execution, it was an incitement to revolt whose price, in case of failure, would have been fatal. In order to protect itself further, the Section des Piques sent a special note to the Convention claiming that "identical letters" had been received and burned "with indignation."

Whatever route the sheet bearing Robespierre's unfinished signature may have taken—and this remains a mystery—the status of these two precise letters *Ro*   and of the blank that followed them immediately provoked a passionate debate. In his *Mémoires*, Barras described his understanding of the circumstances of the letter: "Surprised by the arrival of Merlin de Thionville, frightened by the irruption of the men who accompanied him, completely despairing of his cause, Robespierre did not finish appending his signature and sought, as I have already said, to strike himself so as not to fall in

Figure 9. Maximilien de Robespierre, député d'Artois. Collection and copyright Robert L. Dawson. Detail: representation of Robespierre shot and wounded by the gendarme Merda during the night of 9 Thermidor.

our hands" (p. 301). A close examination of the letter shows, next to Robespierre's incomplete name, a dark spot that was believed to be blood but was not analyzed until many years later. In March 1946, the Service de l'Identité Judiciaire of the Préfecture de Police de Paris, for reasons unknown, became interested in the document and determined that the spot was indeed blood.[17]

This stain, perhaps Robespierre's blood (as he was already wounded when the guards came to arrest him), could be considered as the complement to the incomplete signature, both a sign and an imprint, tragically validating, if not Robespierre's will, at least the document's authenticity. In the historical narrative of this purloined letter, the stain supplements the unfinished signature; it is the indispensable trace allowing for a plausible reconstitution of the events leading to the writing, and the interruption, of the signature.

Another series of documents and testimony, however, greatly complicates the matter, evidence that raises not only the legal question of how and in what circumstances a signature can be validated, but also the question of what *authorizes*, in the strongest sense of the term, that is, what gives authority to, the signing of one's name. Various police reports tell of the discussion that surrounded the interrupted signature. Dulac, a policeman who found himself on duty at the Commune House on 9 Thermidor, described the event as follows: "After having embraced Robespierre, [Couthon] said: 'We must write to the armies.' 'In whose name?' the other replied? 'In the name of the Convention: is it not always wherever we are? And with the armed forces loyal to us, the seditious elements will be dispersed.' Whereupon Robespierre said: 'One must write in the name of the French people.'"[18] The gendarmes Jerôme and Jean-Pierre Javoir reported a similar discussion: "Robespierre and Couthon said aloud, we cannot write to our armies in the name of the Convention, nor in the name of the Commune since it would be stopped. We must write in the name of the French people" (ibid.).

Thus the question intensely discussed in these desperate hours was not just one of strategy, survival, or revenge, but rather the principled question of authority and legitimacy. In whose name can one sign an appeal against the legitimately elected Convention? Robespierre, more concerned than any of the other revolutionaries with the question of legitimacy, could not simply challenge the revolutionary legal system that had been so painfully conquered. In the historical narratives accounting for the tragic night of 9 Thermidor, many writers speculated that Robespierre never completed his signature because one last scruple stopped his hand. It was this last question that had been, in fact, the most important throughout the Revolution: "In whose name?"

In his *Histoire de la Révolution française*, Louis Blanc freely expressed his admiration for Robespierre's hesitation:

"In whose name?" What a sublime expression under the circumstances! Such hesitations are a man's downfall, but they immortalize him. Amidst cannon and pikes, at the sounding of the tocsins, when success depended on FORCE alone, Robespierre could think only of saving the idea of LEGITIMACY. . . . The reason why the [Section des Piques] was prevented from meeting earlier is provided us by the very document to which Robespierre could not resolve to put his signature, and which bears only the first two letters of his name. As he was a member of the Section des Piques, it naturally had to put off answering an appeal from the Commune until Robespierre's name was on the document. They urged him to sign; he wrote *Ro* . . . and could not resolve to finish.[19]

Ernest Hamel, in his 1865 *Histoire de Robespierre*, cited the testimony of Lerebours, whose father had been present on the night of 9 Thermidor and had himself signed the appeal to the Section des Piques. Lerebours quoted his father's account: "It was a matter of obtaining Robespierre's signature. . . . 'But in whose name?' said Maximilien. 'In the name of the Convention,' replied Saint-Just. 'It is wherever we are.' Robespierre persisted in his refusal. Because of Maximilien's long hesitation, all was lost."[20]

A last and different interpretation of the document was published in 1924 by Albert Mathiez, the founder of the *Etudes Robespierristes*. Its explicit aim was to put an end to all the speculations surrounding the unfinished signature of Robespierre, to clarify once and for all the circumstances of its interruption, to fill in all the blanks. Mathiez's theory was original as well as surprising. He contended that the two first letters of Robespierre's name were not the beginning of a signature interrupted either by moral scruples or by the arrival of the Convention troops; it was, simply, a post-scriptum. In support of this theory, he quoted a report from the permanent assembly of the Section des Piques, which mentioned having received a letter "announcing that liberty was found again, and by post-scriptum, that Robespierre had been freed."[21] From these lines, Mathiez deduced that the letter had been written, *completed*, sent to the Section des Piques, received the same night by its addressee, and immediately forwarded to the Convention. In the space of a few hours, this letter flew. The entire content of the post-scriptum, Mathiez argued, was these two letters *Ro*. He added for good measure: "We note that the letter in question was sent in more than one copy. Doubtless another just like it was sent to the civil committee of the Section. It was burned in an auto-da-fé."[22]

This last speculation, far from solving the enigma as Mathiez had claimed, only raises more questions. What of the burned letter, forever out of reach, sacrificed, purified by fire? These letters alone could elucidate the mystery of Robespierre's signature. The hypothesis of a burned letter was intended by Mathiez to dispel two myths. Contrary to witnesses' reports, Mathiez contended, Robespierre did not hesitate to sign in the name of a last scruple. In fact, Robespierre was not signing his name at all; these letters are not the first letters of his name: they are a post-scriptum, and as such, nothing is unfinished. Everything is said, spelled out, closed. Not only that, but it was said and spelled out several times. There is no blank, there is no mystery. It is of course interesting to note that Mathiez, as an historian, is much more at ease with a theory that speculates and is based on a *destroyed* document than with the contemplation of an existing but *unfinished* document. As we shall see, the need for closure in this case even led Mathiez to misread the archives.

If one reads carefully the report written by the clerk of the Section des Piques, one finds, not as Mathiez reported, the word "postscriptum," but another unique creation: *proscriptome*. In this neologism are of course combined two words: *post-scriptum*, that is, what comes *after* the signature (but cannot be defined without the signature) and *proscription*, exile, the act of outlawing someone through writing. At about the same time, or just a few hours before the famous letter was drafted at the Commune House, Robespierre had been declared *proscribed* by the National Convention, an action of which the Section des Piques was not informed until the following day. The clerk's slip therefore suggests—as does the content of the entire text—that the report was not written during the night of 9 Thermidor, but was drafted later and submitted to the Convention after Robespierre's death, in the hope of dispelling the suspicions that would naturally have been directed at the Section des Piques, a Robespierrist stronghold.

The interplay between *post-scriptum* and *proscription* is itself revealing. In the legal practice of writing a will, for example (and in western Europe all legislation surrounding the use and practice of the signature is linked to the legal history of testaments), nothing can be written *after* the signature. More precisely, in the chronologized space of the sheet of paper, everything that is written *below* the signature is invalid, for *the signature must plainly be the last gesture*, validating with a single stroke everything that has been written before. A rigorous temporality gives meaning to the spatial organization of the will. For space is also temporal: "Since the signature's goal is to express the author's approval of the written text, it must chronologically follow this text, and, by consequence, it must be *at the end* of the legal act, because the topographical order reveals generally the chronological order."[23]

As a double consequence, everything written below the signature is thought of as an "afterthought" and cannot be valid. Conversely, any correction or crossing out *above* the signature is considered valid. The respective spatial disposition of the crossings-out and the signature are legally expressed in temporal terms: "Crossings-out *prior to* the writing of the signature are undeniably valid."[24]

The signatory's own presence and intent are the two main concerns that seem to have guided legal decisions related to the validity of texts and, more specifically, of last wills and testaments. This entire jurisdiction is related to the necessity of deciding the authenticity and purpose of the text in the signatory's absence. (In this way, one could argue, there is a strong similarity between the fate of testa-

ments and that of archives.) Laws about testaments must be able,
above all, to enforce the dead signatory's last will and intent. The act
of signing one's name at the bottom of the page is thus always more
important than just the writing of a name, its function being always
to represent one's will after one's death. In this sense, quite literally,
the signature announces the signatory's death.[25] The *blanc-seing* (the
signing of a blank document) was abandoned in the old law because,
since it preceded the text, the signature could not be said to have
represented an approval of the text.

On the other hand, so great is the validating power of a signature
that, in the absence of a new signed document, tearing up a will does
not automatically rescind the dispositions it makes. The spatial disposition of the signature is itself validated by an implicit chronology,
with the signature similar to a line of demarcation between what is
and what is not legal. The afterthought following the signature does
not carry any legal validity. Thus any post-scriptum is proscribed in
the legal interpretation of the relationship between text and signature.

Mathiez, in his consideration of the letter addressed to the Section
des Piques, literally displaces the signature. According to Mathiez,
Ro   is not a signature, not even part of a signature, but a
doubly illegitimate post-scriptum: illegitimate by its endorsement of
a call to arms against the people's legitimate representative, illegitimate by its position below the others' signatures. *Ro*   would
be no more than an afterthought, an addendum without any validating power. Mathiez's displacement and his astonishing theory
leave, of course, many unresolved problems, among them the suggestion that writing the first two letters of one's name could constitute a post-scriptum having an autonomous, complete meaning,
rather than contributing an unfinished signature, and that this would
somehow also explain why Robespierre had *not* signed along with his
friends the message to his own section. During his life, Robespierre
was never known to use an abbreviated signature.

All the narratives attempting to tell the story of the dramatic night
of 9 Thermidor have stumbled over Robespierre's signature in a revealing manner. Some witnesses, revolutionary legislators, and his-

torians repudiate the incompleteness of the signature, either by suggesting that it has been interrupted rather than left incomplete, or simply, like Mathiez, by stating that it was not a signature. Others attempt to find in the blank space that followed *Ro*   a meaning that would fully explain and complete the name. The narratives thus struggle with various strategies of containment and closure. Mathiez is the most radical: there is no blank space, he argues. Against all evidence, he forcefully repudiates the possibility of incompleteness. Louis Blanc, like Michelet, puts together the witnesses' accounts of Robespierre's scrupulous hesitation and this troubling document. Their interpretation gives Robespierre's unfinished signature the gravity of a testament interrupted by his recurring anxiety about the legitimacy of authority: the legitimacy of transferring the authority from the king to the people, from the people to its representatives; or the attempt to save one's life by an illegitimate action.

Above all, the narratives seeking to account for the night of 9 Thermidor testify that the blank following Robespierre's signature is unreadable. We can still observe this blank but we cannot read it. Michelet read three letters, *Rob*, the first syllable of a name that carried a heavy symbolic meaning: Robe-ès-pierre, the "robe" representing the jurist, the law; Robespierre, the jurist of stone, the law engraved in stone.

This is no facetious pun. After Robespierre's execution, the *Moniteur* of 11 Thermidor reported the following:

A fact to be saved for posterity, is the way in which the news of Robespierre's fall was conveyed to the prisoners. . . . Young men, troubled by the movements and the noises they had heard, climbed to the highest point of the jailhouse, and looking in all directions, saw a woman gesturing to them: she saw that they were asking her for news, and, in order to be understood, she showed them a *robe* with one hand, and a *pierre* [stone], and then made an expressive gesture across her neck, which proved to them what the tyrant's end had been.[26]

Barère read two consonants *R.B.*; Mathiez would not read *proscriptome*; and the scrupulous Mitzman translated "Au nom de *qui*?" as "In the name of *what*?"[27] I would suggest that these various accidents in spelling, reading, or translating testify that the *écriture de la fin* is at work: death as agency is disrupting the narrative, undermining the various supplements to an ending, creating a rupture impossible to interpret and to narrate. Robespierre's last question remains unanswered, his signature remains unfinished. He never spoke another word because his jaw had been broken. There are no more clues. This ending, so contrary to formal narrative endings, to the nineteenth century's firm commitment to historical conclusions, generated multiple accounts aiming at completing the unfinished scene—but this could not be done except by *erasing what could not be read, the blank.* How can one describe what failed to take place? How does one account for the pure act of not-signing? How is one to understand it without investing this account with what we know now as the future of this last-word-that-was-not-to-be? In this half-begun signature, or rather what it lacks, the end dissimulates itself; it is both its role and its privilege. "The disaster is the improperness of its name and the disappearance of the proper name," writes Blanchot.[28] Just like death as agency, *l'écriture de la fin* jeopardizes this project; in the threat of imminent disaster, the historian picks up his narrative, no matter whether it is accurate or not. History will never tell.

Michelet thus added these final words: " '*But in whose name?*' He sealed his fate with these words. But he saved himself in history, and for posterity" (*HR*, 2: 980, emphasis in original). These few lines are already, for Michelet, the narrative of a circumscribed ending, that is, a narrative displaying all the signs legitimizing its quality as ending, its closure, its teleology, its historical finality. At the same time, these words recognize in this ending an erasure and, refusing to do away with it, they transform it into a beginning. Robespierre, Michelet argued, refused to *erase* all his life's principles, to cross out with his own hand the idea of law that guided all his actions, and, because of it, he did not die. He was saved. His redemption is now inscribed in history, history as posterity, history also as the historian's fate.

Indeed, Michelet's own fate, his own writing, in the wake of his father's death, is also an echo of the unanswered words: "But in whose name?" Because, at the last moment, Robespierre refused to save his own life, it becomes legitimate for Michelet to give it back to

him. Because Robespierre did not cross out the idea of law, even after
the Convention had declared him an outlaw, the law proceeds and
ironically demands his illegal execution. Thus the legitimate Revolution comes to an end. "He died as a great citizen," Michelet added,
but knowing all the same that, "from that day on, one would no
longer be able to say the word: *Citizen*" (p. 986).

Michelet kept silent about his visit to the "mute earth" where the
remains of the great revolutionaries were buried. A few pages later,
he eloquently rewrote Robespierre's last and unfinished signature so
as to give it a meaning and its place in posterity. Between Michelet's
own silence and his accounting of Robespierre's silence there lies, as
well, a certain vision of history, much like the engraving on a forgotten tombstone.

Around Midnight

"Sans écouter Minuit qui jeta son vain nombre."

The last chapter of the *Histoire de la Révolution française* concludes
with these words:

A few days after Thermidor, a man, who is still living and who was then ten
years old, was taken to the theater by his parents. Leaving the theater, he admired the long line of brilliant coaches which struck him for the first time.
Coachmen in jackets, with their hats off, asked the spectators leaving the theater: 'Do you need a carriage, *master*?' The child did not understand these
new words well. He asked for an explanation, but he was only told that there
had been a great change since Robespierre's death. (p. 990)

In this brief but significant scene, Michelet evokes in one stroke the
superficiality of the regime that followed 9 Thermidor: the reopening
of theaters, the effervescence of the streets, and a disquieting return
to a society where social inequality once again disrupted the pattern
of daily life. The word "citizen" has been replaced by "master." But
the significant time, the boundary, is Robespierre's death. The line is
both drawn and transgressed, since Michelet is speaking from a time
after Robespierre's death, to express better that it is all over. The end

is circumscribed, distance is measured by the "orgy of false mourning" that was to lead France into "the great grave." The end of the book can thus be written, not as silence, but as beginning, as a text yet to come. "The conclusion of this book is itself a book," writes Michelet in the brief conclusion. "I would make it obscure and sterile by compressing it here, in a few pages. It will be published separately, in a free form that will allow it, through the past, *to foresee the future*" (991, emphasis added).

But writing the end is not so simple. The Revolution does not leave Michelet, even though he hoped to be done with it. Two books substantially challenged Michelet's work. Louis Blanc's *Histoire de la Révolution française* and Ernest Hamel's *Histoire de Robespierre* paradoxically criticized Michelet for not having recognized Robespierre's importance and greatness during the historical upheaval. Michelet responded with passion, launching a counterattack in the Preface of 1868. First, he aimed at Louis Blanc: "Certainly, after Robespierre, I am the man who obsessed him the most" (*HR*, 1: 17). But above all— and this is the most interesting element—Michelet repudiated his own work and denied Robespierre. Noting Robespierre's considerable ascendance over the Jacobins, his executive power, his influence over justice and the army, he added: "And all of this, without title, *without writing nor signature*. He did not show up at the Committee of Public Safety, he had colleagues sign his own acts, *and did not sign for them*" (p. 18, emphasis added). We know of course which signature troubled Michelet. Indeed, he specifies just a few pages later: "As to the appeal to arms against the Law that he started writing, but did not complete, it could be explained *by a noble scruple, it was done at midnight*, when he had strength—or *by despair if it was done around one o'clock*, when he was abandoned. No witnesses" (19, emphasis added). Midnight, one o'clock, history takes a new turn, the end is not over, the book is not closed, Robespierre does not sign. No witnesses, says Michelet. Who would have thought of such betrayal?

One year later, Michelet returns to the Revolution once more, and rewrites its end in the form of a new preface to his own work. The 1869 edition of the *Histoire de la Révolution française* includes an introductory preface to book V entitled "The Tyrant." In these

Figure 10. The French People or the Robespierre Regime. Engraving. Cabinet des Estampes. Copyright © Cliché Bibliothèque Nationale de France.

pages, Michelet settles his account, once and for all, with Robespierre and with his own ending of the Revolution. Michelet's new preface was written on January 1st: we thus know that Michelet chose one o'clock, rather than midnight: the dawn of a new day. Last year, before midnight, Robespierre was still perhaps a hero, but in the first hour of this new year he is just a desperate tyrant. Everything rests in the chronology, the beginning and the end. Michelet starts with these words: "Time bears fruit," and he adds: "And this is my verdict as jury: in its troubled form, *this time was a dictatorship*" (*HR*, 2: 1004, author's emphasis).

This, the second of Michelet's denials, is perhaps of his texts the one most filled with hatred. It must be read in the light of what it really denounces, which is both Robespierre and Michelet's own accounting of Robespierre's end, as apotheosis of the great century, and as guarantee of posterity. Michelet is haunted by a familiar thought: "Robespierre did not sign," he repeats (2: 1014). But should one pay heed to his supporters? "To listen to the Robespierrists, *he was nothing, he did nothing*. Truly, this is a joke!" (p. 1015, emphasis in original). Michelet states: "Robespierre strangles and stifles," he is like a "boa constrictor." But if we go back twenty years, we find from Michelet's pen this strange anticipation of a troubled relationship: "I was progressing slowly, like a snake run over by a barrow. Bruised, crushed, it goes on, gathering its remaining strength, pushing forward its miserable and disconnected sections."[29] In 1869, Michelet, judge and jury, indicts Louis Blanc, Ernest Hamel, and the others: "You have a friend in the city, and this friend is Robespierre" (p. 1017). But in the preceding year—before midnight—he himself had admitted: "None of these great actors had left me indifferent. Did I not live with them, did I not follow each of them, through their transformations, in my thoughts like a faithful companion? In the end, I was one of them" (*HR*, 1: 14). He then felt "a kind of kinship" with Camille Desmoulins. In his earliest Preface, that of 1847, in a prophetic vision, he had anathematized the nineteenth century for having "proved false to their friend—nay, their own father, the great eighteenth-century" (p. 3).

By the beginning of this new year, 1869, the family drama has taken quite a new turn: "Did I spare my own father and mother, the great eighteenth-century? ... History must be like Brancaleone, the inflexible statesman, who, before judging, could swear at the gate that he had no parents nor friends in that city" (2: 1016). Michelet's dramatic reversal, a repudiation of what inspired his entire work, from the 1847 Preface to the last words of his *Histoire de la Révolution française*, goes far beyond the polemic that opposed then—as it does today—the various political interpretations of the French Revolution. Michelet's denial, exasperated by his anger against Buchez, Blanc, and Hamel, almost incoherent at times, sought to eradicate further the source of evil. Paradoxically, he wrote, Robespierre's exhumation and rehabilitation was begun under the Restoration, encouraged by "men of letters" and "several octogenarians whose memory was rather confused" (1021). Robespierre's own silence can now be properly judged by Michelet, he who has repudiated his own father and mother, his eighteenth century. For the occasion, he also provided a new form of hereditary transmission, a substitute for the hereditary transmission banished by "our fathers." "The tyrant is born of the tyrant," he concluded (1021).

The 1869 denial is itself undermined by another text that Michelet never disavowed because it was never published. A sort of afterthought; it was written immediately after the *Histoire de la Révolution française*. In these pages, Michelet went back to his visit to the Cemetery of the Terror, so present yet repressed in the text of his *Histoire*, and he meditated on the separation anxiety, the deep pain, he felt when his work was completed. "In this entire history, which was my life and my inner world for ten years, I formed, on the road, many deep bonds of friendship. ... Will you believe it? The greatest void I felt at this whitewood table, from which my book now departs, and where I remain alone, was the departure of my pale companion, the most faithful of them all, who had not left me from '89 to Thermidor; the man of great will, hard-working like me, poor like me, with whom I had, each morning, so many fierce discussions" (p. 995). He refers, of course, to Robespierre.

When Michelet wrote these lines, in 1853, the great century was not yet over for him: tearing himself away from the *Histoire*, he mourned the death of his father, of his faithful companion, Robespierre, and of his own completed work. They were all still painfully present to him. The *écriture de la fin*, the disrupting power of death as agency, which never stops undermining the very texts it constructs, also speaks in these posthumous lines: in Michelet's silence; in his nonpublication, nonsigning of his visit to the Cemetery of the Terror and yet his fascination for this mute land, and for Robespierre, *who never wrote and never signed*.

By 1869, Michelet's mourning has ended. Having repudiated his father and his "faithful companion," his own narrative, he has effectively put an end to his Revolution. The Mallarmean glimmer of Midnight has faded away. It is one in the morning. Robespierre has had his day. The Revolution is over.

6

Graveyard Shift

IN THE YEARS THAT PRECEDED the onset of the Revolution, Paris underwent an urban upheaval of considerable magnitude. From December 1785 to January 1788 the city lived with two permanent demolition sites. By day, the workers pulled down the houses that still sat above the bridges that crossed the Seine River; by night, large tumbrils removed disinterred bodies from the Innocents Cemetery to largely unknown destinations. The decrees that decided to close the largest graveyard in Paris and to demolish the houses that cluttered the bridges were motivated by the same concern: the dismal quality of air in a polluted city, the object of endless complaints from its inhabitants and of shocked wonder from its visitors.

The demolition sites over the Pont Notre-Dame and Pont au Change do not appear to have stirred much controversy. Two paintings, part of the permanent collection of the Musée d'Histoire de la Ville de Paris, commemorate the razing of the dwellings, begun in 1786 to improve the circulation of air over the Seine River. In this case, the living proved to be far less troublesome than the dead. One finds little evidence of protest from the unhappy dwellers who lost their homes to environmental concerns. By contrast, the closing of the Innocents Cemetery and the simultaneous removal of thousands of bodies was mired in a controversy that spanned decades of grievances, inapplicable decrees, and general anxiety over the proper way to bury the dead.

Veüe de l'Eglise et Cimetiere des saincts Innocens a Paris.

Israel siluestre delin. et sculp.   Israel Henriet ex. cum privil. Regis.

Figure II. The church and cemetery of the Holy Innocents. Collection Viollet.

Urban Plights

In her definitive study, *Les Morts, l'église et l'état*, Jacqueline Thibaut-Payen comments on the radical dechristianization of death that occurred during the eighteenth century. Previously, she argues: "[death] had been seen in a Christian perspective." From the eighteenth century on, it "would be seen in an administrative perspective."[1] More specifically, she notes: "In the second half of the century of Enlightenment, new scientific ideas, combined with certain notorious cases of poisoning, drew the attention of the public and the authorities to the problem of hygiene in cemeteries. Cemeteries were accused of breeding epidemics, and the dead suspected of contaminating the living. This is not a case of isolated fright, but of widespread fear" (p. 205). Once a place of religious respect and reverence for the dead, the graveyard is now seen as the most dangerous threat to the health of the living. "Men of the eighteenth century . . . begin to rebel against the fatality of death and strive to find its causes, in order to elude them. A different vision of faith leads to a rejection of death, and finally of cemeteries" (p. 204).

But the dead would not easily be dismissed. The general decree of 10 March 1776 which prescribed the transfer of "insalubrious cemeteries" outside city limits also allowed that Paris was a special and more difficult case, whose resting places quickly became active battlegrounds. A preliminary inquiry had shown, as early as 1763, a catastrophic situation. Thibaut-Payen quotes a report on the Saint-Paul parish in the Marais:

The neighbors have declared that when it thunders or rains, one is disturbed by the effluvia from the cemeteries, and that to know whether it will rain, when the weather heralds it, one only has to stand in a place that has a view on the aforementioned cemetery, and one can see rising from it mephitic vapors, that are a sign of rain. . . . Several neighbors have also declared that the common graves were reopened before the bodies that had been buried there were entirely consumed; that ditchdiggers could be seen breaking up the members of bodies that had been kept there; after which the coffins were burned, which increased the infection. (p. 211)

"The largest, thus the foulest cemetery in Paris, was the cemetery of the Innocents," notes Félix Gannal.[2] More than 2,000 bodies were buried there every year: "Between 150 and 200 bodies received an individual burial place. The bodies of persons for whom no one wanted to undergo this additional expense were piled up in common graves, twenty-five to thirty feet deep. Twelve to fifteen hundred corpses were deposited there *without any layer of soil between the layers of bodies*" (p. 54, emphasis in original). By 1780, when several cellars in the surrounding areas collapsed under the weight of the corpses accumulated in a common grave opened in 1779, the situation had become untenable. "This event, in a neighborhood whose inhabitants had protested for years against the infection caused by the cemetery of the Innocents, created such a stir that the Paris Parliament had to decree that the cemetery would be closed on 1 March 1780" (pp. 57–58).

The church asked for more delays, however, as new resting places proved difficult to find and the transportation of dead bodies through the streets of Paris caused endless problems (this was to become more evident during the revolutionary years). Still, various projects were formed. One of them, approved by Vicq d'Azir,[3] was to replace the cemetery and the church of the Saints-Innocents with an open-air vegetable market. Work began in December 1785. Initially authorities had planned to excavate a four-foot layer of soil, hoping to find no bodies. But, to the general dismay, the closing of the cemetery and its reappropriation by and for the living involved more than twelve months of work and the transfer of 20,000 bodies.

Many of the bodies were taken to Montrouge, far from the center of Paris. Work and exhumations lasted from December 1785 to October 1787, with long interruptions particularly during the summer months. On March 1789, Thouret presented a *Rapport sur les exhumations du cimetière et de l'église des Saints-Innocents* to the Royal Academy of Medicine, meeting in the Louvre, where he described some of the scenes that had haunted Parisians for many months:

There were countless torches lighted everywhere and casting a dismal light; reflections on the surrounding objects; the sight of the Crosses, the Tombs, the Epitaphs; the silence of the night. There was a thick cloud of smoke that surrounded and covered the workplace, in the midst of which the workers, whose activities could not be made out, seemed to move about

like shadows. The varied ruins resulting from the demolition of the struc-
tures, the upheaval of the soil by the exhumations, everything gave the scene
an imposing and lugubrious aspect. This spectacle was compounded by the
religious ceremonies: coffins being transported, in the case of the most distinguished sepultures, with the pomp that accompanied these moves; hearses
and catafalques. There were long lines of funeral wagons, loaded with bones,
and heading at the end of the day toward the new site that had been prepared
outside the walls, for the internment of these sad remains.[4]

The long debates over the unhealthy effects of burial places, and
the dramatic closing of the Innocents Cemetery, help us understand
the Revolution's concern with death and the Convention's expressed
desire to enforce a legislation where the respect due to the dead
would be reconciled with the protection due to the living.[5] Philippe
Muray argues that the nineteenth century really began on 7 April
1786, when the first tumbril of bodies from the Innocents was transferred to the Catacombes, initiating a century-long obsession with
death and the beyond. Although the date and circumstances he describes are debatable, he may be right in his assessment that, to
a certain extent, the Revolution "is perhaps nothing but a case of
cemeteries being filled one after the other, overcrowded, bursting,
and abandoned."[6] Certainly, such an obsession accounts for a double
and contradictory practice: the Revolution's burial of the guillotined
bodies in common graves, nameless, to be forgotten yet unforget-
table; and its glorious transfer of a few great men to the newly dedicated Panthéon.

Where the Dead Rest

In his 1868 essay on the Panthéon, Edgar Quinet reflected on the
vivid way we remember the heroes of the French Revolution: "However dead as they are for us, they are still in the fray. They go on
fighting and hating."[7] But for Quinet, there is something strange
and disturbing in the revolutionaries' continued influence and role in
politics, more than fifty years after their deaths: although their presence is still felt, their remains are nowhere to be found. "Where can
one collect their remains? They have been so thoroughly scattered

Figure 12. Fountain of the Innocents, 1794. Engraving. Collection Viollet.

to the four winds! Go and look for those of Mirabeau, Condorcet, Madame Roland. Try finding those of Voltaire and Rousseau. What has been done with them? We know not" (p. 320).

Indeed, there is no trace of the body of Condorcet, who died in mysterious circumstances.[8] Mirabeau, first buried in the Panthéon, was expelled from the glorious monument when it was discovered that he had conspired with the king against the Revolution. Voltaire and Rousseau, considered as the philosophers whose works most inspired revolutionary fervor, were voted worthy of the Panthéon.[9] Their remains were transferred to the Revolution's most prestigious monument with considerable fanfare, only to be disinterred and cast away by night during the Restoration. As Quinet reported, the Restoration

dared to open the graves of Voltaire and Rousseau, to plunder the remains, and pour them into bags that were thrown away, in I know not what sewer, near the Seine. . . . What would have happened if they had been caught in the act, with their hands in the graves? But with a remnant of prudence that would scarcely seem compatible with such a reckless act, they had chosen the night for their dark deed. The secret of this clandestine victory over human remains was so well kept that it has been revealed only recently, amid the general indifference to which we have grown accustomed. The vaults were still being visited thirty years after they had been emptied. This secret, this fear, this silence, this night, these are our excuse.[10]

The dispersion of Voltaire's and Rousseau's remains ironically duplicated the fate of royal remains, which were traditionally dismembered and distributed according to a complex geographical hierarchy in various parts of France, so that one royal enclosure could claim the heart, while another would contain the head, or again less noble features of the royal corpses.

At any rate, the Panthéon, first built as a church by J.-G. Soufflot and redesigned as a sacred resting place for the great men of France by Quatremère de Quincy during the Revolution, had lost its purpose, its vault vandalized and the spirit that once inspired its dedication now gone forever. And Quinet exclaimed:

To give credit to an ideal Being, the Fatherland, to go so far as to accept the ideal recognition of future generations as payment for our services, who would want such a contract today? Who could even imagine it? Anyone proposing such a thing would be called a mystic. The idea of projecting our thoughts beyond the present, of taking inspiration from the grave, of somehow feeding our great deeds with the lure of a glorious death, of seeking a reason for living beyond life itself, this idea and all others of this kind have been extirpated from the human soul, at the moment I am speaking. They have become so alien and hostile that it is difficult to render them in a persuasive manner! Our present language refuses to express them. Yes, these ideas are dead. (p. 319)

For Quinet, then, the Panthéon remains a symbol of death, no longer this sublime aspiration to an heroic end that once characterized the Revolution, but the death of the Revolutionary spirit itself. Saint-Just, who wrote so movingly of his upcoming death, evoking not the Panthéon of stone that had successively welcomed and expelled so many great men, but a moral Pantheon where sacrifice and gratitude would be forever celebrated, finds an unexpected echo in Quinet, who concludes his essay with these words: "Everything I would have to say supposes a primary Pantheon, a moral edifice, the Pantheon of conscience, of the ideal homeland, of political liberty in the heart and hearth of every man. These ideals would give life to its columns, which would need neither pillars nor iron props to support them in the skies" (p. 320).

The issue of revolutionary burial, whether a celebration of patriotic glory or the disposal of so many victims thrown in anonymous mass graves, raises, indeed, many questions: Where are the dead to be laid to rest? What are the proper grounds for the remains of the great men? Is nature a more appropriate setting than a stone monument? When Marat died, John Goldworth Alger tells us, "the Club des Cordeliers . . . was told that Marat belonged to the entire nation, and that the Commune had no right to dispose of a hair of his head. His heart was, however, buried under a tree in the club garden, 'the true Panthéon,' said Chaumette, 'of the man of nature'."[11]

What would be the role of sculpture and other images in the commemoration of the dead? Would cemeteries be religious or secular grounds? Indeed, all these questions were linked to an essential revolutionary anxiety: how to remember, what place to give memory in a regime that wished above all to do away with every remnant of the past. The problem, in fact, was not to give memory its proper place, but to create, through various resting places, a new form of remembrance: it was to be an invention of memory.

Natural Deaths

In the years that preceded the French Revolution, many projects offered new visions of cemeteries. Added to a general desire to move burial grounds outside of Paris for sanitary reasons, was the wish to create a place of enduring beauty where nature itself would provide a perfect resting place and surround the burial grounds with peaceful melancholy. Richard A. Etlin notes:

> Rousseau's burial at Ermenonville was followed by three important works that set the stage for a new image of the cemetery: Hirschfeld's five-volume-in-quarto treatise on garden design, published simultaneously in German and French between 1779–1785; the Abbé Delille's immensely popular didactic poem *Les Jardins* (1782); and Bernardin de Saint-Pierre's equally popular *Etudes de la Nature* (1784). All three authors shared a common conviction about the moral force of the pastoral and elegiac landscape garden.[12]

Christian Hirschfeld took his readers on pilgrimages to various tombs: "The reader was encouraged to imagine himself leaning on a venerable tree with the moon reflected in the placid waters of the pool and a small rill murmuring at the foot of Sulzer's grave. There was nothing macabre about this 'touching' scene, where 'the idea of death loses all of its frightfulness'" (p. 212). These serene gardens offered a sharp contrast to the much decried cemeteries of Paris, chief among them the Innocents, described by Quatremère de Quincy as "infectious grounds" and "hideous depots of cadavers and skeletons."[13]

All the great architects included a grandiose burial place in their plans for the ideal city. Boullée thought of a colossal pyramidal structure, Lequeu a superposition of cylinders planted with trees, Ledoux, in Michel Vovelle's words "less serene in his explanations, saw in the cemetery 'the last dark abode of greatness.'" And Vovelle adds: "What remains of all these projects and dreams? These very beautiful drawings are enough to suggest the immensity and overwhelming majesty to which they aimed. Yet it's little: perhaps no more than this other form of utopia, experienced for a very brief time, the funereal revolutionary festival." [14]

Both F. A. Aulard and Michel Vovelle [15] have commented on Fouché's decree of 29 September 1793 that simultaneously regulated the freedom of religion and the ceremonies of burials:

Art 4. In every municipality, all dead citizens, no matter their religion . . . will be taken to a common grave, covered with a funereal shroud, painted with a representation of Sleep.
Art. 5. The common grave where their ashes will rest will be isolated from all dwellings, planted with trees, among which will be erected a statue representing Sleep. All the other signs will be destroyed.
Art. 7. All those who, after their death, will be judged by the citizens of their communes as worthy of patriotic recognition, will have a crown of oak sculpted on their tombstone.
Art. 8. On the portal of this field, consecrated by a religious respect for the manes of the dead, will be this inscription: *Death is an eternal sleep*. [16]

These bucolic visions of quiet burial gardens echoed several concerns that remained at the core of the revolutionary attitude toward death. One such concern encompassed a theoretical opposition between nature and architecture. For some, nature alone provided the proper setting for remembering the dead; even at the height of the Panthéon's conversion to a national mausoleum, architects thought of adding gardens to complete the sense of peace indispensable to the quiet contemplation of death. Second, there was a de facto opposition between the crowded charnel houses of Paris—later echoed by the common graves where decapitated bodies would be covered with quicklime—and the solitary monuments dedicated to a few "great men," an uneasy recognition of heroism contrary to the principles of equality so crucial to the revolutionary project.

Anxious to establish a new state, but also to create a collective memory where the people would remember the legitimate ancestors of their newly discovered freedom, the revolutionaries struggled with the question of memorials and the selection—one could say the creation—of their past. The debates surrounding the transfers of Voltaire's and Rousseau's remains to the Panthéon testify to the troubled desire of the Revolution to give itself an ancestry, a legitimacy, that would rival and supplant all forms of repudiated hereditary power.

The logistics of burials, however, were never a simple matter. Etlin remarks:

> One of the paradoxes of the French Revolution, was that while it exacerbated the overcrowding in the cemeteries of Paris, it also set the foundations for the successful implementation of a new order in burials. With the expropriation of church property, the subsequent closing of the churches themselves, the dissolution of the traditional clergy, and the closing of former parish cemeteries, the customary rituals were gravely disrupted. The privileged lost the prerogative of a grave inside the church. (p. 229)

In fact the privilege of being buried inside churches had already been lost, and the mass graves Etlin describes as revolutionary measures were nothing but a continuation of the much decried practices of the Old Regime. The Revolution simply continued to struggle with a century-long problem of space and a desire to protect the living from the dead. The fear of epidemics, the thought of contagion, the contamination of the living by the dead continued to haunt Paris and collectively makes more vivid still the powerful contradiction between the dedication of the Sainte-Geneviève Church as a Panthéon consecrated to the few great men of the fatherland and the quiet desolation of the common graves so powerfully evoked years later by Michelet.

The Panthéon

In April 1791, the Constituent Assembly made official the rededication of the "édifice dit de Sainte-Geneviève" as a monument to the great men of the fatherland. Quatremère de Quincy, who was to be the main architect of this transformation, first criticized the choice of the monument in a letter published in the *Moniteur*. The selection of Sainte-Geneviève was ill-advised, he argued, among other things, "because this example would change our temples back into catacombs, a use already proscribed by reason," and "because, to the man of taste, the inside and outside of the building contrast too strongly with the lugubrious purpose of an hypogeum."[17]

Two recurring elements emerge from these comments: Quatremère held a strong conviction that the dead should not be buried inside churches or temples. (The Decree of 1776 had already severely limited inhumations inside religious buildings.) This belief echoed the already much-favored opinion that nature alone provided the proper resting place for all human remains. Second, beyond the aesthetic argument and the concern with architectural "unity," Quatremère also betrayed a more general reluctance to deal with corpses and burials. Their "lugubrious" character seems incompatible with the architect's wish for a monument that would celebrate not remains, but memory; not death, but immortality. As Mark Deming puts it:

Indeed, for Quatremère the Panthéon was less an "abode of death" than a "temple to immortality," less an "hypogeum" than a "temple dedicated to the cult of great men." This explains why he insisted on separating the funeral and cultural functions of the Panthéon. It was important for him—this, of course, was an old debate—to dissociate the tombs from the statues and commemorative sculptures: it would have been improper for sarcophagi, sad depositaries of human remains, to be associated with the honorific likenesses that will constitute the everlasting assembly of the Fatherland's benefactors. (p. 116)

Still another debate loomed. If it was easy enough to dispose of human remains in a crypt, a space sufficiently separated from the core of the temple to allow for the latter's main function (to keep the memory of great men *alive*) to remain intact, what was the most appropriate way to celebrate immortality? And how could this be reconciled with the growing antireligious movement that denied the possibility of life after death?[18]

The religious issue was adroitly avoided. On 3 Frimaire (23 November 1793) Chaumette, a leader in the dechristianization movement, finalized new rituals for burials. In the funerals, he decreed, a banner would be deployed with the words: "The just man never dies, he lives in the memory of his fellow citizens."[19] Immortality was thus redefined as living memory, and the Panthéon, now freed from any religious intent, could itself become the most glorious expression of human memory.

It is interesting to note that, in his last discourse, Robespierre forcefully challenged this vision of a secular memory. On 8 Thermidor he exclaimed:

I have seen that, in history, all the defenders of liberty were attacked by calumny; but their oppressors died as well! Good and bad people disappear from the earth, but in different circumstances. Frenchmen, don't let your souls be debased by your enemies' shameful doctrine. No, Chaumette, no, Fouché, death is not an eternal sleep. Citizens, erase this maxim from the tombstones: it was engraved by sacrilegious hands. The mourning veil it throws over nature discourages oppressed innocence and insults death itself. Engrave instead this maxim: *death is the beginning of immortality*.[20]

Before Robespierre reintroduced the idea of a Supreme Being in the Revolutionary commemoration of death, however, burials—no matter how glorious—remained a matter of showing respect for the dead. Deming notes: "Thus, by means of allegories that were easy to decipher and excessively symmetrical, the frontispiece of the Panthéon celebrated Revolutionary values. It did not, however, retrace the historical process that had led to their triumph" (p. 130). The elimination of the historical process was determined in part by the Revolution's explicit desire to do away with all representations of a repudiated past. While sculptors were applying themselves with ardor to celebrate the great men of the Panthéon, demolition crews were dismantling the statues of the Kings of Judah that decorated the portal of Notre-Dame.

The Revolution's iconoclastic passion has been well documented.[21] It drew its energy and its fervor from the necessity to do away with all figures of the past, a past that itself had been obsessed with representations, statues, pictorial glorifications of its royal authority. In its iconoclastic zeal, the Revolution also echoed a Rousseauist distrust of images that conflicted nevertheless with the rich allegoric output of the republican regime. Debates surrounding the Pantheon were not exempt from such contradictory desires.[22]

As a sacred cemetery, the Panthéon served conflicting purposes. As we know, it was one of the fundamental principles of all revolutionary festivals that they take place in an open space. This put a severe limitation on the public uses of the Panthéon. Mona Ozouf argues that the symbolic output of the public ceremonies of "pantheonizations" stopped on the steps of the Panthéon.[23] Deming, however, shows that such was not the case. He describes the ceremony organized by David for Le Peletier on 24 January 1793 in these terms:

Since the ceremony was dedicated to a hero killed for the Fatherland, it took on a lugubrious severity in which dramatic intensity took precedence over historical reference. The wounded body, its torso uncovered, was first exposed on the pedestal of the demolished statue of Louis XIV, place des Piques (ex-Vendôme). It was then carried on a ceremonial bed, up to a place beneath the dome of the Panthéon where it was laid on a monumental stage designed by Quatremère. (pp. 143–44)

Thus, the vast enclosed space of the Panthéon also served in the careful ordonnance of public celebrations, but with one difference. This festival was organized primarily as a burial: Lepeletier was put to rest; his loss was deplored, indignation rose over the corpse, his fatal wound visible to all eyes. The tragedy of death eclipsed the concept of eternal fame. Although a glorious burial, it was more a time to grieve than a time to remember.

Mercier, opposed to all forms of pantheonizations, exclaimed repeatedly: "No Idols, no idolatry in our Republic!"[24] His wish was granted: none of the heroes buried in the Panthéon at the time of the Revolution remained there. Vandalism, political transformations, and fanaticism account for much of the disturbances that ultimately left the crypt desolate and empty.

Cemeteries of the Terror

While the Panthéon was being redesigned as a resting temple for a few heroes, the Paris cemeteries continued to overflow. Complaints of overcrowding, already numerous before the onset of the Revolution, became more urgent. Familiar fears of epidemics spread across the city. Michelet described in detail the lugubrious disposal of the dead in one of the last chapters of his *Histoire de la Révolu-*

tion française. In a section entitled "Of the Cemeteries of the Terror,"
he wrote:

Here, I touch upon a melancholy topic; history requires it. Having reached
the highest point of the Terror, I find, as on the top of high mountains, an
extreme aridity, a desert where all life ceases to exist. Everything I am going
to write is literally drawn from the dry administrative acts of the time. Pity
was dying or mute; horror spoke, as did disgust and the anxiety of the great
city in fear of an epidemic. The living took fright, and thought they were
going to be carried away by the dead. What no one dared to say in the name
of humanity, was said in the name of hygiene and salubrity. (2: 923)

In vivid contrast to the concerns surrounding the glorious project of
the Panthéon (how to give the most glorious tomb to a few selected
heroes, how best to keep their memory alive), the Parisian debates
regarding their cemeteries were guided by one overwhelming desire:
to be rid of the guillotined corpses, to have their human remains
taken away, out of sight, out of memory.

It was not—and Michelet is quite explicit on this—that the Terror
was adding dramatically to the number of burials in the city. Rather,
it was a more diffuse and impalpable fear that made the bodies of
the victims more noticeable and a more dangerous presence for the
living.

If one reflects on the scale of the massacres that took place under the Monarchy at various times, without giving rise to similar fears in Paris, one will
marvel at the fact that twelve hundred victims in two months raised concerns
about public health. The Faubourg Saint-Antoine, which, for 150 years, had
buried its dead and those of neighboring areas in the Saint-Marguerite cemetery (thousands of bodies per year), without suffering from this proximity,
declared that it could not bear the addition, which was minimal by compari-
son, of the guillotined. (2: 923)

As John Goldsworth Alger reports: "On the 6th February 1794
the Roule section asked for the closing of the Madeleine cemetery, in
which the King and Queen had been buried. 'The proverb *morte la
bête, mort le venin,*' said the spokesman, 'is falsified, for the aristocrats
are poisoning us even after their death.'"[25] A guillotined body was
no mere corpse; it was a powerfully symbolic enactment of death that
carried with it obscure anxieties not unlike those that surrounded

the bodies of plague victims. To the speculation that their unnatural death had been the result of chance rather than moral retribution was added the fear that they would in turn extract a toll from the living. Michelet adds:

The heat was intense, and doubtless made things worse. It is worth noting however that the complaints had always been the same, in every district, in every season. It was a general trait of the popular imagination. The cemeteries of those killed on the scaffold moved it, worried it, made it fear epidemics even at a time when the very low number of victims added only a truly imperceptible amount to the enormous number of ordinary burials in Paris. (2: 923)

But these far-from-obscure dead refused to be forgotten: "Complaints had started as early as 7 February (19 Pluviôse), in the middle of winter, in the Madeleine district, an area less populated then, and perfectly ventilated. But the King was there, and the Girondins as well; the imagination was preoccupied with them; the neighbors felt sick" (2: 923). These were disturbing corpses: a king and the most fervent of the revolutionaries, thrown together by the prosecution and the grave diggers in a disquieting proximity to each other and the living. The question then arose: not how best to remember them, but how to forget those whose memory haunted the living and whose bodies refused to rest in peace.

Complaints about burial grounds also appeared during the month of Pluviôse in the daily reports sent to the *bureau de l'esprit public*. On 23 Pluviôse (11 February): "Surprise is excited at seeing citizen Launay, a member of the Commune, buried on the boulevard. 'When there is a cemetery,' people say. 'why are not the burials there? . . . If all members of popular societies who die are buried on the highways, the boulevard will soon be covered with tombs.' The grave, moreover, is not deep enough, and it is feared that a fetid odor will exhale."[26] On 30 Pluviôse (18 February): "Many citizens walking in the boulevard du Temple, perceiving the tomb of Delaunay, drew back with horror" (2: 216). The Commune took note.

Hébert and Clootz were the last victims to be buried in the Madeleine cemetery, on 24 March.[27] A new burial ground had been designated in a remote corner of the Monceau plain. Again, in sharp

contrast to the public ceremonies organized by David for the pan-
theonization of heroes, the Commune interred the dead secretly,
shamefully one might say.

> On the 25 [March], the public prosecutor warned the executioner that from
> now on the bodies would go to Monceau. Danton, Desmoulins, Lucile,
> Chaumette, inaugurated this cemetery. Authorities were well aware of the
> love and fanaticism attached to these names. They kept these Monceau buri-
> als secret for a while. The victims were first deposited at the Madeleine
> [cemetery], and were not carried to Monceau until a few days afterwards,
> probably during the night. (2: 924)[28]

The secretive burials had a dual purpose: to prevent a spontaneous
glorification of these martyrs of the Republic, killed by the Revolution itself. Danton, Camille and Lucile Desmoulin, heroes for many,
glorified by a premature and dramatic death, might well have generated spontaneous funeral processions rivaling those carefully prepared for the pantheonized great men. Thus emerged new figures of
quiet patriotic devotion whose images were not transfixed in stone,
but forcefully erased, in the hope they would be forgotten by all.
Revered as they were by many, however, their decomposed bodies
carried with them the same haunting memories of plague-like epidemics. This is also why their burials were undertaken in secret, in a
place concealed from public knowledge. The fear of epidemics was—
as always—also of a moral nature: it was the revulsion created by the
epidemics of deaths that followed the Law of 22 Prairial. The public
clamor against the disposal of bodies can be seen as a public clamor
against the bloodshed itself.

On 21 Prairial (9 June 1794), when the guillotine was moved far
from the center of Paris, first to the Faubourg Saint-Antoine, then
to the Barrière du Trône, a new cemetery was laid out, in one of the
poorest sections of Paris.

> [It] became the slaughterhouse, the cemetery of the Revolution. The con-
> demned prisoners were led alive through the Faubourg, and after their death
> crossed it again, to be buried in the very center of the district, in the middle
> of the Montreuil section, in the Saint-Marguerite cemetery, a cemetery full
> and overflowing. . . . On 26 Prairial [14 June], police administrators wrote
> that the district feared an epidemic if any more victims were added to this

seat of infection. The more than a hundred victims buried there until 4 Messidor [22 June] exacerbated the people's anxiety and irritation. They declared that they could no longer bear the smell. (2: 925–26)

One solution was to throw quicklime over the bodies. But because the victims of the guillotine were buried along with the regular inhabitants of the area, families objected, seized by anxiety at the idea of the unnatural decomposition of their dead. Another solution had to be found: it was to be Picpus, perhaps the strangest location yet proposed for burials. It had been the garden of a convent, seized by the nation along with all religious properties. The convent had been transformed into an asylum where rich and privileged prisoners of both sexes—the Marquis de Sade among them— [29] enjoyed a notorious lifestyle: "Freedom was extreme in these gallant prisons; there was much merriment; the uncertainty of impending fate made hearts tender. Death is a powerful and swift procuress" (2: 927).

Eerie scenes took place in the quiet convent garden, where at dusk common graves were dug:

Each time the overflowing tumbril arrived, the poor suspects had terrible *Memento mori* before their eyes. By night, the most dismal scenes took place. The bodies were stripped in the open air, under the skies, their clothing sent to the river, and from there to the poor houses. The employees writing the reports asked the Commune [on 21 Messidor, 9 July] at least to build them a little shed. For the wind blew out the lights; they were left in the dark of night with their guillotined bodies. (2: 927)

Soon Picpus overflowed. Quicklime was used, but the earth, mostly clay, refused the bodies. "The clay rejected everything, refused to hide anything. Everything remained on the surface. The liquid putrefaction rose and gurgled under the July sun" (2: 928). Another deserted area was found, and, as the architect in charge of the project remarked, perhaps with nostalgia for the peaceful serenity of natural burial grounds, the common graves "will permit us to preserve a beautiful vine and trees whose fruits it would be useful to harvest" (2: 928). But it would take time, and for a few more days, including those that would see the hecatomb of 10 and 11 Thermidor (28, 29 July), the dead were buried at Monceau, the Commune prescribing that thyme, sage, and ginever be burned during the burials. Thus, ironically, incense was perhaps burned, a poor form of incense to be sure, for Robespierre and his friends.

Just as the Revolution tried to create in the Panthéon what Quatremère saw, in Mona Ozouf's terms, as "that which must be ideally the place of collective memory,"[30] it effectively tried to bury its victims in these wastelands, opposing to the public character of the execution the privacy and mystery of nighttime burials, anonymous graves and secretive ceremonies against the backdrop of Parisian clamors for a city freed of corpses.

Remembering

The Panthéon, as we have seen, failed to realize its mission. Mona Ozouf sees in this failure the Revolution's desire to celebrate memory while erasing the past:

The place of collective memory is thus established entirely outside of history. Here is the residence of great men, emptied of all the great men of the past, whether they belonged to Antiquity, the Old Regime or the Revolution. . . . [The Panthéon is] at the same time a consecration of emptiness, a wager on the future, and an invitation to all virtuous citizens (why not thou?), but also the admission of an impossible memory. (p. 155)

Paradoxically, the cemeteries of the Terror, these shameful burial grounds so vividly decried by the revolutionaries themselves, remained for Michelet the most powerful, the most sacred ground of the Revolution. On 19 May 1852, when he visited the "cemetery of the terror" at Monceau—and we know what inspiration he drew from that visit[31]—he noted in his *Journal* that the former Monceau garden had been divided into two sections: a fertile one, that became a public garden, although it "produced nothing" (2: 193), and a barren one.

In this sterile part, there is a place, more sterile still, along the wall, near the barrier, without quite facing it. There, some excavations no more than a few feet deep, meant to lay the foundations for some rabbit sheds, uncovered bones and heads. These are the remains of the victims of the Terror, of those who died Place de la Révolution. . . . These remains are still there. Quicklime was thrown upon the common graves. But, if I believe my cousin Lefebvre, quicklime did not succeed in destroying the bones. There, in this small, abandoned, and sterile corner, in this arid and stony recess, the worst of the worst, there lie the true relics of the Revolution. (2: 193)

For Michelet, there could be no greater contrast than that between this solitary and neglected ground where nothing grows and the powerful spirit of the great revolutionaries who lie there, their relics still intact, if disturbed. Far from encouraging oblivion, this solitude and the sterility of the grounds stirred in Michelet an incomparable emotion.

This cemetery-which-is-not-one, which has erased all traces of its former function, has not erased memory, and Michelet exclaims: "There lie the beautiful and brave Madame Roland, the good and eloquent Vergniaud; there the head from which once came the words: *They are making the Revolution by means of terror; I wanted to do it by love*. There fell Danton's remains, those of the poor Camille and Lucile, and Fabre d'Eglantine, and the sublime and good Anarchasis Clootz, the orator of humanity" (2: 193, emphasis in original). But the contrast is powerful between this silent wasteland and the eloquent voices of those who lie there. "How can the soil that has received and devoured these hearts and these voices remain so cold and silent? Barbarian powers of silence, what have you done to the heart and voice of France that lay within them? Time will pass again and again. One will never be consoled" (2: 193).

Grief and mourning, the interiorization of memory the Panthéon failed to provoke, reached an unparalleled tragic strength in this no-man's-land Michelet could not leave, fascinated by the irony of history:

There, and this is the most bitter, there lie those who killed them and killed themselves as well, there lie these great and heroic men, whatever their sins and furor may have been. There lies he who gave the Revolution its continuity, its intense and profound passion, its immutable soul: the patient, heinous, sober and persevering Robespierre, the sphinx of the Jacobins. There lies, finally, the Revolution's Word, the handsome and terrible Saint-Just, whose words fell like the words of destiny. (2: 193)

The nostalgia, the regrets, the power that these souls exert over Michelet, the emotional visit to the wasteland of Monceau, still illuminate his writings when just a few weeks later he recounts the death of Robespierre and his friends. In the last chapter of the *Histoire de la Révolution française*, Michelet describes the death of Saint-Just with these words: "He died with dignity, seriousness and simplicity. France will never be consoled for losing such a hope" (2: 989).

Michelet mourned. Saint-Just, after all, had found in this sterile and unmarked piece of ground, the moral Pantheon to which he had aspired. For Michelet, the great men of the Revolution, and the great women as well, remained alive there, made more haunting by the civil neglect that, in vain, tried to erase their names and memory. This stony and deserted place, which contrasts so powerfully with what Michelet calls the "hideous tomb" of his father in the Cemetery of the Père-Lachaise, is also evocative of what remains, for Michelet, the most sacred of all the revolutionary spaces: the Champ de Mars. Both empty spaces share a profound and intimate secret, a powerful spirit that could not be contained or expressed by any piece of human architecture: "Although a forgetful generation uses this field as a stage for its vain amusements, imitated from abroad, although the English horse insolently stamps across the ground . . . a great inspiration breathes across the plain; it is nowhere to be felt, it is the Soul, an omnipotent spirit" (1: 1).

There is no mention of the Panthéon in these powerful lines, in which the sandy plain of the Champ de Mars anticipates the vacant lot where the heroes of the Revolution are buried and where the soul of the Revolution also breathes.

The Revolution, as we know, failed to realize a single one of the great architectural projects regularly submitted to its legislators but abandoned for lack of funds, lack of time, or lack of need. One might speculate that the revolutionaries, so uncomfortable and so unsuccessful in the complex transformation of a church into a patriotic temple, might have thought that, just as was the case in revolutionary festivals, nature alone could provide the proper setting for their patriotic endeavors. Or, more obscurely, they may have anticipated the conclusion of Quinet's reflections on the Panthéon: "As long as this monument does not exist within the soul of each Frenchman, let us not even think of reopening the common home of civic glory and immortality. As long as dogma dictates that might makes right, a Panthéon is impossible. Surely, it would remain empty, were it filled to the top with a people made of marble. Tell me, of what use would stone men be to men of stone?" And he added these words, the most appropriate epitaph, perhaps, for all the victims dispersed in mass graves whose memory will continue to haunt the nineteenth century: "The dead are patient; let them wait" (p. 320).

Codicil: The King's New Grave

During the debates of June 1791 on the death penalty, one of the deputies declared: "Interest the hearts of all citizens in the fate of the unfortunate who will come under the sword of justice so that he will be offered solace on every side; and let their miserable remains receive the honors of burial."[32] In fact, we don't know with any certainty where most of the victims claimed by the guillotine were buried, least of all where the body of the king was finally laid to rest.[33] But, in recent years a grandiose memorial has been dedicated, if not directly to the king himself, then to the images of kings brutally destroyed in the violence of revolutionary iconoclasm that followed the execution of Louis XVI.

In a remote corner of the Cluny Museum in Paris, the Eighth Gallery displays a remarkable collection of Gothic sculpture, the last remains of the statues removed from the facade of Notre-Dame in 1793 and 1794. The staging of the exhibit is strikingly dramatic. To the left of the entrance, twenty-one heads rest on high pedestals, to the right, twenty headless bodies stand erect, many of them, like exhumed corpses, still unidentified. The gallery itself, a large space contained on the north and west by the ruins of the Gallo-Roman baths, on the east by a sixteenth-century chapel, and on the south by a recent, nineteenth-century addition, thus offers the most ambitious reconstruction of the Gothic sculpture that originally decorated the Cathedral of Notre-Dame.

Fragments of the statues destroyed by the Revolution were recovered during the nineteenth century, but no discovery was more
dramatic than that of the twenty-one heads of the Galerie des Rois
de Judah, found in 1977 at the headquarters of the Banque Française
du Commerce Extérieur de la Chaussée d'Antin. These heads had belonged to the Tree of Jesse that stretched horizontally across the main
entrance to Notre-Dame.[34] Both as images of kings and as religious
symbols, they had represented a double affront to the revolutionary
ideal and were taken down along with more than one hundred other
sculptures.

The dramatic distribution of the fragments in the gallery—the
careful placing of decapitated heads at an "appropriate height" and
the display of truncated bodies—present the visitor, to quote the Museum brochure, with "an important testimony to the stylistic *revolution that took place brutally* in the years 1230–1240."[35] The historical
significance of this testimony is further enhanced by the arrangement
of the statues in chronological order, and the suggestion that the
mutilated bodies to the visitors' right were "executed at a later date"
than the decapitated heads that greet and startle the visitors as they
first enter. Clearly, several executions are involved here. While the
Eighth Gallery may be the most eloquent repository of the Gothic
statuary that was lost for so long, it confronts the spectator with an
unmistakable rebuke to the excesses of a regime that pursued with
equal violence the execution of Louis XVI and the metaphorical beheading of the Kings of Judah.

In its restaging of the iconoclastic violence of the Terror, the
Eighth Gallery also offers a performance, the ultimate staging of a
failed Revolution. The Cluny Museum tells its own dramatic story,
a tale of Revolution, murder, Restoration and recovery: "As early
as the classical age, serious damage was done to this exceptional en-
semble, before the Revolution would strike the fatal blow" (p. 2).
The remarkable impact of the exhibition, and its most startling effect,
stem from its emphasis on the fact that mutilation took place rather
than on the actual sculptures that were mutilated. As the spectator's
gaze slowly discovers the mutilated heads, the fragmented torsoes,
and the scattered fragments of still unidentified bodies, the serenity of

the Gothic statuary is shattered by an unparalleled sense of inarticulate violence, still and frozen in time. Visitors stand silent. It could be said of this powerful display, created at the time of the Bicentennial of the Revolution, that it represents the last and most dramatic staging of the death penalty, thought of as a spectacle and fit for a king.

Although the body of Louis XVI was never recovered with absolute certainty, it might be fitting that the twenty-one Kings of Judah, beheaded in the early days of the Terror, found their final resting place in the quiet splendor of the Hôtel de Cluny, a unique mausoleum to the royal victims of the Revolution, its only surviving cemetery, a stone Requiem worthy of kings.

* * *

It is no doubt a measure of our conflicting feelings toward the past, particularly the revolutionary past, that we glorify museums as burial chambers, yet remain oblivious to the disappearance of the tragic mass graves that once contained the remains of the great Revolutionary thinkers. The pre-revolutionary anxiety about cemeteries, its clamoring for the expulsion of the dead from the city, has been finally appeased, and not just by a more efficient handling of the dead. A most radical form of officialized memory, which is also a form of collective amnesia, has propelled the creation of these empty graveyards, Cluny, the Panthéon, where no disturbing ghosts will likely haunt the living. Since the Revolution, a few great men have been laid to rest in the large vault of the Panthéon, but the most famous tombs remain empty, and visiting hours are severely restricted.

7

The Legacy of History

There are those who let the dead bury
the dead, and there are those who are forever
digging them up to finish them off.
—J. Baudrillard, *The Illusion of the End*

Portraits

IN 1794, A GERMAN VISITOR to Paris wrote this description of
Robespierre: "He is over six feet tall and bears himself well. . . . Beneath the dark arches of his eyebrows are eyes of a deep blue that
are at once flashing, solemn and reflective and in which the flame of
fanaticism is blended with an indescribably gentle expression. . . .
His dark hair, which is generally allowed to fall freely in light curls,
frames a face whose beauty and agreeable hue are enhanced by the
shadow of his beard."[1] The visitor's judgment, that "Robespierre's
physique entitles him to be considered a handsome man" (p. 81),
is corroborated by various contemporary paintings and engravings.
Soon after his death, however, as Thermidorians set out to revise recent history, they took some pains to disfigure its most recent leader,
both his deeds and his features.

By 1802, an Englishman traveling to Paris was surprised to find in
a "valuable and curious cabinet" a bust of Robespierre "which was
taken of him, a short period before he fell." John Carr noted:

History, enraged at the review of the insatiable crimes of Robespierre, has
already bestowed upon him a fanciful physiognomy, which she has com-

posed of features which rather correspond with the ferocity of his soul, rather than with his real countenance. From the appearance of this bust, which is an authentic resemblance of him, his face must have been rather handsome. His features were small, and his countenance must have strongly expressed animation, penetration and subtlety. This bust is a real curiosity. It is very likely that not another is now to be found. Mons. le G. is permitted to preserve it, without reproach on account of his art.[2]

The traveler's naive admiration for the handsome face of Robespierre was as rare as portraits of the revolutionary leader, most of them having been taken out of circulation soon after Thermidor.[3] But as early as 1802, as Carr noted, the fanciful physiognomy inspired by the "ferocity of his soul" had supplanted images of "his lively and subtle expression."[4] Indeed, nineteenth-century writers made a point of reminding the reader that, in all cases, the monstrous killers of the king had been monstrous to behold.

One can read in the fate of revolutionary portraits the vagaries of historical interpretations. In a recent essay entitled "Icon and Symbol: The Historical Figure Called Maximilien Robespierre," Ann Rigney examines Robespierre as "a cultural unit," interpreting the elaborate construction of his physical appearance as a way to "increase his rhetorical force as a spokesman" and relate him to "the program and the constituency he stands for."[5] Through such portraits as well, one can find the genesis of historical thought, tightly interwoven with literary legends.

Revolutionary Monsters

In a footnote to his *Histoire de la Révolution française*, Michelet reported this anecdote: "A young man . . . one day asked old Merlin, of Thionville, how he had brought himself to sentence Robespierre. The old man seemed to experience some remorse. But then, rising suddenly with a violent movement, he exclaimed: 'Robespierre! Robespierre! . . . Ah! if you had seen *his green eyes*, you would have sentenced him just as I did.'"[6]

By the time Merlin remembered Robespierre's eyes for posterity,

Figure 13. Robespierre. Oil. Eighteenth-century school, Versailles.
Collection Viollet.

much had already been written on Robespierre's fateful physiognomy. In her 1818 *Considérations sur la Révolution française*, Madame de Staël described Robespierre in the following terms: "I once spoke with Robespierre at my father's house in 1789. He was then known as a lawyer from Artois, very exaggerated in his democratic views. His features were repulsive, his complexion pale, his veins a shade of green. . . . There was something mysterious in his manner, something that suggested an unspoken terror in the midst of the visible terror his government advocated."[7]

Robespierre, who was then thirty-one years old, is presented like a ghost: the paleness of his face and the green color of his veins betray the contemporary fascination with vampires, and would become integral part of his legend.[8] These details are reproduced, with variations, in countless works on the Revolution. In fact, they may have been inspired not only by Madame de Staël's unlikely encounter with Robespierre but also by a Thermidorian engraving, done by Tassart and showing Robespierre "drinking blood."[9]

In 1821, the Marquis de Ferrières described Robespierre as follows: "He was somber, mournful, suspicious, irascible, vindictive, considering events only in relation to himself. His face had something of the cat and the tiger about it."[10] The feline characteristics of Robespierre's face were taking hold of both the popular and aristocratic imagination. They echoed a Thermidorian expression according to which the last months of Robespierre's political life were a "tigrocratie."[11] The demonic quality of Robespierre's gaze was meant to express, better than any political argumentation, both Robespierre's remarkable ascendancy over the Revolution — an hypnotic, mesmerizing effect — and the necessity of destroying him for posterity.

By 1831, when Nodier drew his physical portrait, Robespierre, once observed as measuring over six feet, had become "a fairly small, spindly man." "His gaze, was an indescribable shaft of light that flashed from a wild eye, between two convulsively retractile eyelids," Nodier added, "a shaft of light that wounded when it struck. . . . With his dreadful good faith, his naive thirst for blood, his pure and cruel soul, Robespierre was the Revolution incarnate."[12] Robespierre's "retractile eyelids" clearly suggest a bird of prey, a thought later echoed by Michelet when he wrote of Robespierre: "He swooped down like a hawk on an already paralyzed bird, and bit the tender flesh."[13]

In his 1847 *Histoire des Girondins*, Lamartine contributed as well to the construction of Robespierre's monstrosity:

> Robespierre was small of stature; his limbs were puny and angular, his walk jerky, his attitudes affected . . . his rather sharp voice sought for oratorical effects but found only fatigue and monotony. . . . His eyes, very much veiled by the eyelids, and very piercing, were deeply embedded in their sockets; they had a bluish look, rather soft but vague, like steel gleaming in a bright light . . . his mouth was big, his lips thin and disagreeably contracted at the corners, his chin short and pointed, his complexion a deadly yellow, like that of a sick man, or one exhausted by night watches and meditations.[14]

We can see in these lines the simultaneous shrinking of Robespierre's physique and the progression of his monstrosity.[15] The eyes in particular have kept their animal quality but a new element has been invoked; they gleam like steel, a direct evocation of the guillotine, one that Michelet will also repeat a few years later: "His anxious eyes . . . casting a pale gleam of steel" (2: 61). In the popular imagination fired by early accounts of the French Revolution, Robespierre, like Frankenstein's creature, was death among the living, an unnatural being betrayed by his green veins and his yellow skin, his deep eye sockets and his mechanical gestures. "His automatic gait was that of a man of stone," Michelet would add, punning on Robespierre's name (61).[16]

By the end of the nineteenth century, Robespierre's metamorphosis was complete, and he was unrecognizable. Hippolyte Taine, in his passionate hatred of Robespierre, may have given us the most fantastic vision of the revolutionary thinker. Describing Robespierre's withdrawal from the political scene during the months of the Great Terror, he wrote:

> In vain he detaches himself from the action, and raises his preacher's eyes to heaven, he cannot help hearing and seeing all around him, beneath his immaculate feet, a cracking of bones and a flowing of blood, the insatiable gaping mouth of the monster he has trained and he bestrides. This mouth grows more ravenous each day, and needs a more ample feast of human flesh, and it is good, not only to let it eat, but even to supply it with food, often with

his own hands. . . . This butchery awakens destructive instincts that civilization had long held in check. His cat's physiognomy, which was at first that of a worried, but fairly gentle house cat, became the ferocious expression of a tiger-cat.[17]

The now-familiar feline qualities of the portrait are meant to suggest an untamable creature, a man-eating tiger with a suggestion of rabid disease, "foaming at the mouth when he speaks."

The Sphinx

Like monsters of Antiquity, Robespierre was thus constructed as a composite, mythical beast. For Nodier, he was a predator, a hyena with the tawny eyes of a bird of prey; for Taine, a rabid tiger; but for all, indeed (and Michelet would use the word freely) a sphinx. A feline body with a human face, Robespierre was a dramatic reincarnation of the monster who devoured the young men of Thebes. But, as the Sphinx of the Jacobins, Robespierre became a monster whose riddle was never quite solved. Michelet describes his strategy as "so obscure Robespierrists were constantly misled" (2: 596).

Historians have striven to understand the enigma of the sphinx, with varying degrees of success. As Jean-Joseph Goux remarks: "The Sphinx is a 'head-chopper'. This gives us something to reflect upon. She kills by decapitation to take the soul beyond."[18] The Sphinx, one recalls, was a female monster—*le sphinx* or *la sphinge*—and Robespierre, the man who would soon be represented as the dictator responsible for all the beheadings of the Terror, was also endowed by posterity with an enigmatic sexuality. Known for his austere and celibate life, he became feminized by writers and historians alike. Michelet described him as "more delicate and more feminine" than his sister (2: 61).

Although his clothes were not the topic of much discussion during his life (during the course of the Revolution, he apparently owned no more than three coats), the extraordinary emphasis given by all writers to his habit of dress also suggests the feminization of the monster. Madame de Staël notes: "He was not badly dressed; on the contrary, he alone wore a powdered wig and his clothes were

Figure 14. Miniature, possibly a portrait of Robespierre. Collection
and copyright Robert L. Dawson.

neat" (pp. 140–41). Ferrières noted that Robespierre "dressed and
powdered with immaculate elegance" (p. 135). Nodier, more mali-
ciously and more explicitly, wrote: "Add to this all the trappings of
stuffy, prudish, pouting coquetry, and you will almost have him"
(pp. 191–92). Hilaire Belloc dedicated a long page to Robespierre's
sober elegance and concluded with words that could apply to an Ancien Regime marquise: "A figure slight but erect and sufficiently well
filled, a little dainty and always exquisitely fitted, not disdainful of
color but contemptuous of ornament." [19]

The feminization of Robespierre's voice also deserves consideration. It is ironic that one of the most successful orators of the Revolution was alleged to have had such a strange mode of speech, "hoarse when low, false when the tone was high, and which in moments of intense excitement or anger turned into a howling rather like that of hyenas."[20] A howling perhaps, yet a chant impossible to escape. The seductiveness of Robespierre's strange voice and eloquence, although unexplained, was begrudgingly acknowledged. Nodier admits, in another reference to Antiquity: "The sirens caused the death of the lovers who were drawn to them by the charm of their concerts; but antiquity does not accuse them of having sung badly" (p. 187). Taine, less willing to be seduced, would write that Robespierre could only "moan" or "foam with rage" (3: 210).

These uneasy accounts of Robespierre's strange voice also echo the inexpressible voice attributed to the Sphinx when she called on the young men she was about to devour. It was an indescribable sound, comparable to "a rhapsody," "a song difficult to understand," notes Marie Delcourt.[21] In Euripides's words it was "a song without a lyre, strange to the Muses," sometimes compared to a muffled rumbling of thunder.[22] In a few decades the posthumous construct of Robespierre's identity took place: he had become a devouring monster whose voice, simultaneously seductive and horrifying, would lead the country to a bloodbath.

The Minotaur

Every monster needs an antidote. Robespierre's deadly sphinx was contrasted with a being who, through his appetite for life and his unequivocal human desires, both counteracted and amplified the funereal qualities of his enemy. Thus was born the legend of Danton. It could be said that Danton was invented by nineteenth-century writers to offset and dramatize Robespierre's quiet and deadly stillness. But nineteenth-century writers could not simply make Danton—a more resolute regicide than Robespierre ever was, and the main architect of the fearful Revolutionary Tribunal—into a glorified victim or a fallen hero; so he too became monsterized, a form of monstrous answer to a monstrous enigma.[23]

From the beginning, it seems that Danton's character and thus his physical description were developed chiefly as a response to Robespierre's. Whereas Robespierre was a hypocrite, Madame de Staël argues, "Danton was factious." Where Robespierre wanted power, "Danton wanted only pleasure" (p. 141).

Michelet, who repeatedly described Danton as "a sublime monster," wrote of Danton at the time of the September massacres: "As I have said, there was something of a lion in this man, but also something of a mastiff, and a fox. And this fellow kept the lion's skin at any price" (1: 1073). Later Michelet acknowledged a strange metamorphosis: "Those who are familiar with portraits of Danton, in particular the sketches David drafted during the Convention's nightly sessions, know how a man can sink from the lion to the bull—indeed fall as low as the boar, a somber and degraded character, with a distressing sensuality" (2: 446). The mixed animal metaphors that were meant to express Danton's ruthless character and instincts would slowly become fused into the mythical image of the Minotaur.

Belloc gave the best account of the composite features that metonymically created the revolutionary myth:

He was tall and stout, with the forward bearing of the orator, full of gesture and of animation. He carried a round French head upon the thick neck of energy. His face was generous, ugly, and determined. With wide eyes and calm brows, he yet had the quick glance which betrays the habit of appealing to an audience. His upper lip was injured, and so was his nose, and he had been further disfigured by the small-pox, with which disease that forerunner of his, Mirabeau, had also been disfigured. His lip had been torn by a bull when he was a child, and his nose crushed in a second adventure, they say, with the same animal. In this the Romans would have seen a portent; but he, the idol of our Positivists, found only a chance to repeat Mirabeau's expression that his "boar's head frightened me." [24]

It is said that Danton himself once soberly acknowledged his powerful ugliness by saying that nature had endowed him with "the harsh physiognomy of liberty." But a more colorful legend took over. Carlyle described Danton sitting "erect with a kind of internal convulsion struggling to keep itself motionless; his lips curling in Titanic scorn" (p. 250).

A later essayist commented:

GEORGES JACQ . DANTON

Député à la Convention Nationale.

Né à Arcis, Dépt de l'Aube le 26. 8bre 1759.

A Paris de l'Imprimerie du Cercle Social.

Figure 15. Danton. Engraving. Cabinet des Estampes. Copyright © Cliché Bibliothèque Nationale de France.

[Danton] was enormous; his colossal height dominated the Assembly; his wide shoulders; his bull's neck; his pock-marked face; his thick hair brushed straight back; his high forehead; his piercing eyes; his large, flat, snout-like nose; the scar, which he owed to his adventurous youth, and which swept his face in a sneering grin,—all helped to impress people, all contributed to his air of insolent audacity, of threatening, passionate tumult. . . . His whole appearance brought an assurance of strength which his contemporaries tried to embody in the most diverse phrases: "Gigantic Revolutionary," "King of the Revolution," "*real* tribune of the people," "Creator of the Republic," "Cyclops," "Atlas of the Party," "Titan," "Stentor," "Hercules"—such were the various epithets applied to Danton.[25]

As we can see from these portraits, Danton is meant to be in every detail, height, forehead, nose, eyes, voice, gesture, the opposite of Robespierre. As Robespierre shrinks in size, Danton grows to gigantic proportions.

Taine, whose hatred for Robespierre led him unexpectedly to glorify Danton, contributed in turn the following vision:

In temperament and character, he is a *barbarian* and a barbarian born to command his fellows. . . . A colossus with the face of a "tartar" scarred by smallpox, tragically and terribly ugly, he had the distorted mask of a growling "bulldog," tiny eyes sunken beneath the enormous furrows of a throbbing forehead, a thundering voice, a brawler's gestures, overflowing and seething with blood, anger and energy, the outbursts of a force that seems unlimited like those of nature; his declamation was wild *like the roaring of a bull*, whose sound carried through closed windows as far as fifty steps into the street, with immoderate images, sincere bombast, quivers and shouts of indignation, vengeance, and patriotism, capable of awakening the ferocious instincts in the calmest of souls and the generous instincts in the most brutish; with curses and coarse words, and a cynicism, not monotonous and deliberate like that of Hébert, but gushing forth spontaneously and naturally, frightfully coarse remarks, worthy of Rabelais, a streak of jovial sensuality and cheeky goodheartedness.[26]

As for Lamartine, anticipating perhaps such descriptions, he had dismissed Danton with unmistakable aristocratic scorn: "Everything in him was athletic, coarse and vulgar like the masses" (p. 176).

Robespierre's and Danton's transformation into mythical monsters would not have been complete without a correlated account of their lifestyles and sexuality. Robespierre's surname, "l'Incorrup-

Figure 16. Danton. Drawing by David. Collection Viollet.

tible," was given to him during his lifetime. His austerity was prov-
erbial and no one knew him to have any mistresses. By contrast, historians and commentators, in spite of all evidence to the contrary,
have emphasized Danton's unbridled sexuality and taste for life. John
Goldworth Alger wrote: "Danton's philosophy, whether or not he
uttered the phrase, was 'It is now our turn for riotous living'." [27]
Taine noted that Danton spoke to the instincts, the powerful voice
of nature. In him, Taine wrote: "There are no repugnances. He has
no moral or physical distastes. . . . He can fraternize with drunkards"
(p. 180). However, as Belloc duly noted: "Upon the faith of some
who did not know him he acquired the character of a debauchee.
For the support of this view there is not a tittle of direct evidence.
He certainly loved those pleasures of the senses which Robespierre
refused, and which Roland was unable to enjoy; but that his good
dinners were orgies or of any illegitimate loves (once he had married
the woman to whom he was so devotedly attached) there is not a
shadow of proof" (p. 56).

Certainly the image of Danton emerging from nineteenth-century
readings seems incompatible with the Danton who was so wretched
over the death of his wife that, like Emerson a few decades later, he
had her casket reopened to look at her once more some time after her
death. But, when Michelet recast the scene, the romantic gesture of
despair took a different tone as Danton "roaring with pain, reopened
the earth to kiss" his wife a last time (2: 444). [28]

Sexual Politics

Although twentieth-century historiography slowly abandoned the
practice of historical narratives organized around dominating figures, Danton and, above all, Robespierre continued to haunt the historical imagination. [29] More revealing still are the popularized images
of the revolutionary drama that were staged again a few years before the Bicentennial. For our purpose, the most interesting, perhaps
inevitable, post-Freudian reappraisal of Robespierre's and Danton's
characters took place in Andrzej Wajda's 1987 film *Danton*. [30]

Adapted from a play by Stanislawa Przybyszewska, *The Danton Case*, the film capitalizes on the familiar and contrasting figures of Danton and Robespierre. In contrast to Danton's exuberant, larger-than-life physique (Danton is played by a robust Depardieu), Robespierre (brilliantly played by Wojciech Pszoniak) is true to his legend: a thin man with cold, inexpressive features, except for a frown of permanent resentment. In our first encounter with him, we see him sick, rising painfully from bed to meet his hairdresser. His head is carefully hidden behind a mask and a wig that serve as exteriorization of a complex, inscrutable personality. Robespierre lives in a curious household, under the adoring eyes of the "maid Duplay," whose shy advances he systematically rejects with undisguised revulsion. In another correlated scene, striking in its detached cruelty, Duplay coldly beats a naked child (who would appear to the uninformed spectator to be her son) for his inability to memorize his revolutionary catechism. (Ironically, at the time the scene is supposed to take place, the Commune had just passed a decree forbidding masters, fathers, and mothers to inflict corporal punishment on children.) [31] Duplay is made to appear as a revolutionary, unnatural, harsh mother; only in the end is the spectator told that the abused child is in fact Duplay's little brother.

By contrast, Danton is presented as a force of nature. Of vigorous disposition, he is shown to prefer a night with a woman to an urgent meeting with his friends and political allies. He invites Robespierre to a sumptuous dinner, only to throw away fine dishes, glasses, and carefully prepared food when Robespierre declines to eat. Danton represents life, waste, and excess. He lives luxuriously while the people beg for bread; he is rich and wasteful, but redeemed by a devastating sincerity. In Wajda's tale, Danton is fully exonerated.

Consequently, the reasons for Danton's fall are no longer attributed to political corruption but to the capriciousness of irrational politics and, more specifically, to Robespierre's unpredictable character. Two momentous scenes seal Danton's and Camille Desmoulins's fate. The first takes place when Danton, having invited Robespierre to eat with him, loses his temper and screams at the Incorruptible: "What do you know of the people? Nothing! Look at yourself! You don't drink wine! You faint at the sight of a naked sword! And they say you've never screwed a woman! So? . . . You want the happiness of men and you are not even a man." This explosion of anger makes explicit what the movie has already gone to some pain to emphasize. First, that Robespierre lives in an isolated world, entirely detached from the people, or, we should say, what the word "people" is supposed to mean. Second, Danton's judgment emphasizes what remains, in Wajda's eyes, Robespierre's most deplorable sin: his effeminacy. Already connoted by powder, make-up, and wig, Robespierre's femininity takes a more decisive and, for Wajda, more deplorable turn. It becomes a physical cowardice crudely associated with Robespierre's personal sexual failures. In what may have been an unintentional comment on this scene, the national secretary of the French Socialist party, Marcel Debarge, declared during the Bicentennial: "I like Danton because I have always had a weakness for people who live, who screw. . . . The visionary side of Robespierre sends shivers down my spine."[32] In Wajda's account of the French Revolution, sexuality and politics are inseparable, or rather, sexuality serves to emphasize the fact that Robespierre cannot serve the people adequately. Wajda's feminization of Robespierre amounts to an indictment. As Danton makes clear, Robespierre is unfit to lead the nation.

In a second scene, both more cruel and pathetic, Robespierre, who has come to plead with Camille Desmoulins (Patrice Chéreau) to abandon Danton, is rejected by Desmoulins and his friends, in the midst of laughter and derision. Robespierre, alone in the corridor, hears the mockery and leaves, humiliated, resentful, more than ever determined to see them all executed. Wajda's argument, that Robespierre was in love with Camille Desmoulins—made more explicit in a previous scene where Robespierre tenderly puts his arms around Desmoulins's shoulders but does not succeed in moving the journalist—also serves to show two irreconcilable visions of the Revolution: Danton and his friends offer images of conspicuous consumption, delighting both in domestic bliss and decadent feasts. Most of all, they are *undisguised*. Unlike Robespierre, who is first seen being made up, Danton keeps throwing away his disheveled wig.

By contrast, in Wajda's eyes, Robespierre's repressed sexuality symbolizes how far the Revolution had strayed from its course. Everything that comes in contact with him is anomalous, from the strange domestic arrangement at the Duplay house to the repeated visits of a caricatural Saint-Just, sporting a single earring, heavy make-up, flowers, and speaking with obscene violence. In the concluding scene, after Danton and Desmoulins have been executed, Robespierre lies alone, still sick and in bed, covering his face, in shame or despair, with a white shroud-like sheet.

Of course, Wajda's film was meant first of all as a political fable on contemporary Poland, a nation struggling with Communism (embodied by Robespierre's rigid austerity), seduced by the lure of Capitalist decadence (whose excesses and appeal are represented by Danton) under the watchful camera-eye of a Catholic Church worried about family values.[33] As Raymond Lefebvre comments:

It has been said that Robespierre's impassive face was reminiscent of Jaruzelski's mask, and that Danton had expressions similar to those of Walesa. It is true that [in the film] parable takes precedence over historical analysis. As Wajda himself put it: "If one is under the impression that my sympathies lie with Danton, it's because it is difficult not to side with the victim of a political trial."[34]

In economic terms—and we should remember that these legends were first forged in the early days of liberal capitalism—Danton is redeemed as an emblem of productive economic activity. He could just as well have emerged from a Balzac novel. He takes bribes, gambles, borrows, spends, squanders, wastes, invests, and gets rich, immensely rich, before dying. The Minotaur rides a bull market; he is a figure of greed, high investment, and profit. In contrast, Robespierre is further castigated as a figure of sterility, withdrawal, austerity, shrift, and fruitless hoarding.[35]

But Wajda's film is exemplary in another important way. Like all movies and popular novels about the French Revolution, its underlying concern is not the personal rivalry between Danton and Robespierre, but their relationship to this ultimate and deadly signifier, the guillotine, and what the guillotine stands for, the Terror. The culmination of the film is what we have known and expected from the first scene: Danton's death, filmed with documentary precision. Lefevre notes "the removal of the black sheet, the straw where the blood will gush forth," and calls it a "horribly effective" conclusion (p. 144). Ultimately, as we shall see, the creation of Danton and Robespierre's legends also served to account for the Terror.

Revolution and Its Discontent

In an recent essay entitled *La Révolution fratricide*, Jacques André proposed an analysis of the French Revolution that throws some light on the process by which Danton and Robespierre were recreated as monstrous embodiments of the Revolution and, more importantly, on the role the Terror has played in these posthumous interpretations. André sought to analyze the Revolution in the light of Freud's theories, with a view to exploring a "psychoanalysis of the social bond as such." In *Totem and Taboo*, Freud's account of the beginning of society, and, to a lesser degree, in *Moses and Monotheism*, André finds the key to an understanding of the Revolution as a privileged moment when the origins of society are briefly revealed. "In terms of these ageless questions, the French Revolution constitutes an exceptional circumstance. It is part of one of those historical movements in which an aspect of the origins of society is played out anew, is staged to the point of exposing itself—before quickly burying itself and again becoming imperceptible to us."[36]

The reader will recall Freud's account of the formation of social bonds in "The Infantile Recurrence of Totemism." "One day, the expelled brothers joined forces, slew and ate the father, and thus put an end to the father horde." From the resulting guilt emerged the fundamental taboos of totemism, the prohibition against killing the totem/father, and the taboo of incest with the mother that "correspond to the two repressed wishes of the Oedipus complex." Moreover, we find in moral precepts

the consequences of the tender impulses towards the father as they are changed into remorse. . . . The social and fraternal feelings on which this great change is based, henceforth for long periods exercises the greatest influence upon the formation of society. They find expression in the sanctification of the common blood and in the emphasis upon the solidarity of life within the clan.[37]

Certainly *Totem and Taboo* provides a compelling framework for an analysis of the Revolution as replay of the origins of society. In *The Family Romance of the French Revolution*, Lynn Hunt remarks that "the French killed the father in an act that comes as close as anything does in modern history to a ritual sacrifice."[38] André himself proposes a different theory based on a rereading of *Totem and Taboo*. He argues that the incest taboo is not successfully integrated into Freud's text, because "the horde itself is not incestuous . . . and there is nothing before the horde." On the basis of Freud's observation that the brothers "kept the organization that had made them strong and which may have relied on homosexual feelings and practices that had become established among them at the time of their exile," André speculates that the originary social bond was based, not on the father's murder, but on the brothers' love. *"From love addressed to the father to reciprocal attachment, fraternal homosexuality and the state of society develop through the same impulse"* (p. 26, emphasis in original). Consequently, in André's rereading of Freud, the brothers did not kill the father in order to lay claim to the women, but because *"he does not respond to the request for love,* that he nonetheless elicits" (p. 27, emphasis in original).

This conceptual shift from a social tie founded on parricide and the resulting incest taboo to a social tie based on homosexual love and the concurrent exclusion of the feminine leads André to argue that the execution of Louis XVI was in no way the "founding" act of the Republic. André writes: *"the murder of the father-tyrant is not a drama, or a phantasm, that haunts the brothers of the Revolution, supplying the final meaning for their acts, but a scenario they construct, in an attempt to bind the anxiety and violence that threatens to dissolve the social order 'in every direction'"* (p. 130, emphasis in original). In this, André is closer to René Girard than to Freud.[39] As Lynn Hunt notes: "In a Girardian account [of the King's sacrifice], the emphasis would not be on the King's position as father of his people. The brothers do not kill him because they want to share his power but rather because the French fear their own capacity for violence and need a ritual in order

Figure 17. Act of Justice, 9–10 Thermidor. Engraving after Viller. Collection Viollet.

to reinstate community boundaries" (p. 11). Interestingly, there is no founding act in André's analysis, just the replay of an originary model ("there was nothing before the horde").

The sacrifice of the king is "a failed sacrifice," André contends, since it failed to diminish the violence and disorder that threatened the successful outcome of the Revolution. By contrast, 9 Thermidor, he asserts, is a "successful sacrifice":

Unlike the execution of the King, or the elimination of the Girondins and other members of the Convention, the sacrifice of Robespierre, Saint-Just, Couthon and their partisans is a successful sacrifice—the word does not prejudge of the appreciation one can make on the following period. The sacrifice is successful in that it absorbs, if not all the violence that threatens the social body, at least that which, under the name of Terror, does instead of government and serves as social bond. (pp. 184–85)

Finally, André notes, "the Freudian thesis positing a deep complicity between paranoia and unconscious homosexuality—in both the collective and individual orders—finds a remarkable confirmation in the Terror, and in the Terror's best spokesman, the *Incorruptible*" (p. 242). In Robespierre's last discourse, André finds a "classic example of the rhetoric of persecution" (p. 242). Quoting Robespierre's words: "One hides, one dissimulates, one misleads, thus one conspires," as an expression of paranoia, he adds: "But this is not its originality." Indeed, he argues, one has to go back to the discourse attacking Danton to see that "on that occasion [Danton's elimination], the enemy is named, isolated, and the dialectic of accusation is still that of antagonism; an antagonism that contains the principle of its own resolution: the restoration of the One through suppression of everything opposed to it" (p. 242).

For our purpose, the most revealing part of André's brilliant and controversial analysis lies not in its suggestive interpretation of Terror as pathology (p. 137), or its reevaluation of the marginalization of women by the Republic ("the feminine danger," p. 204, "the hatred of women," p. 206),[40] but rather in its inescapable return to the dominating figure of Robespierre, which concludes the study, and its accompanying reduction of the revolutionary process to the unfolding of Terror. Indeed, although the book takes the entire Revolution to task, none of its relevant achievements are discussed. The Revolution appears as a succession of "murders" and inescapable bloodshed. Even André's discussion of David's painting is embedded in a rhetoric of violence, where the brothers' love yields a deep hatred of women.

The Terror

André's appraisal further emphasizes what has been clear from two centuries of agonized accounts of the troubled creation of the Republic. That, central to its elaboration, central to the construction of Danton and Robespierre, lies the Terror; that every analysis of the Revolution seems compelled, first and foremost, to take the Terror into account, explain it, or else explain it away. Nineteenth-century historians, like Aulard, saw the Terror as unavoidable response to growing threats mounting against the Republic. The Terror was a desperate response to outside pressure. Taine, on the other hand, saw in the Terror the proof of revolutionary evil. As Donald Greer put it, for Taine, "the Terror was a political philosophy written in blood. The Philosophy was that of Rousseau, and the Terror was an inter-lude of Jacobin paranoia induced by the virus of the *Social Contract*— a crime committed collectively by the dregs of society which this poisonous leaven had brought to the top for a brief reign of destruc-tion." [41] For their part, the Bicentennial's revisionist historians left the horror intact in its tragic unfolding while simultaneously producing what Jean Baudrillard calls "a perfectly pious *vision* of the Revolu-tion, cast in terms of the Rights of Man. Not even a nostalgic vision, but one recycled in the terms of postmodern intellectual comfort. A vision which allows us to eliminate Saint-Just from the *Dictionnaire de la Révolution*. 'Overrated rhetoric', says François Furet, perfect his-torian of the repentance of the Terror and of glory." [42]

Although it accounted for fewer victims in Paris than the Saint-Barthélémy massacre (when 3,000 persons were killed in a single night),[43] royal reprisals against peasant insurrections in the seven-teenth and eighteenth centuries, or the Bloody Week of the Com-mune, the Terror still appears as unprecedented violence. It exerts on readers and historians alike the fascination elicited by senseless serial murders.[44] Even more singular is the fact that, under the word "Terror" are collapsed many distinct events, some preceding what is strictly called the Terror (which is associated with the creation of the Revolutionary Tribunals), others related to the civil war in Ven-dée. Unlike the September massacres, that cost a greater number of lives but have failed to arouse among commentators the angst and the horror provoked by the decisions of the Revolutionary Tribunal, the Terror was not an unmediated, irrational act of violence. Why are these deaths more disturbing? Certainly, when the law appears to promote the Terror, the citizen is no longer afforded the protection the law is meant to provide; and it may be this visible failure of the legal structure that made the Terror more horrifying than unpremeditated scenes of mob violence.

Politically, the Terror has been amplified and dramatized in order to discredit the republican process. Nineteenth-century chroniclers of the Revolution relied heavily on the theatrical horror of the guillotine to show how far the Revolution had strayed from its original goal and, by extension, to cast the most serious doubts on the possibility that what they viewed as an illegitimate republican government could establish a wise and orderly rule. It did not matter that the guillotine replaced deaths by hangings, burning at the stake, often preceded by horrendous torture. Little consideration has been given to the fact that the Revolution did away with the most revulsive aspects of arbitrary justice under the Old Regime. The Terror appears as an act of personal revenge enacted by a blood-thirsty government first against the supporters of the king, then against their own friends and followers.

Beyond the partisan politics that one unavoidably encounters in any account of the Revolution, however, there remains an underlying anxiety that cannot be explained solely by political prejudices. It is worth noting that the Terror's victims, unlike those of the Saint-Barthélémy massacre, have names and personal histories that have become known to us. Beginning with the royal family, victims of the Terror have haunted posterity with their tragic individual destinies. A striking example is Marie-Antoinette's posthumous representations, as censurable though hapless queen, or as a queen who was above all a mother and wife.[45]

Most forceful among the touching accounts of scenes that took place on the way to the scaffold were scenes of shattered *domestic* happiness: "The Royal family cell at the Temple prison," long the subject of a special exhibit at the Musée Carnavalet; Marie-Antoinette's wrenching separation from the Dauphin, recorded many times on canvas; Camille and Lucile Desmoulins's destroyed domestic bliss, or André Chénier's last verses to his beloved, written on the tumbril that led him to his death. These far-from-unknown victims have left

indelible marks on the popular imagination, historical accounts of
the Revolution, and generations of French pupils.[46] With the excep-
tion of Robespierre who was made into a decidedly fantastic, unfeel-
ing being, all victims of the guillotine, whatever their past or identity, have been made to appear *familiar*, in all the senses of the word.
In his hugely popular *Citizens*, Simon Schama introduced his story
of the Terror with an account entitled "Death of a Family."[47] Books
have been published that contain diaries written from prisons, farewell letters to one's family, and more scenes of shattered domestic
innocence.[48] The Terror remains terrifying in its uncanny familiarity
in that, as it is recounted to us, it was not directed against a recognizable Other, an enemy coming from the outside,[49] but against the
very people who contributed to the revolutionary process. Far from
taking a toll on a threatening Other, the horror specific to the Terror,
and expressed in different ways, lies in its destruction of the Same.
The Same kills the Same. The brothers kill each other. The Revolution devours its own children.

The pre-Thermidorian victims of the guillotine have been exonerated by posterity. Where revolutionary fervor could not fully be invoked, domestic values relieved them from all political guilt. Danton
was a regicide and a terrorist, Michelet notes, but also a devoted husband. Although some of these images may have faded from contemporary historical accounts of the Revolution, a rapid bibliographical
survey indicates that the Terror, the guillotine, and the family (royal
and other) still occupied center stage during Bicentennial revisita-
tions.[50] Its domestic quality suggests that the Terror, our image of the
Terror, has been embedded, not so much with the originary murder
of *Totem and Taboo*, but with Freud's definition of the *unheimliche*. If
Freud is to be invoked, Freud's analysis of the Uncanny would offer
the best guide to the way we have both emphasized and tamed the
horror of the guillotine.

With the Terror, historiography argues, no one is safe. Furet calls it
"an *ubiquitous* form of government" whose effects took gigantic proportions.[51] Dismissing the carefully documented numbers produced
by Georges Lefebvre, and revising his previous assessment that the
revolutionaries "were not these blood-drinkers created by royalist

legends,"[52] Furet speaks of 16,600 victims and of close to a half million arrests, to which must be added, he notes, the "tens of thousands of deaths" resulting from the actions of Carrier in Nantes and Turreau in Vendée.[53] As Furet's source specifies, but Furet omits to mention, these numbers (based on a "statistical method") result from distinct factors (including deaths from disease), yet they are largely imputed by Furet to the "Dictatorship of Year II." The repeated mentions of dramatic, largely unverifiable numbers, and the concurrent disclosures of a "Revolutionary holocaust" (or a "génocide vendéen"),[54] lend support to the thesis that the Bicentennial of the Revolution served largely to occult the fiftieth anniversary of the 1939 defeat and the more recent Holocaust to which Vichy France contributed.

Finally, André's essay provides another and more complex answer to our undiminished anxiety about the Terror. In the concluding lines of *La Révolution fratricide*, he writes that with Robespierre's death "Terror ceases to be on the agenda: on the agenda of democracy, of which it could be a fundamental, and necessarily unrecognized, element" (p. 243). That Terror may be an unavoidable component of the democratic process, that the origin of the modern state should be tainted with bloodshed that would be part and parcel of Revolution itself, is a question all historians—of all political stripes—have labored hard to elude. Anxiety about an origin necessarily founded in violence may in turn account for the necessity historians have felt, either to ascribe the origin of such a violence to *outside* factors (the war, the effects of the European coalition against France), or to put the blame for the Terror on an *extra-ordinary* individual. This anxiety may explain how and why the posthumous image of Robespierre was created.

Carrying the Burden

Louis XVI, André argues, was created in order to explain, and atone for, the unchecked violence that already marred the revolutionary process in September 1792: "The tyrant is a *construct* of the Revolution, a figure that it elaborates at a turning point in its own history"

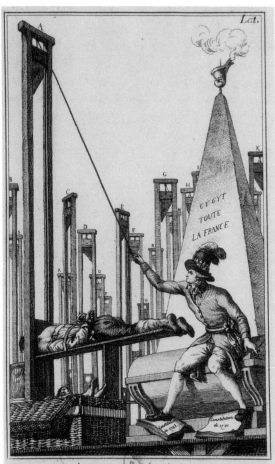

Figure 18. "Robespierre executing the executioner after executing all the Frenchmen." Engraving. Cabinet des Estampes. Copyright © Cliché Bibliothèque Nationale de France. Similar engravings were circulated with different legends, one with the name of Fouquier-Tinville substituted for that of Robespierre.

(p. 122). By killing the tyrant, the Revolution would cleanse itself of the senseless violence that had tainted its unfolding. Lynn Hunt notes: "The King had to be transformed into a kind of sacred monster, whose expulsion will return the community to itself" (p. 11). But similarly, one might add, generations of historians and commentators have *constructed* a second, duplicate tyrant, Robespierre, to account for the bloody Terror of 1793–94.[55] In this vertiginous *mise-en-abîme*, it is interesting to note, Robespierre is not just a monster, but a *royal* monster.[56] The recurring chapter headlines that have become common currency ("The Reign of Terror," "The Reign of Robespierre," "Robespierre the Tyrant") illustrate better than any argument that the making of Robespierre into a scapegoat duplicates the revolutionaries' attempts to create and destroy an image of royal tyranny. In fact, the expression "bloodthirsty tiger" was used to describe first the king, then Robespierre. In his study of the fate of Robespierre's image during the Bicentennial in France, Steven Kaplan suggestively speaks of a "totemic Robespierre."[57]

Once the Terror can be ascribed to an individual, an extraordinary one, it can also be contained and rationalized. Furthermore, by being represented as the ultimate despot, Robespierre removed a fundamental anxiety; he served to separate Terror from the Republic, from the social tie that was formed over the decapitated body of the king. André has shown how the king was feminized in images produced at his trial and in representations of his death. In André's view, the king's feminization and execution served also to express and appease the revolutionary brothers' "hatred" of the feminine.[58] It is significant that the very elements that served to construct Louis XVI as royal despot worthy of death were used in turn by commentators of the Revolution to construct Robespierre as a revolutionary tyrant worthier of death than his direct predecessor. To both are attributed the responsibility for senseless violence and excess, together with a disquieting femininity.

Robespierre's feminization, which made him look to posterity like an Ancien Régime marquise and sound like a siren while destroying all around him, ultimately refers to the more archaic image of the feminine as chaos. Ewa Lajer-Burcharth has shown how post-

Figure 19. Head of Robespierre, executed 10 Thermidor. Wood engraving. Musée Carnavalet. Collection Viollet. "Maximilien Robespierre known as the modern Catilina." Inspired by a well-known image showing the decapitated head of Louis XVI.

Figure 20. Allegory of Terror. Copyright © Cliché Bibliothèque Nationale de France.

Thermidorian caricatures portrayed a feminized Terror, closely associating the disorder of revolutionary history with the fury of women.[59] Robespierre's femininity as well refers to disorder and destruction. His femininity is that of the devouring sphinx.

The Anxiety of Origin

Indeed, such mythical and fanciful images could not have taken hold had they not responded to a deep anxiety regarding both the inevitability of the Revolution and its dramatic unfolding as origin of the modern state. And this is why the figure of Robespierre as Sphinx takes on a special urgency. In his analysis of the origin of the political state, Mitchell Greenberg quotes these lines from Stephen Heath: "For Hegel, the Sphinx stands at the beginning of the history of consciousness. . . . Oedipus solves the riddle, flings the Sphinx over the rock, gets rid of the monstrous."[60] And Greenberg adds: "The politics that the Oedipus myth represents, the politics that is condensed in and on the figure of the riddle-solving perpetrator of parricide and incest, is also the originary moment of Western masculine hegemony."[61] There also rests the enduring power of the revolutionary legend, which reads[62] at times like a modern version of the Oedipus myth: it combines the haunting memories of the parricide/regicide with the plague and the chaos that preceded the Sphinx's encounter with Oedipus. From this perspective, the transformation of Robespierre the statesman, the regicide, the theoretical founder of the Republic, into the man-eating Sphinx, the feminine figure of archaic chaos and disorder, forcefully expresses a repudiation of the modern state on the part of the early royalist manufacturers of the revolutionary legend and, as Baudrillard puts it, a "boundless *ressentiment*" on the part of more recent commentators (p. 22).

For Michelet, a Republican mourning the Revolution, the legend of the Sphinx pervaded the history of the Revolution, but he added a correlated element. Describing Danton's emergence on the political stage, he exclaimed: "What is most terrifying about [Danton] is that he has no eyes; at least one hardly sees them. Indeed! will this terrible blindman be the guide of nations?" (1: 505) and a few lines later, he commented: "He is a devoted Oedipus, who, possessed by his riddle, carries the terrible sphinx within himself, so as to be devoured by it" (1: 505).[63] From Michelet's point of view, the Revolution failed because Danton, both its Minotaur and its Oedipus, internalized his hidden enemy, the sphinx-like Robespierre, and was blinded *before* he had an opportunity to rid the city of the plague. He would die, but still, Michelet repeatedly argued, he ultimately triumphed over the winged monster and ultimately caused its death. Indeed, Robespierre was doomed from the moment he sentenced Danton/Oedipus, and the devouring sphinx would perish for it: "Billaud threw Danton to him, a meal *fit for a king* [*royal morceau*], but that was difficult to digest, and became deadly for Robespierre" (2: 1014, emphasis added).

The Sphinx herself, of course, was sent to Thebes as punishment for a parricide. Similarly, although nineteenth-century writing made him primarily into the devourer of young lives, Robespierre was seen as both agent and punishment for the king's death. It is significant as well that no one among the Thermidorians would arise as the riddle-solver, the parricide hero, founder of a new order. For the legend of Robespierre as Sphinx also posited that the chaotic unfolding of the Revolution could not lead to a new order. Nor did Robespierre's death single-handedly check revolutionary violence. On the contrary, the Terror continued,[64] and Robespierre's fall precipitated France into another twenty years of tyranny and war.

Varying accounts suggest that the Sphinx either threw herself to her death or was killed by Oedipus after he solved her riddle. With striking similarity, history has it that either Robespierre tried to kill himself just before he was arrested or the gendarme Merda, a most unlikely hero, shot and wounded him. The sphinx was dead, to be sure, but because no riddle-solver emerged, chaos remained. Thus Robespierre had to be killed again, explained, "anatomized," to use Michelet's expression, resolved, in the endless representations of his revolutionary legend.

The pervasive presence of the legend in nineteenth-century accounts of the Revolution also reminds us that the discipline of history in France was developed in part as an attempt to solve the riddle of the Revolution. History emerged as a new science whose dual goal was to account for the past and, at the same time, indefinitely to ponder the moment when the Sphinx plunged to her death unvanquished, her enigma unsolved, and the illuminating encounter with Oedipus, as well as the birth of the modern state, indefinitely postponed.[65] We might apply to these efforts to decipher the Revolutionary past what Lamartine once wrote of Robespierre: "He was the last word of the Revolution, but nobody could read him" (p. 41).

Notes

Introduction

1. Louis-Antoine de Saint-Just, *Oeuvres complètes*, ed. Michèle Duval (Paris: Gérard Lebovici, 1984), p. 979. This note is found among various unfinished texts posthumously regrouped under the title "Fragments d'institutions républicaines."

2. In *Prelude to Terror*, Norman Hampson briefly wonders about the relationship between the Revolution's ideology and the failure of its political goals. His chapter on the question is suggestively entitled "The Unhelpfulness of Ideology." *Prelude to Terror: The Constituent Assembly and the Failure of Consensus, 1789–1791* (London: Basil Blackwell, 1988), pp. 99–110.

3. Jean Baudrillard, *The Illusion of the End*, trans. Chris Turner (Stanford, Calif.: Stanford University Press, 1994), p. 23.

4. Most historians agree that the Revolution ended with the fall of Robespierre (27 July 1794).

5. Maximilien Robespierre, *Oeuvres de Maximilien Robespierre*, ed. Marc Bouloiseau, Jean Dautry, Georges Lefebvre, and Albert Soboul (Paris: Presses Universitaires de France, 1958), 9: 495.

6. The question of the Revolution's debt to the philosophers of the Enlightenment has been discussed by Daniel Mornet in his classic *Les Origines intellectuelles de la Révolution française* (Paris: Armand Colin, 1933). For a recent examination of the question, see Roger Chartier, *The Cultural Origins of the French Revolution*, trans. Lydia G. Cochrane (Durham, N.C.: Duke University Press, 1991); and Dena Goodman, *The Republic of Letters: A Cultural History of the French Enlightenment* (Ithaca, N.Y.: Cornell University Press, 1994).

7. Jean-Jacques Rousseau, *On the Social Contract*, ed. Roger D. Masters, trans. Judith R. Masters (New York: St. Martin's Press, 1978), p. 46.

8. Dominick LaCapra, "History and Memory," paper given at the 1994 meeting of the Modern Language Association, p. 5. I quote with gratitude from this unpublished paper.

9. For a comprehensive analysis, see Linda Orr, *Headless History: Nineteenth-Century French Historiography of the Revolution* (Ithaca, N.Y.: Cornell University Press, 1990).

10. Baudrillard, *The Illusion of the End*, pp. 22–23.

Chapter 1

1. A Neufchastel, 16: 413. The author quotes Newton, Wallis and Chambers in this article and associates the conflagration of lightning with that of gunpowder.

2. On Franklin's experiments with electricity, see Alfred Owen Aldridge, *Benjamin Franklin, Philosopher and Man* (Philadelphia: Lippincott, 1965), chapter 9, "The Electrical Years," pp. 91–101. See also Esmond Wright, *Franklin of Philadelphia* (Cambridge, Mass.: Belknap Press of Harvard University Press, 1986), pp. 62–70. Wright briefly mentions the lightning rod trial, p. 68. *The Experiments and Observations on Electricity* was translated into French by François Thomas Dalibard and published by Durand in Paris in 1752. On the French reception of Franklin's discovery, see the Abbé Nollet, *Lettre sur l'électricité* (Paris, 1753). Nollet expresses serious doubts concerning the lightning rod. M. de Romas's *Mémoire sur les moyens de se garantir de la foudre dans les maisons*, published by Bergeret in Bordeaux in 1776, reports on the author's experiments with the electrical kite.

3. A Amsterdam, 4: 948–49 (emphasis in original). Morveau refers to two important *Mémoires* on the question: the *Mémoire* of Le Roy, published in the Collection of the Royal Academy of Sciences in 1770, and the *Mémoire* of M. de Saussure on lightning rods, published in Geneva.

4. Louis-Bernard Guyton-Morveau wrote thirteen articles for the *Encyclopedia*. Born in Dijon in 1737, he served for 21 years as avocat-général in the Burgundy Parliament, then resigned his charge to dedicate himself entirely to his studies in chemistry. He published *Eléments de chimie théorique et pratique* in 1776–77. He was elected to the Legislative Assembly and later to the Convention. He sat on the first Committee of Public Safety from April to July of 1793. He oversaw the fabrication of armaments during the Terror and participated in the battle of Fleurus. In November 1793, he proposed a republican chess, where the king, queen, knight, bishop, and other pieces would be renamed after military titles. He survived the Revolution and received from Napoleon the title of Baron. He died in 1816. See John Lough, *The Contributors to the Encyclopédie* (London: Grant and Cutler, 1973).

5. See Maximilien Robespierre, *Oeuvres de Maximilien Robespierre*, ed. Marc Bouloiseau, Jean Dautry, Georges Lefebvre, and Albert Soboul (Paris: Presses Universitaires de France, 1926–67), 1: 20.

6. Letter from M. de Vissery to Antoine-Joseph Buissart, quoted in Vellay (note 8 below), p. 28.

7. Antoine-Joseph Buissart, born in Arras in 1737, was admitted to the bar in 1761 and elected to the Arras Academy in 1767. He was the king's commissioner for primary assemblies in 1790 and was elected justice of the peace in 1791. He withdrew from public life after Robespierre's execution. He was

one of the most respected physicists in Amiens. See Vellay (note 8 below), p. 28.

8. A detailed account of this trial was given by Charles Vellay in "Robespierre et le procès dit du paratonnerre," *Annales Révolutionnaires* (January–March 1909): 25–37; (April–June 1909): 201–19. See also Des Essarts, *Causes célèbres, curieuses et intéressantes de toutes les cours souveraines du Royaume avec les jugements qui les ont décidées* (Paris, 1783), 99: 3–110; 103: 125–36. Ernest Hamel, Robespierre's most devoted biographer, speaks of the trial, although he tends to exaggerate Robespierre's role and the fame he acquired from it. See his *Histoire de Robespierre* (Paris: Lacroix, Verboeckhoven, 1865), 1: 38–42. In his *Robespierre* (Paris: Gallimard, 1961), Gérard Walter also discussed the trial and emphasized Buissart's contributions. But Walter underestimated the friendship between Buissart and Robespierre when he accused Robespierre of having stolen some of the fame that should have gone to the older man. See Georges Michon's edition of the *Correspondance de Maximilien et Augustin Robespierre* (Paris: Alcan, 1926).

9. See Vellay, pp. 206–7.

10. Robespierre, *Plaidoyers pour le sieur de Vissery de Bois-Valé, appellant d'un jugement des échevins de Saint-Omer, qui avait ordonné la destruction d'un Par-à-tonnerre élevé sur sa maison* (Arras: Imprimerie de Guy Delasablionnière, 1784). The *Mercure de France* spoke of the trial on several occasions. In an article of 21 June 1783, it applauded the victory of science and hailed the worth of Buissart, with a flattering note on Robespierre's merit. On 1 May 1784, it duly noted the publication of Robespierre's speeches at the trial.

11. Library of the University of Pennsylvania. The letter was published for the first time in France by Vellay, "Robespierre et le procès," p. 215.

12. Anne Robert Jacques Turgot, Baron of L'Eaulne (1727–1781) had first envisioned joining the church. Instead he became a friend of the philosophers and contributed to the *Encyclopedia*. He was an habitué of the salon of Madame Helvétius. His publications include *Lettres sur la tolérance* (1754) and *Réflexions sur la formation et la distribution des richesses* (1776). He was appointed comptroller general in 1774, but his reforms quickly made him unpopular with the aristocracy and he was dismissed in 1776. Interestingly enough, the article he wrote for the *Encyclopedia* was dedicated to etymology. He is considered a physiocrat, although he differed from them on questions of industry and economic exchange.

13. Alfred Owen Aldridge speaks at length of this epigram and its success in *Franklin and His French Contemporaries* (New York: New York University Press, 1957), pp. 124–42.

14. Roland Mortier, *Clartés et ombres au siècle des Lumières* (Geneva: Droz, 1969). See in particular pp. 13–60.

15. Although Furetière could still write that "The Enlightenment of Faith

and the Gospels have dissipated the shadows and the blindness of the human race," the word was already inscribed in a semantic system that associated it with reason opposed to ignorance. Examples are frequent in Malebranche, himself a scientifically inclined priest. Quoted in Mortier, *Clartés*, p. 16.

16. Turgot, who was to become friendly with Franklin in Paris, evolved from thinking that he could preach the reconciliation of church, royalty, and Enlightenment, to thinking that Enlightenment led to a natural religion. Enlightenment acquired a resolutely profane meaning. Alone outside this movement, Rousseau would strive to reopen the question of Enlightenment as opposed not to ignorance and superstition but to the notions of virtue and truth. The debate would continue unabated throughout the French Revolution, itself deeply divided between the republic of letters and sciences, and the republic of virtue.

17. Robespierre, *Plaidoyers*, pp. 75, 26, 28, 71, emphasis added.

18. On the important question of chance and its resonance in eighteenth-century philosophical debates, see Thomas M. Kavanagh, *Enlightenment and the Shadows of Chance* (Baltimore: Johns Hopkins University Press, 1993).

19. Robespierre, *Plaidoyers*, p. 27, emphasis added.

20. Jean-Jacques Rousseau's influence on Robespierre is well known. For a recent evaluation, see Carol Blum, *Rousseau and the Republic of Virtue: The Language of Politics in the French Revolution* (Ithaca, N.Y.: Cornell University Press, 1984). In this instance, however, Robespierre detaches himself completely from Rousseau in his appreciation of human progress. His belief that science advanced civilization remained intact through his last great speeches of 1794.

21. Robespierre, *Plaidoyers*, p. 20.

22. On the question of blindness and Enlightenment, see William R. Paulson, *Enlightenment, Romanticism, and the Blind in France* (Princeton, N.J.: Princeton University Press, 1987).

23. Quoted by Ronald Paulson, *Representations of Revolution, 1789–1820* (New Haven, Conn.: Yale University Press, 1983), p. 44. Wollstonecraft also evokes "the rumblings of the approaching tempest" and the "gathering storm."

24. Paulson, *Representations of Revolution*, p. 58. Paulson's analysis of the metaphors organized around the idea of storm, light that smashes to bits, and the tempest is especially interesting here, as is all of Chapter 3, entitled "Burke, Paine and Wollstonecraft: The Sublime and the Beautiful," pp. 57–87. Of particular interest is the idea Burke presented in 1757 in his *Philosophical Enquiry into the Origin of the Sublime and the Beautiful*: although, in Paulson's words, "Darkness is sublime, light is not," "extreme light," Burke noted, "by overcoming the organs of sight, obliterates all objects, so as in its effects exactly resembles darkness" (p. 59). See also Paulson's remark that, for Burke, "the true sublime in government is a mixture of fear and awe or admiration,

whereas the false sublime . . . generates only fear and a grotesque energy" (p. 66). Burke's views on the tragicomic, grotesque character of the French Revolution are well known. Indeed, few English thinkers misunderstood the French Revolution so thoroughly while being so deeply fascinated by its unfolding. Nevertheless, the concept of the sublime that Robespierre associates with the Cult of the Supreme Being is not far from Burke's own thoughts.

25. For a recent appraisal, see *Representing the French Revolution: Literature, Historiography, and Art*, ed. James A. W. Heffernan (Hanover, N.H.: University Press of New England, 1992).

26. On the general reactions to Franklin's death in revolutionary France, see Aldridge, *Franklin and His French Contemporaries*, pp. 212–34, and Gilbert Chinard, *L'Apothéose de Benjamin Franklin* (Paris: Alcan, 1955).

27. Reprinted in Chinard, *L'Apothéose*, p. 161. Like Robespierre and Condorcet, Vicq d'Azir died in 1794. He had been Marie-Antoinette's personal physician and an influential voice in the decision to remove cemeteries from the cities for hygiene purposes. See below, chapter 6.

28. Condorcet, *Oeuvres*, ed. Condorcet O'Connor and M. F. Arago (Paris, 1847), "Eloge de Franklin," 3: 404.

29. See *Couplets civiques* for the inauguration of the busts of Franklin, Voltaire, Buffon, Jean-Jacques Rousseau, Marat, and Le Peletier in the hall of the popular republican society of Avre-Libre, by Citizen Dourneau-Demophile (Paris, Year II).

30. Jacques-Pierre Brissot (1754–1793) came from a rich bourgeois family of Chartres. One of his most interesting prerevolutionary projects was to establish in London an international academy of writers and philosophers that would make itself known through a prestigious publication. Although Brissot was able to find financial support, the project turned into a fiscal disaster and Brissot was briefly jailed for bad debts. Back in France, suspected of having written a pamphlet against Marie-Antoinette, he was sent to the Bastille. But, as soon as he was freed, he became the secretary of the Duke of Orleans. In 1788, a trip to the United States, financed by a banker from Geneva, allowed him to meet Franklin. Brissot returned to France full of enthusiasm for the young Republic. Elected to the Legislative Assembly, he became a leader of the Girondins and spoke with fervor in support of the declaration of war. See the bibliographical notes by Gérard Walter in his edition of Jules Michelet, *Histoire de la Révolution française* (Paris: Gallimard, 1952), 2: 1242–45. On Brissot's London project and his contributions to the revolutionary republic of letters, see Dena Goodman, *The Republic of Letters: A Cultural History of the French Enlightenment* (Ithaca, N.Y.: Cornell University Press, 1994), pp. 281–300.

31. See François Hincker and Monique Hincker's introduction to Condorcet, *Des Progrès de l'esprit humain* (Paris: Editions Sociales, 1971), p. 58.

32. *Plaidoyers*, p. 55.

33. In 1774 Condorcet had been named, on Turgot's recommendation, Inspecteur des Monnaies. Condorcet was also a member of the Académie Française and the Royal Academy of Sciences. Keith Baker notes: "In 1789, the marquis de Condorcet was, as Sainte-Beuve remarked, one of the most serious ornaments of the Old Regime." See *A Critical Dictionary of the French Revolution*, ed. François Furet and Mona Ozouf, trans. Arthur Goldhammer (Cambridge, Mass.: Harvard University Press, 1989), p. 204.

34. Condorcet, "Eloge de Franklin," p. 404.

35. Robespierre, *Oeuvres*, 8: 309–10.

36. Condorcet, *Des Progrès de l'esprit humain*, p. 248.

37. Robespierre, *Oeuvres*, 10: 444. Dibutade (or Dibutades) was a legendary artist to whom, according to Pliny, a Corinthian tradition attributed the invention of terra cotta sculpture.

38. Rousseau considers the definitions of moral and natural law and their relationship to the idea of right. Not unpredictably, he notes: "Knowing nature so little, and agreeing so poorly upon the meaning of the word *law*, it would be very difficult to agree on a good definition of natural law." Jean-Jacques Rousseau, *The First and Second Discourses*, ed. Roger D. Masters, trans. Roger D. Masters and Judith R. Masters (New York: St. Martin's Press, 1964) pp. 94–95.

39. Quoted in Aldridge, *Franklin and his French Contemporaries*, p. 135.

40. Quoted in Chinard, *L'Apothéose*, pp. 158–59 (emphasis added).

41. Robespierre, *Oeuvres*, 9: 466.

42. After being declared subject to arrest, Condorcet hid for a time in Paris, then left the city on 25 March 1794. It was only after 9 Thermidor (27 July) that Madame Condorcet instituted inquiries about a man who was found starved to death in the Meudon Forest. See the chapter Michelet devotes to Condorcet in his *Histoire de la Révolution française*, 2: 815–21, as well as Gérard Walter's corrections in the appendix. On Condorcet's contributions to science see Keith Michael Baker, *Condorcet: From Natural Philosophy to Social Mathematics* (Chicago: University of Chicago Press, 1975) and Baker's analysis of Condorcet's failures to come to grips with the revolutionary movement, in *A Critical Dictionary of the French Revolution*, ed. Furet and Ozouf, pp. 204–12.

43. In D. A. F. de Sade, *Français encore un effort, L'Inconvenance majeure par Maurice Blanchot* (Paris: J. J. Pauvert, 1965), pp. 35–36. In his introduction, Blanchot compares texts by Saint-Just and Sade. He discusses Sade's view that "a new republic will have the means to survive by its virtues, . . . but an already old and corrupted nation, which bravely throws off the yoke of monarchical government to adopt a republican one, will be able to preserve itself only by many crimes" (pp. 30–31). It might be added that this idea is directly related to Rousseau's description of the political state. In the

Discourse on the Origin and Foundations of Inequality, he wrote: "Despite all the labors of the wisest legislators, the political state remained ever imperfect because it was almost the work of chance, and because, as it began badly, time in discovering faults and suggesting remedies could never repair the vices the constitution." *The First and Second Discourses*, p. 162.

44. Sade, *Les Infortunes de la vertu* (Paris: J. J. Pauvert, 1968), p. 185.

45. Sade, *The Complete Justine, Philosophy in the Bedroom and Other Writings*, comp. and trans. Richard Seaver and Austryn Wainhouse with introduction by Jean Paulhan and Maurice Blanchot (New York: Grove Press, 1965), p. 742. The first version of *Justine, Les Infortunes de la vertu* was probably written in 1787. It was discovered and published in 1930. *Justine ou les malheurs de la vertu* dates from 1791. The third version, *La Nouvelle Justine*, was written in 1797. Justine does not die at the end, but becomes the audience of the *Histoire de Juliette*. The prosperity of vice might be seen to function as a metaphorical thunderbolt.

46. Lucienne Frappier-Mazur, *Writing the Orgy: Power and Parody in Sade*, trans. Gillian C. Gill (Philadelphia: University of Pennsylvania Press, 1996), p. 125. On Sade and the French Revolution, see also Marcel Hénaff, *L'Invention du corps libertin* (Paris: Presses Universitaires de France, 1978); Gilles Deleuze, *Masochism, Coldness, and Cruelty*, trans. Jean McNeil (New York: Zone, 1989); Lynn Hunt, *The Family Romance of the French Revolution* (Berkeley: University of California Press, 1992).

47. Nancy Miller, *French Dressing: Women, Men, and Ancien Régime Fiction* (New York: Routledge, 1995), pp. 122, 130.

48. Sade, *Français, encore un effort*, p. 75, emphasis added.

49. Blanchot, *L'Inconvenance majeure*, p. 37.

50. Quoted by Blanchot, *L'Inconvenance majeure*, p. 37.

51. *Français, encore un effort*, p. 81.

52. Ibid. It might be worth noting that, at the beginning of the Festival of the Supreme Being, a giant statue "representing" Nothingness (*le Néant*) was ceremonially burned by Robespierre. See below, chapter 2.

Chapter 2

1. Quoted by Joseph Butwin, "The French Revolution as *Theatrum Mundi*," *Research Studies* 43, 3 (September 1975): 148 (translation modified).

2. See also Marvin A. Carlson, *Theater of the Revolution* (Ithaca, N.Y.: Cornell University Press, 1966); and Marie-Hélène Huet, *Rehearsing the Revolution: The Staging of Marat's Death, 1793–1797* (Berkeley: University of California Press, 1982).

3. See Huet, *Rehearsing the Revolution*, pp. 53–58.

4. Jules Michelet, *Histoire de la Révolution française*, ed. Gérard Walter (Paris: Gallimard, 1952), 2: 843.

5. Quoted in Francis Scarfe, *André Chénier: His Life and Work 1762–1794* (Oxford: Clarendon Press, 1965), p. 309. André Chénier, who, unlike his brother Marie-Joseph, repeatedly attacked the revolutionary regime, was executed in July 1794, three days before Robespierre.

6. Quoted in Ronald Paulson, *Representations of Revolutions, 1789–1820* (New Haven, Conn.: Yale University Press, 1983), p. 57.

7. Quoted in Carlson, *Theater of the Revolution*, p. 170.

8. Quoted in Frederick Brown, *Theater and Revolution: The Culture of the French Stage* (New York: Viking, 1980), "The Speechless Tradition," p. 80. (Brown mistakenly attributes the quote to Claude-François's brother, Joseph Payan.)

9. *Moniteur*, XX, 151, quoted in François-Alphonse Aulard, *Le Culte de la raison et de l'être suprême (1793–1794)* (Paris: Félix Alcan, 1909), p. 246.

10. See Maximilien Robespierre, *Oeuvres de Maximilien Robespierre*, ed. Marc Bouloiseau, Jean Dautry, Georges Lefebvre, and Albert Soboul (Paris: Presses Universitaires de France, 1926–67), 10: 465. Many historians have interpreted Robespierre's commitment to the Cult of the Supreme Being as a political gesture meant, among other things, to secure his leadership as great priest of the new religion. But this view does not take into account Robespierre's deeply religious beliefs. He had been thoroughly opposed to the de-Christianization campaign, and so hated materialism that he had a statue of Helvetius smashed at the Jacobins Club (see *Oeuvres*, 10: 442).

11. Mona Ozouf, who goes to great lengths to minimize both the importance of the Festival of the Supreme Being and the clarity of the message it conveyed ("The Festival of the Supreme Being . . . is always saying, like Marx's petty bourgeois, on the one hand this, on the other that") acknowledges, however, that the ritual burning of idols was duplicated in many provincial celebrations. *Festivals and the French Revolution*, trans. Alan Sheridan (Cambridge, Mass.: Harvard University Press, 1988), p. 112.

12. Discourse to the Jacobins, 1 Frimaire, Year II, Robespierre, *Oeuvres*, 10: 196, emphasis in original.

13. Jules Michelet, *Histoire de la Révolution française*, 2: 869–70.

14. André Chénier's younger brother, Marie-Joseph Chénier (1767–1811), was a better-known poet at the time of the Revolution. Elected to the Convention, he became an active member of the Committee on Public Instruction. He welcomed the fall of Robespierre as well as Bonaparte's 18 Brumaire. Gérard Walter sees in Marie-Joseph Chénier a "perfect specimen of these 'leftist' intellectuals, sincerely enthusiastic, but weak and impulsive, whose attachment to the revolutionary cause will never be durable nor profound" (in Michelet, *Histoire de la Révolution française* 2: 1285).

15. J. M. Chénier, *Oeuvres de J. F. Ducis, suivies des oeuvres de J. M. Chénier* (Paris: Ledentu, 1839), p. 689. For a description of the Festival of the Supreme Being, the main source is the account given in *Le Moniteur*, XX, 700. For recent commentaries, see Carol Blum, *Rousseau and the Republic of Virtue: The Language of Politics in the French Revolution* (Ithaca, N.Y.: Cornell University Press, 1986), pp. 238–59; and Lynn Hunt, *Politics, Culture, and Class in the French Revolution* (Berkeley: University of California Press, 1984), pp. 52–119.

16. Mishelet, *Histoire de la Révolution française*, 2: 268.

17. Quoted in Aulard, *Le Culte de la raison*, pp. 328–29. This decree and the following injunction were published in *Le Moniteur*, XXI, 210. In an unusually serene evocation of the festival, Charles Nodier forgot all the clouds and showers, and commented at length on the "radiant weather," "the transparent firmament" of this "pure summer day," a rare salute to revolutionary moments on the part of one of the most dedicated of royalists. See *Portraits de la Révolution et de l'Empire* (Paris: Tallandier, 1988), 1: 193.

18. Published in *Le Moniteur*, XXI, 210, and reproduced in Aulard, *Le Culte de la raison*, pp. 327–30.

19. See Aulard, *Le Culte de la raison*, particularly chapter 22, "Robespierre and Jean-Jacques Rousseau," to which Mona Ozouf's analysis ("The Power of Images," pp. 203–11) is very much indebted.

20. See Claude Lévi-Strauss, *The Savage Mind* (Chicago: University of Chicago Press, 1966), p. 32.

21. (Paris: Louvet, 20 Prairial, Year III).

22. Here, I agree with Michelet's view that the French Revolution ended with the fall of Robespierre in July 1794. On this question, see below, chapter 5.

23. Discourse of 25 Floréal, Year II to the Convention, quoted by Aulard, *Le Culte de la raison*, pp. 282–88. Claude-François de Payan came from an old aristocratic family from the Dauphiné. He was named to the jury of the Revolutionary Tribunal and played an important role in the administration. He was one of the signatories of the appeal of 9 Thermidor and died with Robespierre and Saint-Just on 10 Thermidor. See below, chapter 5.

24. Immanuel Kant, *The Critique of Judgement*, trans. James Creed Meredith (Oxford: Clarendon Press, 1911), p. 92.

25. In *La Révolution française*, quoted by Aulard, *Le Culte de la raison*, p. vi.

26. Mona Ozouf stresses the fact that "the organizers of festivals rejected that which constitutes the reality of the spectacle—masks, make-up, and machinery" (*Festivals and the French Revolution*, p. 207), but, at the same time, costumes were readily used and the unfolding of the festivals could not help recall a perfect or not-so-perfect staging.

27. Robespierre, *Oeuvres*, 10: 458.

28. Stendhal, *Vie de Henry Brulard*, in *Oeuvres intimes* (Paris: Gallimard, 1982), 2: 941–42.

29. Marie-Joseph Chénier, *Oeuvres*, p. 688. The last stanza declares: "Sur tes pas, austère sagesse / Amenant l'aimable gaîté, / Des Arts la troupe enchanteresse / Vient couronner la Liberté." ("Following your steps, austere wisdom / Bringing amiable gaiety, / The enchanting troop of Arts / comes to crown Liberty.")

30. Quoted in Aulard, *Le Culte de la raison*, p. 83. As Aulard comments, for Hébert the Cult of Reason was more of "a joke on priests than the advent of a new thought."

31. Quoted by Mona Ozouf, *Festivals and the French Revolution*, p. 101.

32. *Discours républicain prononcé le dernier décadi frimaire, jour de l'inauguration du temple de la Raison, par le citoyen Jacques-Antoine Brouillet, prédicateur de morale nommé par la Société des Amis de la République une et indivisible, séante à Avize, et l'un de ses membres* (Bibliothèque de Grégoire: an II) quoted by Aulard, *Le Culte de la raison*, p. 88.

33. Salaville's long analysis is superbly commented by Aulard, *Le Culte de la raison*, p. 96. Salaville's objections to the Cult of Reason are all the more remarkable as he was a dedicated atheist.

34. Quoted in Aulard, *Le Culte de la raison*, p. 284. Payan's discourse is particularly interesting in that it traces a sort of history of the theatrical practices of degenerated religions: "Priests transformed religion into bizarre ceremonies and superstitious emblems." Elsewhere Payan denounced the "comedies played by the priests" (p. 283).

35. Jean-Joseph Goux, *Les Iconoclastes* (Paris: Seuil, 1978), pp. 12–13.

36. Archives Nationales. AF 11, 66, written in Couthon's hand, notes Aulard, who adds in his commentary: "Robespierre's *report* is considered as a sacred text" *Le Culte de la raison*, p. 250.

37. *Le Moniteur*, XX, 653.

38. Stanley J. Idzerda, "Iconoclasm During the French Revolution," *American Historical Review* 60 (1954): 13–26.

39. See Louis Marin, *Portrait of the King*, trans. Martha M. Houle (Minneapolis: University of Minnesota Press, 1988).

40. The Place de la Concorde, or Place de la Révolution, where the guillotine stood for most of the Revolution, had long been associated with a tragic event: in 1770, on the day of Dauphin's wedding, 120 persons were trampled to death.

41. Quoted in John Goldworth Alger, *Paris in 1789–1794* (London: George Allen, 1902), p. 240.

42. Georges Lefebvre, *The French Revolution: From 1793 to 1799*, trans. John Hall Stewart and James Frigulietti (New York: Columbia University Press, 1964), p. 125. These numbers do not include the Thermidor hecatomb: 22 executions on 10 Thermidor, 71 on 11 Thermidor, 12 on 13 Thermidor.

43. See Carol Blum, *Rousseau and the Republic of Virtue*, p. 257. Blum notes: "The juxtaposition of these two documents, the prescriptive scenario of the festival of the Supreme Being and the Law of 22 Prairial, has offered difficulties to the interpreters, who, finding a fundamental disparity between them, concluded that the author must have undergone a radical metamorphosis" (p. 258). She sees in this juxtaposition (and I agree with her) "the two facets of the same phenomenon, the republic of virtue" (p. 259).

44. See Gérard Walter's edition of Michelet's *La Révolution française* 2: 1537.

45. Kant, *Critique of Judgement*, p. 127.

46. On the much-debated question of Rousseau's suspicion of *écriture*, see Jean Starobinski, *La Transparence et l'obstacle* (Paris: Plon, 1958); Jacques Derrida, *Of Grammatology*, trans. Gayatri Chakravorty Spivak (Baltimore: Johns Hopkins University Press, 1974), pp. 165–92; Thomas Kavanagh, *Writing the Truth: Authority and Desire in Rousseau* (Berkeley: University of California Press, 1987), pp. 51–77; Marie-Hélène Huet, "Le Défaut de l'Histoire: écriture et paternité chez Rousseau," *Modern Language Notes* (1989): 804–18. On Rousseau and the Revolution, see Jean Starobinski, *1789, Les emblèmes de la raison* (Paris: Flammarion, 1979), pp. 175–79; Carol Blum, *Rousseau and the Republic of Virtue*; Gérard Walter, *Robespierre*, 2 vols. (Paris: Gallimard, 1961). See also *Robespierre: écrits présentés par Claude Mazauric* (Paris: Messidor/Editions Sociales, 1989).

47. Germaine de Staël, *Considérations sur la Révolution française* (Paris: Delaunay, Bossange et Masson, 1818), 2: 143.

48. Nodier, *Portraits de la Révolution*, 1: 189.

49. Michel Vovelle, *La Mentalité révolutionnaire* (Paris: Messidor/Editions Sociales 1985), p. 168. See also his *Les Métamorphoses de la fête en Provence, 1750–1830* (Paris: Flammarion, 1976).

50. See F. A. Aulard, *Paris pendant la réaction Thermidorienne et sous le Directoire* 3 vols. (Paris: Cerf, 1889), 1: 1–15.

51. Paul Thureau-Dangin, *Royalistes et républicains* (Paris: Plon, 1888), p. 1.

52. Jean-Luc Nancy, *Du Sublime* (Paris: Belin 1988), p. 7.

53. See below, chapter 7.

54. Michel de Certeau, *L'Ecriture de l'histoire* (Paris: Gallimard, 1978), p. 312.

55. Did Robespierre really go to Ermenonville, as has been often suggested, to gather from the philosopher's last abode inspiration for his last discourse? Probably not. Why did he remain so long without speaking at the Convention? This question has not been answered.

56. Gérard Walter, notes to chapter X, in Michelet, *Histoire de la Révolution française*, II, p. 1138.

Chapter 3

1. Terry Eagleton, *The Ideology of the Aesthetic* (Oxford: Basil Blackwell, 1990), p. 3.

2. How Kant's *Critique of Judgement* should lead to an analysis of political thought has been recently illustrated by Dana Villa in his study of Hannah Arendt's theory of political action and, more precisely, "her idiosyncratic appropriation of Kant's third *Critique*." In "Beyond Good and Evil: Arendt, Nietzsche, and the Aestheticization of Political Action" (*Political Theory* 20, 2 [May 1992]: 274–308), Villa remarks:

> To do justice to political action, to redeem the meaning potentially disclosed by words and deeds in the public realm, the judging spectator must be able to assume an attitude similar to Kant's *uninteressiertes Wohlgefallen*. Without it, nonsovereign political action would lose its revelatory capacity. . . . To appreciate the "play of the game" that characterizes a genuinely agonistic politics, the audience must be "released from life's necessity" and in a position to bracket such interests. . . . This is why Kant's formulation of aesthetic or taste judgments is an appropriate model for political judgment, for "tastes judges the world in its appearance and its worldliness." (p. 294)

Stressing the contemplative character of Kant's aesthetics, his insistence on the point of view of the spectator, Villa adds:

> While the question of the nature and degree of "abstraction from interest" appropriate to the political realm is a perplexing one, it is important to see the thrust of Arendt's reliance on Kant. Agonistic, virtuoso political action threatens to fragment the polis. One way of avoiding this is to cultivate an ethos whereby actors are more committed to playing the game than to winning. (p. 294)

In this analysis, particular emphasis is placed on the character of representation that presides over aesthetic and political judgment. For Arendt, "Political thought is representative." Furthermore, and I quote Villa's article:

> As Arendt says in "The Crisis in Culture": taste judgments (unlike demonstrable facts or truths demonstrated by argument) "share with political opinions that they are persuasive; the judging person—as Kant says beautifully—can only 'woo the consent of everyone else' in hope of coming to an agreement with him eventually." (p. 297)

These words could well serve as an opening for a study of the politics of persuasion, public deliberation, and political exchange at the time of the Revolution. For the first time in the history of French politics, a stage is set for debates and, most of all, for the all-important audience. There would be, of course, considerable irony in imagining a disinterested spectator, one removed enough from passion to be persuaded as well as persuasive, or in the ultimate hope of a shared vision of taste and politics. But, for our purpose, we are more interested in the moment when Kant's aesthetic ceases to be spectator-oriented, that is, when the experience ceases to be communicable, rising beyond words and representation, thus signaling perhaps also the limits of political intent.

3. Saint-Just, *Oeuvres complètes*, ed. Michèle Duval (Paris: Gérard Lebovici, 1984), p. 457. Unless otherwise indicated, all translations are by Jay L. Caplan.

4. Maximilien Robespierre, *Oeuvres de Maximilien Robespierre*, ed. Marc Bouloiseau, Jean Dautry, Georges Lefebvre, and Albert Soboul (Paris: Presses Universitaires de France, 1926–67), 10: 351.

5. See Robespierre, *Oeuvres*, 10: 167ff.

6. Jean-Paul Marat, *Textes choisis*, ed. Lucien Scheler (Paris: Editions de Minuit, 1945), p. 79.

7. Immanuel Kant, *The Critique of Judgement*, trans. James Creed Meredith (Oxford: Clarendon Press, 1911), p. 179.

8. Philippe Lacoue-Labarthe, "Sublime Truth," in *Of The Sublime: Presence in Question*, pp. 71–107, trans. Jeffrey S. Librett (Albany: State University of New York Press, 1993), p. 104.

9. For comments on this event, see Daniel Hamiche, *Le Théâtre et la Révolution* (Paris: Union Générale d'Editions, 1973); Jacques Hérissay, *Le Monde des théâtres pendant la Révolution* (Paris: A. Perrin, 1922); Ernest Jauffret, *Le Théâtre révolutionnaire* (Paris: Furne, Jouvet, 1869), and the *Journal des Spectacles*.

10. *Oeuvres*, 10: 556.

11. See Stanley J. Idzerda, "Iconoclasm During the French Revolution," *American Historical Review* 60 (1954): 13–26, and E. H. Gombrich, "The Dream of Reason: Symbolism of the French Revolution," *British Journal For Eighteenth-Century Studies* 2, 3 (1979): 187–205.

12. See below, chapter 6.

13. Quoted in F. A. Aulard, *Le Culte de la Raison et de l'Etre Suprême, (1793–1794)* (Paris: Félix Alcan, 1909), p. 287.

14. Rousseau, *On the Social Contract*, ed. Roger D. Masters, trans. Judith R. Masters (New York: St. Martin's Press, 1978), p. 46, emphasis added.

15. See Carol Blum, *Rousseau and the Republic of Virtue: The Language of Politics in the French Revolution* (Ithaca, N.Y.: Cornell University Press, 1986).

16. See Kant, *The Critique of Judgement*, pp. 94–109.

17. In that context, it is interesting to read Paul de Man's notes on the mathematical sublime in Kant ("Phenomenality and Materiality in Kant," in *The Textual Sublime: Deconstruction and Its Differences*, ed. Hugh Silverman and Gary E. Aylesworth [Albany: State University of New York Press, 1990], pp. 87–108). Of particular interest is de Man's insistence on the lack of articulation: "Because the infinite is not comparable to any finite magnitude, the articulation cannot occur. It does not, in fact, ever occur and the *failure* of the articulation becomes the distinguishing characteristic of the sublime" (p. 92).

18. Patrice Guéniffey, *Le Nombre et la raison: la Révolution française et les élections* (Paris: Editions de l'Ecole des Hautes Etudes en Sciences Sociales, 1993).

19. According to Guéniffey, Montgilbert was inspired by Montesquieu's *De l'esprit des lois*. Like Montesquieu, he advocated a "tirage au sort", chance drawing. For our purpose, it is interesting to note that, on several occasions, the "tirage au sort" was called, in official reports, "the blind goddess" (p. 124). At issue here are two slightly different concepts. Guéniffey is considering the legitimacy of selecting candidates, of having citizens propose themselves as worthier of public office than their compatriots. Robespierre is concerned with the sovereign relinquishing its inalienable power to the hands of a few elected citizens.

20. This is one of the areas where Saint-Just takes a point of view radically opposed to that of Robespierre. On 26 Germinal, Year II, he warns: "Patriots, if you believe me, you will hate and recognize as enemies those who decry representation: a patriot never has any solid reason to decry representation, for there is no fatherland without it" (*Oeuvres complètes*, p. 814).

21. In his comments on Kant's *Critique of Practical Reason*, Gilles Deleuze adds these illuminating comments on the idea of inscrutable freedom: "In so far as we consider phenomena as they appear under the conditions of space and time, we find nothing which resembles freedom. . . . Freedom . . . is defined by its power to 'begin a state *spontaneously*.' . . . When the moral law is the law of the will, the latter finds itself entirely independent of the natural conditions of sensibility which connect every cause to an *antecedent* cause. . . . This is why the concept of freedom, as Idea of reason, enjoys an eminent privilege over all other Ideas." *Kant's Critical Philosophy: The Doctrine of the Faculties*, trans. Hugh Tomlinson and Barbara Habberjam (Minneapolis: University of Minnesota Press, 1993), pp. 29–31, emphasis in original.

22. Terry Eagleton is quoting Ernst Cassirer, *Kant's Life and Thought* (New Haven, Conn. and London: Yale University Press, 1981), p. 318.

23. Jean-François Lyotard, *Leçons sur l'analytique du sublime* (Paris: Galilée, 1991), p. 74.

Chapter 4

1. Jules Michelet, *Histoire de la Révolution française* (Paris: Gallimard, 1952), 2: 73. Unless otherwise indicated, all translations are by Jay L. Caplan.

2. This portrait has had a lasting influence on historians. On Saint-Just see Albert Ollivier, *Saint-Just et la force des choses*, preface by André Malraux (Paris: Gallimard, 1954); Marc Eli Blanchard, *Saint-Just et Cie: La Révolution et les mots* (Paris: Nizet, 1979); Maurice Dommanget, *Saint-Just* (Paris: Editions du Cercle, 1971); Yves Ladret, *Saint-Just ou les vicissitudes de la vertu* (Lyon: Presses Universitaires de Lyon, 1989); Yves Michalon, *La Passion selon Saint-Just* (Paris: Albin Michel, 1981); Albert Soboul, *Saint-Just, ses idées politiques et sociales* (Paris: Editions Sociales, 1937).

3. Historians of the Bicentennial have been in similar awe of Saint-Just. His name was missing from the first edition of François Furet and Mona Ozouf's *Dictionnaire critique de la Révolution française*. This absence created an outcry, and an additional entry was hastily added to the paperback edition of the book. This new entry, however, does not do justice to Saint-Just. Rather, it reads as a series of reasons why Saint-Just was not included in the initial version of the *Dictionnaire*.

4. On the posthumous feminization of revolutionary leaders and, more specifically, on the link between this feminization and the Terror, see below, chapter 7.

5. On the king's trial, the most relevant documents have been published and edited by Albert Soboul in *Le Procès de Louis XVI* (Paris: Julliard, 1966).

6. Saint-Just, *Oeuvres complètes*, ed. Michèle Duval (Paris: Gérard Lebovici, 1984), pp. 376–78.

7. François Furet and Mona Ozouf, eds., *Dictionnaire Critique de la Révolution française* (Paris: Flammarion, 1992), p. 276. Saint-Just was not reinstated in the Dictionary in time for the English translation.

8. Albert Soboul, Avant-Propos, *Actes du colloque Saint-Just* (Paris: Société des Etudes Robespierristes, 1968), p. 6.

9. Quoted by Maurice Blanchot in "L'Inconvenance majeure," preface to Sade, *Français, encore un effort* (Paris: Jean-Jacques Pauvert, 1965), pp. 34, 36.

10. Gilles Deleuze, *Masochism, Coldness, and Cruelty*, trans. Jean McNeil (New York: Zone, 1989), p. 86.

11. Miguel Abensour, "La Théorie des institutions et les relations du législateur et du peuple selon Saint-Just" in *Actes du Colloque Saint-Just*, p. 258.

12. Jacques Lacan, *Ecrits I* (Paris: Gallimard, 1966), p. 278.

13. In this, he anticipates Sartre's well-known aphorism: "There is no good father, that's the rule. Don't lay the blame on men but on the bond of paternity, which is rotten." Jean-Paul Sartre, *The Words*, trans. Bernard Fretchman (New York: George Braziller, 1964), p. 19. See also Robert Har-

vey, *Search for a Father: Sartre, Paternity and the Question of Ethics* (Ann Arbor: University of Michigan Press, 1991).

14. Michel Foucault, *Discipline and Punish: The Birth of the Prison*, trans. Alan Sheridan (New York: Vintage Books, 1979). The Terror has obscured the extraordinary judicial reform of 1791. As a result of this reform, torture was banned and horrendous public executions were replaced by what was seen as the more dramatic yet more humane guillotine. Part of what may have made the people of Paris more tolerant of the guillotine is that it replaced infinitely more dreadful spectacles of agonized suffering.

15. Foucault, *Discipline and Punish*, p. 29.

16. Miguel Abensour offers a detailed and exhaustive description of Saint-Just's theory of institutions in "La Théorie des institutions," pp. 239–90. See also Maurice Dommanget's analysis, *Saint-Just*, pp. 149–74.

17. Before fully developing the concept of institutions as replacement of laws, Saint-Just had already thought out the paternal/maternal structuring of the legal system: "Let the law be stiff and inflexible towards the enemy of the country, let the law be maternal and soft towards the citizens!" (p. 814).

18. There is much to say about Saint-Just's vision of language and terror. He makes a clear association between misleading speech, treason, and unchecked violence. This is also the moment when the Revolution goes astray and duplicates the symbolic order it had meant to repudiate. To this distrusted language, Saint-Just, like Robespierre, opposes the sublime and eloquent silence of truth: "La vérité brûle en silence dans tous les coeurs, comme une lampe ardente dans un tombeau." ("Truth shines silently in all hearts, like a burning lamp inside a tomb.") (Second discourse on the judgment of Louis XVI, p. 401.)

19. Saint-Just was charged by the Committee of Public Safety to present the case against Danton. Robespierre's own hesitations and remorse are well known to historians who sometimes point out that Robespierre both admired Danton and "sacrificed" him, so to speak, to the more violent factions of the Convention. Saint-Just had no such qualms, writes Michelet. He notes Saint-Just's extraordinary "cynical morality" when, a few days after Danton's death, he alluded in a discourse to his resting place. "This passage leads us to believe—we know the man well—that, indeed, he himself went to consult the dead; that, fortified by his sincerity, he asked the advice of those he had killed, and that, from their very tombs, he brought back his revolutionary thought" (2: 850).

20. *Oeuvres de Maximilien Robespierre*, ed. Marc Bouloiseau, Jean Dautry, Georges Lefebvre, and Albert Soboul (Paris: Presses Universitaires de France, 1926–67), 10: 357.

Chapter 5

1. Stéphane Mallarmé, *Oeuvres complètes* (Paris: Gallimard, 1965), p. 435.

2. Maurice Blanchot, *The Writing of the Disaster*, trans. Ann Smock (Lincoln: University of Nebraska Press, 1986), p. 1.

3. In his essay "Michelet and the French Revolution," Lionel Gossman discusses Roland Barthes's suggestion that Michelet shared with Nietzsche the idea that "we are in the time of the end of history." In *Representing the French Revolution: Literature, Historiography, and Art*, ed. James A. W. Heffernan (Hanover, N.H.: University Press of New England, 1992), pp. 81–105. On the modes of historiographical narrative, particularly that of the nineteenth century, see Lionel Gossman, *Between History and Literature* (Cambridge, Mass.: Harvard University Press, 1991); and Hayden White, *Metahistory: The Historical Imagination in Nineteenth-Century Europe* (Baltimore: Johns Hopkins University Press, 1973). Conversely, it is interesting to see history interpreted by fiction: see Sandy Petrey, *Realism and Revolution: Balzac, Stendhal, Zola and the Performances of History* (Ithaca, N.Y.: Cornell University Press, 1988).

4. Jules Michelet, *History of the French Revolution*, trans. Charles Cocks, ed. by Gordon Wright (Chicago: University of Chicago Press, 1967), pp. 6–7, translation modified, emphasis added. This is a translation of the first three books of Michelet's *Histoire de la Révolution française*.

5. Michelet's original text ("*L'injuste transmission du bien*, perpétuée par la noblesse; *l'injuste transmission du mal*, ou la flétrissure civile des descendants du coupable") plays on the double meaning of the word "bien", which means good in opposition to evil as well as material goods or property. Descendants of great criminals were forever barred from some of their civil rights. In some cases, they lost their names, made too infamous by their forefather's crime to be allowed to survive with future generations. After Ravaillac assassinated Henry IV in 1610, no one was permitted to bear his name.

6. Jules Michelet, *Journal*, ed. Paul Viallaneix (Paris: Gallimard, 1959), 1: 656–57. Unless otherwise indicated, all translations are by Jay L. Caplan.

7. Arthur Mitzman, *Michelet, Historian: Rebirth and Romanticism in Nineteenth-Century France* (New Haven, Conn.: Yale University Press, 1990), pp. 117–34.

8. Jules Michelet, Avant-Propos, *Histoire de la Révolution française*, ed. Gérard Walter (Paris: Gallimard, 1952), 1: xxii.

9. Michelet's course at the College de France had been suspended in April 1851 because his teaching was judged too controversial. In 1852, along with Edgar Quinet, Michelet lost his position at the College de France. Two months later (June 1852) Michelet refused to take the oath, an obligation for all public servants during the Second Empire. On the same day, he left

his position as director of the Archives historical section, a position he had occupied for 22 years. He left for Nantes a few days later.

10. This text is commented on at greater length in chapter 6.

11. Blanchot, *The Writing of Disaster*, p. 37.

12. Albert Mathiez, *La Réaction thermidorienne* (Paris: Colin, 1919), pp. 3–4.

13. Quoted by Gérard Walter, *La Conjuration du neuf Thermidor* (Paris: Gallimard, 1974) p. 121.

14. Again, testimonies contradict each other. Some suggest that Robespierre attempted to kill himself, others that he was wounded by the guards. Gérard Walter believes that the second hypothesis is the most probable. However, the thesis that Robespierre was wounded by the gendarme Merda rests entirely on his own account, for there were no witnesses. Merda claimed that he walked alone toward the room where Robespierre and his fiends were standing, that he walked straight to Robespierre and shot him when he refused to surrender. Merda later published his account of the events under a slightly less embarrassing name. See C.-A. Méda, *Précis historique des événements qui se sont passés dans la soirée du 9 Thermidor, adressé au Ministre de la Guerre* (Paris: Baudoin, 1825).

15. Paul-François, Vicomte de Barras, *Mémoires*, in *Bibliothèque des mémoires relatifs à l'histoire de France pendant le XVIIIe siècle* (Paris: Firmin-Didot, 1875) p. 302. Barras, an aristocrat turned revolutionary, had distinguished himself during the siege of Toulon, where he demonstrated some courage and made the acquaintance of Bonaparte. Gérard Walter notes, however, that Barras's cruelty toward the people exasperated Robespierre who had previously expressed his objection to Carrier's exercise of terror in Nantes. Robespierre's role in trying to protect populations from terrorist abuse was certainly one reason for his fall. This role, however, was carefully erased by the Thermidorians, and few historians had been willing to set the record straight. See Gérard Walter's edition of Michelet, *Histoire de la Révolution française*, 2: 1198–99, 1262–63.

16. Published in *Le Moniteur*, 14 Thermidor, 314. Born in 1755, Bertrand de Barère was elected to the Etats-Généraux but did not gain preeminence until the time of Louis XVI's trial, over which he presided. He led many attacks against Marat and was elected to the first and second Committee of Public Safety. He did not participate in the plot to overthrow Robespierre and joined the movement at the last minute, by presenting the decrees that made Robespierre and his friends outlaws. Because of his attachment to Robespierre, he remained suspect to the Thermidorians and was arrested, but escaped and on 18 Brumaire joined Bonaparte. He worked for the Emperor and, like other regicides, exiled himself in 1815. He came back to France in 1830 when he became a member of the Conseil Général of his department. He died in 1841.

17. I wish to thank the Curator of the Musée Carnavalet, who kindly opened to me the dossier of documents related to Robespierre's letter. The dossier contained the entire report of the 1946 "Service de l'Identité Judiciaire," but no documents suggesting what may have prompted this analysis.

18. Archives Nationales, Dossier F7 4432.

19. Louis Blanc, *Histoire de la Révolution française* (Paris: Pagnerre, Furne et Cie, 1864), 11: p. 257.

20. Ernest Hamel, *Histoire de Robespierre* (Paris: Lacroix, Verboeckhoven, 1865), 2: 789–90.

21. This document is at the Archives Nationales, Dossier F7 4478.

22. Albert Mathiez, *Annales historiques de la Révolution française* (1924), 2: 289–94.

23. André Plas, *La Signature, condition de forme et manifestation de volonté* (thesis, Université de Poitiers, 1938) p. 93. Peggy Kamuf has written a compelling analysis on the meaning of signature and authorship. But if one takes the signature at face value, so to speak, that is, as a mark historically and legally legislated, one cannot agree with her statement that the signature "is not . . . a line of division, nor a dividing line." From our perspective, in the specific instance we are considering, the signature functions as a line of demarcation between what is legitimate and what is not. This precision is not incompatible with her analysis of the relationship between the signature and the author. See *Signature Pieces: On the Institution of Authorship* (Ithaca, N.Y.: Cornell University Press, 1988), p. 12.

24. Plas, *La Signature*, p. 95, emphasis added.

25. See Jacques Derrida, "Signature, Event, Context," *Glyph* 1 (1977): pp. 172–97. On the practice of signature, see Jean-François Lyotard, *Dérive à partir de Marx et Freud* (Paris: Union Générale d'Editions, 1973), pp. 2–3. See as well Jean-Claude Lebensztejn's commentaries on Stella's signature in *Zigzag* (Paris: Aubier Flammarion, 1981), p. 69.

26. *Le Moniteur*, 11 Thermidor, 311, p. 3, note 1.

27. Arthur Mitzman, *Michelet, Historian*, p. 238. In an extraordinary statement, Mitzman adds to his obvious mistranslation that "Michelet can be forgiven his wrong interpretation of the evidence." This generous pardon, the *erasure* of the sin, is based on the fact that, according to Mitzman, Michelet did not have access to the Archives and probably relied on Lamartine.

28. Blanchot, *The Writing of Disaster*, p. 40.

29. Quoted by Gérard Walter, Avant-Propos, Michelet, *Histoire de la Révolution française*, 1: xvi.

Chapter 6

1. Jacqueline Thibaut-Payen, *Les Morts, l'église et l'état: Recherches d'histoire administrative sur la sépulture et les cimetières dans le ressort du parlement de Paris au XVIIe et XVIIIe siècles* (Paris: Fernand Lanore, 1977), p. 9.

2. Félix Gannal, *Les Cimetières depuis la fondation de la Monarchie française jusqu'à nos jours* (Paris: Muzard, 1884), p. 54.

3. On Vicq d'Azir, see chapter 1. Vicq d'Azir also published in 1778 an *Essai sur les lieux et dangers de sépulture*.

4. Quoted by Madeleine Foisil in "Les Attitudes devant la mort au XVIIIe siècle: sépultures et suppressions de sépultures dans le cimetière parisien des Saints-Innocents," *Revue Historique* (April 1974): 303–30.

5. In *La Civilisation de l'Europe des Lumières* (Paris: Arthaud, 1971), Pierre Chaunu emphasizes the role of the philosophers in the eighteenth-century reevaluation of burying places, or, rather, he blames the philosophers for having attempted to destroy the religious piety due to the immortal souls of the departed. "What monstrous progress indeed the new systems have made that reduce everything to matter, extinguishing all religious devotion and hence the Catholic cult of prayer to the dead" (p. 167). "What they are trying to affect through these purification measures, is piety toward the dead which they consider a prejudice," notes Madeleine Foisil, "Les Attitudes devant la mort," p. 323).

6. Philippe Muray, *Le Dix-neuvième siècle à travers les âges* (Paris: Denoël, 1984), p. 48.

7. Edgar Quinet, "Le Panthéon," in *Guide par les principaux écrivains et artistes de France* (Paris: Lacroix, Verboeckhoven, 1868). Reproduced in the collective work, *Le Panthéon: Symbole des Révolutions* (Paris: Picard, 1989), p. 320. Unless otherwise indicated, all translations are by Jay L. Caplan.

8. Condorcet spent the last months of his life in Paris, finishing his *Tableau des progrès de l'esprit humain*. Michelet's description of Condorcet's end, how he fled Paris after having received an anonymous letter, was arrested, and committed suicide, is inexact. For a long time, Condorcet was thought to have escaped and reached Switzerland. He appears to have died near Paris. On this still mysterious death, see Gérard Walter's footnote in Jules Michelet, *Histoire de la Révolution française* (Paris: Gallimard, 1952), 2: 1306.

9. Voltaire's remains were brought to the Pantheon on 10 July 1791, Rousseau's on 11 October 1794.

10. Edgar Quinet, "Le Panthéon," p. 319.

11. John Goldworth Alger, *Paris in 1789-1794* (London: George Allen, 1902), p. 123.

12. Richard A. Etlin, *The Architecture of Death: The Transformation of the Cemetery in Eighteenth-Century Paris* (Cambridge, Mass.: MIT Press, 1984), pp. 209–10.

13. Antoine-Chrysostôme Quatremère de Quincy, *Encyclopédie méthodique* (1788), article "Cemetery" quoted in Etlin, *The Architecture of Death*, p. 216.

14. Michel Vovelle, *La Mentalité révolutionnaire* (Paris: Messidor/Editions Sociales: 1985), p. 229.

15. See Vovelle, *La Mentalité révolutionnaire*, pp. 217–20.

16. Aulard noted that Fouché had been inspired by a 1792 brochure entitled *Accord de la religion et des cultes*, signed by De Moy. See F. A. Aulard, *Le Culte de la Raison et de l'Etre Suprême, 1793–1794* (Paris: Alcan, 1909), pp. 28–29.

17. *Le Moniteur Universel*, VIII, 13 April 1791, pp. 109–10. Quoted by Mark K. Deming in "Le Panthéon révolutionnaire," *Le Panthéon: Symbole des révolutions*, pp. 95–150.

18. Several projects were put forth. One involved placing a gigantic statue of *Renommée* (Fame) on top of the Panthéon dome, a suitable allegory for a monument dedicated to men worthy of the greatest fame the fatherland could bestow on them. This project was abandoned, but a new frontispiece by Jean-Guillaume Moitte exalted the triumph of Virtue, Genius, Philosophy, and Liberty over errors and Despotism. In Deming's words: "Fatherland, the 'primary divinity' of the temple, stands in the center, surrounded by the symbols of France. She holds a crown in each hand, and with her arms spread wide apart, she seems to encourage emulation. . . . To the left, Virtue, a young maiden recognizable by her 'shy expression' and 'modest bearing' waits for her crown; to the right, Genius, a proud, winged young man, armed with a club, snatches the reward presented to him. . . . Behind Virtue soars Liberty, driving a chariot decorated with the emblems of all the virtues; lying in her wake, Despotism agonizes among ruins" (p. 129). Clearly, the frontispiece, as well as the ultimately unsuccessful project for the *Renommée*, meant a triumph of right over wrong, as well as life over death. The function of the Panthéon as burial ground was erased, to celebrate not the remains hidden in the crypt but the memory that kept them alive, or the ideological victory presumably made possible by the devotion and heroism of the men buried inside.

19. See Aulard, *Le Culte de la raison*, p. 65.

20. Maximilien Robespierre, *Oeuvres de Maximilien Robespierre*, ed. Marc Bouloiseau, Jean Dautry, Georges Lefebvre, and Albert Soboul (Paris: Presses Universitaires de France, 1926–67) 10: 567.

21. See Stanley J. Idzerda, "Iconoclasm During the French Revolution," *American Historical Review* 60 (1954): 13–26.

22. It is not our purpose to describe or assess the well-documented and numerous architectural transformations the Panthéon underwent during the Revolution. But the suppression of twenty-nine windows, the resulting austerity of the building, the coldness, and what Deming describes as the "zeni-

thal light" now falling only from above, also transformed the Panthéon into a closed space, ideologically incompatible with the Revolutionary dreams of large open public spaces where the people would gather to express patriotic fervor. More comparable to a large tomb, how could it become and remain the space of glorious celebrations?

23. See Mona Ozouf, "Le Panthéon," in *Les Lieux de Mémoire*, ed. Pierre Nora (Paris: Gallimard, 1984), 1: 139–66.

24. Quoted in Deming, "Le Panthéon révolutionnaire," p. 140.

25. Alger, *Paris in 1789–1794*, p. 147.

26. Signed by Béraud, quoted by Alger, *Paris in 1789–1794*, p. 214. The *bureau de l'esprit public* was created by Garat in March 1793 to gather information on public opinion.

27. According to Alger, however, Hébert and Clootz were the first to be buried in the Monceau plot. See *Paris in 1789–1794*, p. 147.

28. Nothing remains of this cemetery. Alger notes: "When the northern end of the rue Miromesnil was made, some of the bones of the victims were discovered. As late as 1896, a dingy one-story liquor-shop at the corner of the rue Monceau stood on part of the cemetery, but it is now all covered with lofty houses, in constructing the cellars of which every vestige of 1794 must have been destroyed" (*Paris in 1789–1794*, p. 147).

29. See Gilbert Lely, *Vie du marquis de Sade* (Paris: Pauvert, 1965), pp. 497–578. Sade was transferred from Saint-Lazare to Picpus on 27 March 1794 (7 Germinal, Year II) and freed on 15 October 1794.

30. Ozouf, "Le Panthéon," p. 150.

31. See Michelet, *Journal*, ed. Paul Vialleneix (Paris: Gallimard, 1962), 2: 193, and chapter 5.

32. Session of the National Assembly, 3 June 1791, *Le Moniteur*, p. 154.

33. During the Restoration, Louis XVI's remains were taken from the common grave at the Madeleine and transported to the royal enclosure at Saint-Denis. But an enduring story alleges that the remains now in Saint-Denis are, in fact, not those of the king, but those of a regicide. According to Gaston Lenotre, Barras first spread the story, during the Restoration, of a royal exhumation "so poorly directed that they dug in the precise spot where the bodies of Robespierre and other Thermidor victims had been thrown. And thus, he said, Hanriot, the former servant, the charlatan of suburban fairs, Robespierre's lackey, rests—unexpected epilogue to his stupefying history—in the King's tomb, restored by the pious Bourbons in order to receive him." *Vieilles maisons, vieux papiers* (Paris: Perrin, 1906), 3: 330.

During the Bicentennial, the *Figaro* published a reader's letter expressing his belief that Robespierre himself had been buried at Saint-Denis. According to this reader, the mistake had been caused by the fact that, all the bodies having been made unrecognizable by quicklime, the diggers had identified the king's body thanks to his shoe buckles. But, the reader states, Robespierre also wore shoe buckles, hence the horrendous error. Although identification of the king's body may have been indeed difficult, neither Hanriot nor Robespierre was buried in the Madeleine Cemetery.

34. In *Signs and Symbols in Christian Art* (New York: Oxford University Press, 1961), George Ferguson gives the following description of the Tree of Jesse:

> The genealogy of Christ, according to the Gospel of St. Matthew, is frequently shown in the form of a tree which springs from Jesse, the father of David, and bears, as its fruit, the various ancestors of Christ. Usually, the tree culminates with the figure of the Virgin Mary bearing her Divine Son in her arms. The representation of the Tree of Jesse is based on the prophecy of Isaiah II:1–2, "and there shall come forth a rod out of the stem of Jesse, and a branch shall grow out of his roots: And the spirit of the Lord shall rest upon him." The presence of the crucified Christ in the Tree of Jesse is based on the medieval tradition that the dead tree of life may only become green again if the Crucified Christ is grafted upon it and revives it with His blood. (p. 39)

35. *Les Sculptures de Notre-Dame* (Paris: Editions de la Réunion des Musées Nationaux), p. 12, emphasis added. The brochure also offers a brief history of "revolutionary destructions," p. 2.

Chapter 7

1. Quoted in *Robespierre*, ed. George Rudé (Englewood Cliffs, N.J.: Prentice-Hall, 1967), p. 81.

2. John Carr, *The Stranger in France; or a Tour from Devonshire to Paris* (Brattleboro, Vt.: Isaiah Thomas, 1806), pp. 244–45. The book was first published in London in 1803.

3. There were numerous engravings of Robespierre done between 1792 and 1794, now disseminated in the various collections of the Cabinet des Estampes. They show him to have been a rather handsome man. At the end of the nineteenth century, contemplating an image of Robespierre by A. Lefèvre (1792), Hippolyte Buffenoir exclaimed in turn: "One is struck by the nobility of his carriage. Faced with so much dignity . . . the most biased observer, if he is endowed with sincerity, senses the mountains of calumny and error that still surround the personality of Robespierre." *Les Portraits de Robespierre, Etude iconographique et historique* (Paris: E. Leroux, 1909), p. 17. Unless otherwise indicated, all translations are by Jay L. Caplan.

4. In 1803, the Abbé Proyard, in a book dedicated to Louis XVI, already speaks of Robespierre as a monster: "From this school, [Louis-le Grand] will emerge a monster with a human face, a monster of a ferocity unknown to barbarian antiquity; a monster who, after having brought out his king's murder more than anyone else, will himself reign over you and your families . . . will drink the blood of a million men. . . . The name of this monster, his execrable name, is Robespierre." Quoted by Gérard Walter in *Robespierre* (Paris: Gallimard, 1961), 1: 20. As Walter reflects, Proyard's "allegations are always more or less inexact, his way of presenting facts reflects an obvious bias" (p. 21).

5. Ann Rigney, "Icon and Symbol: The Historical Figure Called Maximilien Robespierre," in *Representing the French Revolution: Literature, Historiography, and Art*, ed. James A. W. Heffernan (Hanover, N.H.: University Press of New England, 1992), pp. 106–22.

6. Jules Michelet, *Histoire de la Révolution française*, ed. Gérard Walter (Paris: Gallimard, 1952), 2: 61, emphasis in original. This extraordinary reply was widely circulated in the nineteenth century and is reported, with minor variations, by different writers.

7. Germaine de Staël, *Considérations sur les principaux événements de la Révolution française* (Paris: Delaunay, Bossange et Masson, 1818), 2: 140–41.

8. Ann Rigney discusses the pallor of Robespierre's face in Louis Blanc's account of the Revolution, and shows how it is interpreted as a sign of his willingness to sacrifice himself. For Michelet, she suggests, it supports his view of Robespierre as a man of "colorless talent" ("Icon and Symbol," p. 113).

9. Engraving by Tassart, collection De Vinck, Bibliothèque Nationale, Cabinet des Estampes.

10. Charles-Elie de Ferrières, *Mémoires*, 3 vols. (Paris, Baudoin: 1821–1822), 1: 343–44. Quoted in E. L. Higgins, *The French Revolution as Told by Contemporaries* (Cambridge, Mass.: Riverside Press, 1938), p. 135.

11. See the engraving in the Collection De Vinck: "Miroir du passé pour sauvegarder l'avenir / Tableau parlant du Gouvernement cadaverofaminocratique de 93, sous la *Tigrocratie* de Robespierre et Compagnie." Paris, Germinal, Year V. Bibliothèque Nationale, Cabinet des Estampes.

12. Charles Nodier, *Portraits de la Révolution et de l'Empire* ed. Jean-Luc Steinmetz (Paris: Tallandier, 1988), vol. 1, p. 191.

13. Michelet, *Histoire de la Révolution française*, 2: p. 667.

14. Alphonse de Lamartine, *Histoire des Girondins* (Paris: Hachette, 1870) 1; pp. 41–42. I quote the translation published by Henri Béraud, *Twelve Portraits of the French Revolution*, trans. Madeleine Boyd (Boston: Little, Brown, 1928), p. 66.

15. Moreover, if Lamartine's description sounds vaguely familiar, it may

also be because, in its style, it echoes the description of Frankenstein's monster, published a few years before: "His yellow skin scarcely covered the work of muscles and arteries beneath; his hair was a lustrous black, and flowing; his teeth of a pearly whiteness; but these luxuriances only formed a more horrid contrast with his watery eyes, that seemed almost of the same color as the dun white sockets in which they were set." Mary Wollstonecraft Shelley, *Frankenstein or the Modern Prometheus: The 1818 Text*, ed. James Rieger (Chicago: University of Chicago Press, 1982), p. 52.

16. Thomas Carlyle himself would be influenced by the now-familiar monstrous legend. Commenting on the terrible days that preceded Thermidor, he describes "a seagreen Robespierre converted into vinegar and gall." *The French Revolution: A History* (London: J. M. Dent, 1906), 2: 329.

17. Hippolyte Taine, *Les Origines de la France contemporaine: La Révolution* (Paris: Hachette, 1885), 3: pp. 209–10.

18. Jean-Joseph Goux, *Oedipe philosophe* (Paris: Aubier, 1990), p. 63.

19. Hilaire Belloc, *Robespierre* (New York: Charles Scribner's Sons, 1902), p. 11.

20. Nodier, *Portraits de la Révolution*, 1: 191.

21. Marie Delcourt, *Oedipe ou la légende du conquérant* (Paris: Droz, 1944), p. 133.

22. Jean-Joseph Goux gives an illuminating analysis of the Sphinx's voice in *Oedipe philosophe*, pp. 53–55.

23. Even Gérard Walter, usually so restrained in his comments, describes the four-year-old Danton as follows: "He was a sort of little monster." See Michelet, *Histoire de la Révolution française*, 2: 1321.

24. Hilaire Belloc, *Danton: A Study* (New York: Charles Scribner's Sons, 1902), p. 53.

25. Béraud, *Twelve Portraits*, pp. 38–39, emphasis in original.

26. Taine, *Les Origines*, 3: 179, emphasis added.

27. John Goldworth Alger, *Paris in 1789–1794* (London: George Allen, 1902), p. 455. Alger also notes that, in earlier days, "with evident desire to creep into aristocratic rank," Danton had signed his name d'Anton. He was not the only revolutionary to have entertained such ambitions. In 1784, adds Alger, the Roland had applied, unsuccessfully, for *lettres de noblesse*. See pp. 43–44.

28. Michelet described how Danton, shattered by the death of his wife, had the coffin reopened a week after her death, so as to have a last look at her. Six months later he remarried. His fifteen-year-old bride, Michelet noted, had been chosen by his dying wife (2: 444).

29. The physical descriptions linking the revolutionaries' monstrous features to their monstrous deeds were transmitted, largely unchallenged, to the twentieth century. In a 1937 essay entitled *Robespierre: The First Modern*

Dictator (London: Macmillan, 1937), Ralph Korngold reproduced in great detail the legendary features and habits of dress attributed to Robespierre, from "his green-gray eyes" with a "steely" gleam, to his clothing "immaculate, almost to the point of elegance" (pp. 20–21). A cursory survey of books dedicated to the Revolution show the fanciful portraits of Danton and Robespierre faithfully reproduced.

30. Andrzej Wajda, *Danton*, a 1987 Gaumont production, based on the play, *L'Affaire Danton*, by Stanislawa Przybyszewska.

31. This decree did not receive unanimous support from the public, however. Alger quotes reports attributing children's mischievousness to Chaumette's abolition of corporeal punishment. *Paris in 1789–1794*, pp. 212, 218.

32. Quoted by Steven Laurence Kaplan, *Farewell Revolution: Disputed Legacies, France 1789/1989* (Ithaca, N.Y.: Cornell University Press, 1995), p. 449.

33. Initially, Przybyszewska's play had been meant to reflect Soviet Russia. Robespierre emerged as a solitary, tragic hero. See Craig Ziner's fascinating essay on a recent production of the play, "Staging Stanislawa Przybyszewska's *The Danton Case*," in *Fictions of the French Revolution*, ed. Bernadette Fort (Evanston, Ill.: Northwestern University Press, 1991), pp. 163–79.

34. Raymond Lefevre, *Cinéma et révolution* (Paris: Edilig, 1988), p. 144.

35. Lest we believe that modern historiography itself has successfully discarded the monstrous legend created after the Revolution, in *A Critical Dictionary of the French Revolution* (ed. François Furet and Mona Ozouf, trans. Arthur Goldhammer [Cambridge, Mass.: Harvard University Press, 1989]), Mona Ozouf in turn acknowledges the powerful couple formed by Danton and Robespierre. Far from dismissing the fable so coarsely crafted by decades of popular, conservative, and liberal thinking alike, she reinforces it: "Robespierre has been compared to Danton as virtue to vice, incorruptibility to venality, industriousness to indolence, faith to cynicism. . . . But, one might equally well contrast the two men as sickly to strong, suspicious to generous, feminine to masculine (or more accurately, female to male), abstract to concrete, written to oral, deadly systematizer to lively improviser—such is the Dantonist version" (pp. 213–14).

This series of characterizations, "sickly, suspicious, feminine, abstract, written," and the punch line "deadly systematizer," undermine the positive qualities previously listed. "Virtue and incorruptibility," "industriousness and faith," point to the debilitating sterility of a man who had no known mistresses, a surprising indictment of his capacity to lead the nation. If we add up the characteristics of Danton, "strong, generous, masculine, concrete, oral, lively improviser," we find no less than a forceful rehabilitation of the monstrous Minotaur, saved by his coarse but appealing sensuality, his natural appetites guaranteeing that, had he been given a chance, this bull would have yielded much profit to the beleaguered Revolution.

36. Jacques André, *La Révolution fratricide* (Paris: Presses Universitaires de France, 1993), pp. 11–12.

37. Sigmund Freud, "Totem and Taboo" in *The Basic Writings of Sigmund Freud*, trans. A. A. Brill (New York: Random House, 1938), pp. 915–18.

38. Lynn Hunt, *The Family Romance of the French Revolution* (Berkeley: University of California Press, 1992), p. 9.

39. See René Girard, *Violence and the Sacred*, trans. Patrick Gregory (Baltimore: Johns Hopkins University Press, 1977).

40. I would not endorse André's view that the revolutionaries "hated" women. Much has been written recently on the complex political status of women before and during the French Revolution. See, in particular, Paule-Marie Duhet, ed., *Cahiers de doléances des femmes en 1789 et autres textes* (Paris: Des Femmes, 1981); Madelyn Gutwirth, *The Twilight of the Goddesses: Women and Representation in the French Revolutionary Era* (New Brunswick, N.J.: Rutgers University Press, 1992); Joan B. Landes, *Women and the Public Sphere in the Age of the French Revolution* (Ithaca, N.Y.: Cornell University Press, 1988); and Sara E. Melzer and Leslie W. Rabine, eds. *Rebel Daughters* (New York: Oxford University Press, 1992).

41. Donald Greer, *The Incidence of the Terror During the French Revolution: A Statistical Interpretation* (Cambridge, Mass.: Harvard University Press, 1935), p. 5.

42. Jean Baudrillard, *The Illusion of the End*, trans. Chris Turner (Stanford, Calif.: Stanford University Press, 1994) pp. 23–24.

43. During the night of August 23rd to August 24th, 1572, the troops of Charles IX systematically killed the Protestant population of Paris. The blame for this bloodshed has been squarely laid at the feet of the Queen Mother, Catherine de' Medici.

44. See, for example, Daniel Arasse, *La Guillotine et l'imaginaire de la Terreur* (Paris: Flammarion, 1987).

45. The Bicentennial has done more for the posthumous image of the queen than for any other character of the Revolution. See Chantal Thomas, *La Reine scélérate: Marie Antoinette dans les pamphlets* (Paris: Seuil, 1989); Pierre Saint-Amand, "Terrorizing Marie-Antoinette," *Critical Inquiry* 20 (1994): 379–92; Lynn Hunt, "The Bad Mother" in *The Family Romance of the French Revolution*, pp. 89–123; Sara Maza, *Private Lives and Public Affairs: The Causes Célèbres of Prerevolutionary France* (Berkeley: University of California Press, 1993); and Jacques Revel's entry on Marie-Antoinette in Furet and Ozouf, eds., *A Critical Dictionary of the French Revolution*, pp. 252–64.

46. Particularly interesting is the recasting of the royal victims of the guillotine as an ordinary family of simple habits and ordinary, authentic emo-

tions. The countless images of Louis XVI, Marie-Antoinette, and the Dauphin in the Temple jail as *simple folks* could have illustrated any nineteenth-century popular journal. Shorn of their royal attributes, simply dressed, their gestures and faces expressing sweet resignation and tenderness, they are made into a recognizable version of the typical nineteenth-century petit-bourgeois family.

47. Simon Schama, *Citizens: A Chronicle of the French Revolution* (New York: A. Knopf, 1989), pp. 822–27.

48. For a recent example of these publications, see Olivier Blanc, *Last Letters: Prisons and Prisoners of the French Revolution, 1793–1794*, trans. Alan Sheridan (New York: Farrar, Straus and Giroux, 1987).

49. When discussing the Terror, many historians stress the fact that aristocratic victims, even the royal family, were ineffective threats against the Republic.

50. A full bibliographical account would be tedious, but it is worth mentioning that Norman Bryson entitled his history of the French Revolution *Prelude to the Terror*. The title is fully explained in his introduction, where he states simply that he would like to know why, two years after claiming a "triumph for humanity . . . these same Frenchmen were at each other's throats and the country was heading for civil war and the Terror." *Prelude to the Terror: The Constituent Assembly and the Failure of Consensus, 1789–1791* (London: Basil Blackwell, 1988), p. x.

51. François Furet, *Terror* in *A Critical Dictionary of the French Revolution*, ed. Furet and Ozouf, p. 140.

52. François Furet and Denis Richet, *La Révolution française* (Paris: Fayard, 1973), p. 233.

53. *A Critical Dictionary*, p. 143. Furet invokes the authority of Donald Greer, *The Incidence of the Terror During the French Revolution: A Statistical Interpretation*. It should be pointed out that Greer's numbers do not result from new archival research but from the compilation of previously published data. On the reliability of such sources, Greer himself acknowledges that they are often tainted by partisan politics. Indeed, some of the published sources quoted are reliable, others are not. Finally, Greer proposes to produce a *statistical* estimate, rather than an historical figure. Knowing the limitations of his method, Greer is extremely prudent in advancing his numbers; Furet is much less so in reproducing them. I am not interested in the probability or improbability of such numbers, however, but in their symbolic value. It is enough to emphasize here the extraordinary *disparity* in modern accounts of the Terror.

54. The word "holocaust" was used repeatedly in the press. The *Figaro-Magazine*, in particular, made numerous references to "l'holocauste vendéen," with mentions of one million deaths.

55. In his essay on the Terror, Furet does not refer to Robespierre by name, but to the "Dictatorship of Year II."

56. Furet, for example, speculates that the Terror may ultimately have imitated the violence of aristocratic society itself. Thus, in an extraordinary replay, "the Terror may have stemmed from an egalitarian fanaticism born of an inegalitarian pathology in the old society" (p. 150).

57. Steven Laurence Kaplan, *Farewell Revolution*, p. 455. During the Bicentennial, Kaplan notes: "The Incorruptible remained Incooptable. . . . His name served to epitomize every deviation. . . . In his anniversary aggiornamento more than ever before, Robespierre was Modern Evil, Totalitarianism, Stalinism, Hitler, Pol Pot. In unconscious mimesis of the worst brand of Jacobinism scapegoating by association and anachronism, *Le Figaro* resolved the issue expeditiously: 'Lenin pronounced himself a Robespierrist'" (p. 444). Kaplan sums best the official view of Robespierre during the Bicentennial celebrations when he writes: "Robespierre did not fit into a strategy for the celebration of the 'luminous side' of the Revolution" (p. 450).

58. See André, "La tête de Méduse," pp. 123–30, a brilliant though debatable analysis of the king's execution.

59. See Ewa Lajer-Burcharth's remarkable essay, "*Les Sabines* ou la Révolution glacée," in *David contre David*, ed. Régis Michel (Paris: La Documentation Française, 1993), pp. 471–547.

60. Stephen Heath, "The Ethics of Sexual Difference," *Discourse* (Spring-Summer 1990): 128, quoted by Mitchell Greenberg in *Canonical States, Canonical Stages: Oedipus, Othering and Seventeenth-Century Drama* (Minneapolis: University of Minnesota Press, 1994), p. xxxiii.

61. Greenberg, *Canonical States, Canonical Stages*, p. xxxiii.

62. It may be necessary to emphasize the obvious fact that the Revolution cannot possibly be the replay of Freud's imaginary scenario, nor that of the Oedipus myth. But it *reads* as such. Our own assessment of the Revolution, our narratives of the Revolution have also taken as models these other narratives where we believe we *recognize* the origins of state and society.

63. In a remarkable essay on Michelet's fascination for monsters, Gilles Marcotte argues that the *History of the French Revolution* contrasts Danton, as sublime monster, to Robespierre, "a man, only a man." Marcotte also quotes Michelet on Danton's oedipean blindness. See "L'Amour du monstre: Michelet, la sirène, Danton;" *Etudes Françaises* 30, 1 (1994): 122–31.

64. The Thermidorian terror is not a subject discussed at length by conservative historians, as it would invalidate the construction of Robespierre as scapegoat and diffuse the guilt among *ordinary* citizens.

65. Donald Greer wrote of the Terror that it "was the translation, perhaps garbled in the process, of the chaotic instincts of the people, of popular borborygmies." Donald Greer, *The Incidence of Terror*, p. 125. History also

undertook the task of translating this inchoate speech, still inarticulate and made more frightening by its incoherent sounds, into a recognizable narrative, one that carried, however, in its unfolding an unsolved enigma. Greer adds at the end of his study, "The Terror, after all, was inevitable; but it was operated by a small group of men who, for a few months at least, lived in that dangerous world where ideas, principles, or dreams count more than anything else" (p. 128).

Selected Bibliography

Abensour, Miguel. "La Théorie des institutions et les relations du législateur et du peuple selon Saint-Just." Pp. 239–90 in *Actes du colloque Saint-Just*. Paris: Société des Etudes Robespierristes, 1968.

Aldridge, Alfred Owen. *Benjamin Franklin, Philosopher and Man*. Philadelphia: Lippincott, 1965.

———. *Franklin and His French Contemporaries*. New York: New York University Press, 1957.

Alger, John Goldworth. *Paris in 1789–1794*. London: George Allen, 1902.

André, Jacques. *La Révolution fratricide*. Paris: Presses Universitaires de France, 1993.

Arasse, Daniel. *La Guillotine et l'imaginaire de la Terreur*. Paris: Flammarion, 1987.

Aulard, François-Alphonse. *Le Culte de la raison et de l'Etre Suprême, 1793–1794*. Paris: Félix Alcan, 1909.

———. *Paris pendant la réaction thermidorienne*. 3 vols. Paris: Cerf, 1899.

Baker, Keith Michael. *Condorcet: From Natural Philosophy to Social Mathematics*. Chicago: Chicago University Press, 1975.

Barras, Paul-François. *Mémoires*. In *Bibliothèque des Mémoires relatifs à l'histoire de France pendant le XVIIIe siècle*. Paris: Firmin-Didot, 1875.

Barthes, Roland. *Michelet par lui-même*. Paris: Seuil, 1965.

Baudrillard, Jean. *The Illusion of the End*. Trans. Chris Turner. Stanford, Calif.: Stanford University Press, 1994.

Belloc, Hilaire. *Danton: A Study*. New York: Charles Scribner's Sons, 1902.

———. *Robespierre*. New York: Charles Scribner's Sons, 1902.

Béraud, Henri. *Twelve Portraits of the French Revolution*. Trans. Madeleine Boyd. Boston: Little, Brown, 1928.

Blanc, Louis. *Histoire de la Révolution française*. 15 vols. Paris: Pagnerre, Furne et Cie, 1864.

Blanc, Olivier. *Last Letters: Prisons and Prisoners of the French Revolution, 1793–1794*. Trans. Alan Sheridan. New York: Farrar, Straus and Giroux, 1987.

Blanchard, Marc-Eli. *Saint-Just et Cie: La Révolution et les mots*. Paris: Nizet, 1979.

Blanchot, Maurice. *L'Inconvenance majeure*. Paris: J. J. Pauvert, 1965.

———. *The Writing of Disaster*. Trans. Ann Smock. Lincoln: University of Nebraska Press, 1986.

Blum, Carol. *Rousseau and the Republic of Virtue: The Language of Politics in the French Revolution*. Ithaca, N.Y.: Cornell University Press, 1986.

Brown, Frederick. *Theater and Revolution: The Culture of the French Stage*. New York: Viking, 1980.

Bryson, Norman. *Prelude to the Terror: The Constituent Assembly and the Failure of Consensus, 1789–1791*. London: Basil Blackwell, 1988.

Buffenoir, Hippolyte. *Les Portraits de Robespierre, Etude iconographique et historique*. Paris: E. Leroux, 1909.

Butwin, Joseph. "The French Revolution as *Theatrum Mundi*." *Research Studies* 43, 3 (September 1975): 141–52.

Carlson, Marvin A. *Theater of the Revolution*. Ithaca, N.Y.: Cornell University Press, 1966.

Carlyle, Thomas. *The French Revolution: A History*. 2 vols. London: J. M. Dent, 1906.

Carr, John. *The Stranger in France; or a Tour from Devonshire to Paris*. Brattleboro, Vt.: Isaiah Thomas, 1806.

Cassirer, Ernst. *Kant's Life and Thought*. New Haven, Conn.: Yale University Press, 1981.

Certeau, Michel de. *L'Écriture de l'histoire*. Paris: Gallimard, 1978.

———. "L'Histoire, science et fiction." Pp. 19–39 in *Philosophy of History and Contemporary Historiography*, ed. D. Carr, W. Dray, and T. Geraets. Ottawa: University of Ottawa Press, 1982.

Chartier, Roger. *The Cultural Origins of the French Revolution*. Trans. Lydia G. Cochrane. Durham, N.C.: Duke University Press, 1991.

Chaunu, Pierre. *La Civilisation de l'Europe des Lumières*. Paris: Arthaud, 1971.

Chénier, J. M. *Oeuvres de J. F. Ducis, suivies des oeuvres de J. M. Chénier*. Paris: Ledentu, 1839.

Chinard, Gilbert. *L'Apothéose de Benjamin Franklin*. Paris: Alcan, 1955.

Condorcet, Jean-Antoine-Nicolas Caritat. *Des Progrès de l'esprit humain*. Ed. François and Monique Hincker. Paris: Editions Sociales, 1971.

———. *Oeuvres*, ed. Condorcet O'Connor and M. F. Arago. Paris: 1847.

Delcourt, Marie. *Oedipe ou la légende du conquérant*. Paris: Droz, 1944.

Deleuze, Gilles. *Masochism, Coldness, and Cruelty*. Trans. Jean McNeil. New York: Zone, 1989.

de Man, Paul. "Phenomenality and Materiality in Kant." Pp. 87–108 in *The Textual Sublime: Deconstruction and Its Difference*. Ed. Hugh Silverman and Gary E. Aylesworth. Albany: State University of New York Press, 1990.

Deming, Mark K. "Le Panthéon révolutionnaire." Pp. 95–150 in *Le Panthéon: Symbole des révolutions*. Paris: Picard, 1989.

Derrida, Jacques. "Signature, Event, Context." *Glyph* (1977): 172–97.

Des Essarts. *Causes célèbres, curieuses et intéressantes de toutes les cours souveraines du Royaume avec les jugements qui les ont décidées*. Paris, 1783.

Dommanget, Maurice. *Saint-Just*. Paris: Editions du Cercle, 1971.

Duhet, Paule-Marie, ed. *Cahiers de doléances des femmes en 1789 et autres textes*. Paris: Des Femmes, 1981.

Eagleton, Terry. *The Ideology of the Aesthetic*. Oxford: Basil Blackwell, 1990.

Etlin, Richard A. *The Architecture of Death: The Transformation of the Cemetery in Eighteenth-Century Paris*. Cambridge, Mass.: MIT Press, 1984.

Ferguson, George. *Signs and Symbols in Christian Art*. New York: Oxford University Press, 1961.

Ferrières, Charles-Elie de. *Mémoires*. 3 vols. Paris: Baudoin, 1821–22.

Foisil, Madeleine. "Les Attitudes devant la mort au XVIIIe siècle: sépultures et suppressions de sépultures dans le cimetière parisien des Saints-Innocents." *Revue Historique* (April 1974): 303–30.

Foucault, Michel. *Discipline and Punish: The Birth of the Prison*, trans. Alan Sheridan. New York: Vintage Books, 1979.

Frappier-Mazur, Lucienne. *Writing the Orgy: Power and Parody in Sade*. Trans. Gillian C. Gill. Philadelphia: University of Pennsylvania Press, 1996.

Freud, Sigmund. *The Basic Writings of Sigmund Freud*. Trans. A. A. Brill. New York: Random House, 1938.

Furet, François and Mona Ozouf, eds. *A Critical Dictionary of the French Revolution*. Trans. Arthur Goldhammer. Cambridge, Mass.: Harvard University Press, 1989.

———. *Dictionnaire critique de la Révolution française*. Paris: Flammarion, 1992.

Furet, François and Denis Richet. *La Révolution française*. Paris: Fayard, 1973.

Gannal, Félix. *Les Cimetières depuis la fondation de la Monarchie française jusqu'à nos jours*. Paris: Muzard, 1884.

Girard, René. *Violence and the Sacred*. Trans. Patrick Gregory. Baltimore: Johns Hopkins University Press, 1977.

Gombrich, E. H. "The Dream of Reason: Symbolism of the French Revolution." *British Journal for Eighteenth-Century Studies* 2, 3 (1979): 187–205.

Goodman, Dena. *The Republic of Letters: A Cultural History of the French Enlightenment*. Ithaca, N.Y.: Cornell University Press, 1994.

Gossman, Lionel. *Between History and Literature*. Cambridge, Mass.: Harvard University Press, 1991.

———. "Michelet and the French Revolution." Pp. 81–105 in *Representing the French Revolution: Literature, Historiography, and Art*. Ed. James A. W. Heffernan. Hanover, N.H.: University Press of New England, 1992.

Goux, Jean-Joseph. *Les Iconoclastes*. Paris: Seuil, 1978.

———. *Oedipe philosophe*. Paris: Aubier, 1990.

Greenberg, Mitchell. *Canonical States, Canonical Stages: Oedipus, Othering and Seventeenth-Century Drama*. Minneapolis: University of Minnesota Press, 1994.

Greer, Donald. *The Incidence of Terror During the French Revolution: A Statistical Interpretation*. Cambridge, Mass.: Harvard University Press, 1935.

Guéniffey, Patrice. *Le Nombre et la raison: La Révolution française et les élections*. Paris: Editions de l'Ecole des Hautes Etudes en Sciences Sociales, 1993.

Gutwirth, Madelyn. *The Twilight of the Goddesses: Women and Representation in the French Revolutionary Era*. New Brunswick, N.J.: Rutgers University Press, 1992.

Hamel, Ernest. *Histoire de Robespierre*. 3 vols. Paris: Lacroix, Verboeckhoven, 1865.

———. *Histoire de Saint-Just député à la convention nationale*. Paris: Poulet-Malassis et de Broise, 1859.

Hamiche, Daniel. *Le Théâtre et la Révolution*. Paris: Union Générale d'Editions, 1973.

Hampson, Norman. *Prelude to Terror: The Constituent Assembly and the Failure of Consensus, 1789–1791*. London: Basil Blackwell, 1988.

Harvey, Robert. *Search for a Father: Sartre, Paternity and the Question of Ethics*. Ann Arbor: University of Michigan Press, 1991.

Hénaff, Marcel. *L'Invention du corps libertin*. Paris: Presses Universitaires de France, 1978.

Hérissay, Jacques. *Le Monde des théâtres pendant la Révolution*. Paris: A. Perrin, 1922.

Higgins, E. L. *The French Revolution as Told by Contemporaries*. Cambridge, Mass.: Riverside Press, 1938.

Huet, Marie-Hélène. *Rehearsing the Revolution: The Staging of Marat's Death, 1793–1797*. Berkeley: University of California Press, 1982.

Hunt, Lynn. *The Family Romance of the French Revolution*. Berkeley: University of California Press, 1992.

———. *Politics, Culture, and Class in the French Revolution*. Berkeley: University of California Press, 1984.

Idzerda, Stanley J. "Iconoclasm During the French Revolution." *American Historical Review* 60 (1954): 13–26.

Jauffret, Ernest. *Le Théâtre révolutionnaire*. Paris: Furne, Jouvet, 1869.

Kamuf, Peggy. *Signature Pieces: On the Institution of Authorship*. Ithaca, N.Y.: Cornell University Press, 1988.

Kant, Immanuel. *The Critique of Judgement*. Trans. James Creed Meredith. Oxford: Clarendon Press, 1911.

———. *Kant's Critical Philosophy: The Doctrine of the Faculties*. Trans. Hugh Tomlinson and Barbara Habberjam. Minneapolis: University of Minnesota Press, 1993.

Kaplan, Steven Laurence. *Farewell Revolution: Disputed Legacies, France 1789/1989*. Ithaca, N.Y.: Cornell University Press, 1995.

Kavanagh, Thomas. *Enlightenment and the Shadows of Chance*. Baltimore: Johns Hopkins University Press, 1993.

Korngold, Ralph. *Robespierre: The First Modern Dictator*. London: Macmillan, 1937.

Lacan, Jacques. *Ecrits I*. Paris: Gallimard, 1966.

LaCapra, Dominick. "History and Memory." Paper given at Modern Language Association, annual meeting, December 1994.

Lacoue-Labarthe, Philippe. "Sublime Truth." In *Of the Sublime: Presence in Question*. Trans. Jeffrey S. Librett. Albany: State University of New York Press, 1993.

Ladret, Yves. *Saint-Just ou les vicissitudes de la vertu*. Paris: Presses Universitaires de Lyon, 1989.

Lajer-Burcharth, Ewa. "*Les Sabines* ou la Révolution glacée." Pp. 471–547 in *David contre David*. Ed. Régis Michel. Paris: La Documentation Française, 1993.

Lamartine, Alphonse de. *Histoire des Girondins*. Paris: Hachette, 1870.

Landes, Joan B. *Women and the Public Sphere in the Age of the French Revolution*. Ithaca, N.Y.: Cornell University Press, 1988.

Lebensztejn, Jean-Claude. *Zigzag*. Paris: Aubier Flammarion, 1981.

Lefebvre, Georges. *The French Revolution*. Vol. 1: *From Its Origins to 1793*. Trans. Elizabeth Moss Evanson. New York: Columbia University Press, 1962.

———. *The French Revolution*. Vol. 2: *From 1793 to 1799*. Trans. John Hall Stewart and James Frigulietti. New York: Columbia University Press, 1964.

Lefevre, Raymond. *Cinéma et révolution*. Paris: Edilig, 1988.

Lély, Gilbert. *Vie du Marquis de Sade*. Paris: J. J. Pauvert, 1965.

Lenotre, Gaston. *Vieilles maisons, vieux papiers*. 3 vols. Paris: Perrin, 1906.

Lévi-Strauss, Claude. *The Savage Mind*. Chicago: University of Chicago Press, 1966.

Lough, John. *The Contributors to the "Encyclopédie"*. London: Grant and Cutler, 1973.

Lyotard, Jean-François. *Dérive à partir de Marx et Freud*. Paris: Union Générale d'Editions, 1973.

———. *Leçons sur l'analytique du sublime*. Paris: Galilée, 1991.

Mallarmé, Stéphane. *Oeuvres complètes*. Paris: Gallimard, 1965.

Marat, Jean-Paul. *Textes choisis*. Ed. Lucien Scheler. Paris: Minuit, 1945.

Marcotte, Gilles. "L'Amour du monstre: Michelet, la sirène, Danton." *Etudes Françaises* 30 (1994): 122–31.

Marin, Louis. *Portrait of the King*. Trans. Martha H. Houle. Minneapolis: University of Minnesota Press, 1988.

Mathiez, Albert. *La Réaction thermidorienne*. Paris: Colin, 1919.

Maza, Sara. *Private Lives and Public Affairs: The Causes Célèbres of Prerevolutionary France*. Berkeley: University of California Press, 1993.

Mazauric, Claude. *Robespierre, Ecrits présentés par Claude Mazauric*. Paris: Messidor/Editions Sociales, 1989.

Méda, Charles-André. *Précis historique des événements qui se sont passés dans la soirée du 9 Thermidor, adressé au Ministre de la Guerre*. Paris: Baudoin, 1825.

Melzer, Sara E. and Leslie W. Rabine, eds. *Rebel Daughters*. New York: Oxford University Press, 1992.

Michalon, Yves. *La Passion selon Saint-Just*. Paris: Albin Michel, 1981.

Michelet, Jules. *Histoire de la Révolution française*. Ed. Gérard Walter. 2 vols. Paris: Gallimard: 1952.

———. *History of the French Revolution*. Trans. Charles Cocks, ed. Gordon Wright. Chicago: University of Chicago Press. 1967.

———. *Journal*. Ed. Paul Viallaneix. 2 vols. Paris: Gallimard, 1962.

Miller, Nancy. *French Dressing: Women, Men, and Ancien Régime Fiction*. New York: Routledge, 1995.

Mitzman, Arthur. *Michelet, Historian: Rebirth and Romanticism in Nineteenth-Century France*. New Haven, Conn.: Yale University Press, 1990.

Mornet, Daniel. *Les Origines intellectuelles de la Révolution française*. Paris: Armand Colin, 1933.

Mortier, Roland. *Clartés et ombres au siècle des Lumières*. Geneva: Droz, 1969.

Muray, Philippe. *Le Dix-neuvième siècle à travers les âges*. Paris: Denoël, 1984.

Nancy, Jean-Luc. *Du Sublime*. Paris: Belin, 1988.

Nodier, Charles. *Portraits de la Révolution et de l'Empire*. Paris: Tallandier. 1988.

Nollet, Abbé. *Lettre sur l'électricité*. Paris, 1753.

Ollivier, Albert. *Saint-Just et la force des choses*. Paris: Gallimard, 1954.

Orr, Linda. *Headless History: Nineteenth-Century French Historiography*. Ithaca, N.Y.: Cornell University Press, 1990.

Ozouf, Mona. *Festivals and the French Revolution*. Trans. Alan Sheridan. Cambridge, Mass.: Harvard University Press, 1988.

———. "Le Panthéon." *Les Lieux de Mémoire*, ed. Pierre Nora. Paris: Gallimard, 1984. 1: 139–66.

———, ed. *A Critical Dictionary of the French Revolution*. Trans. Arthur Goldhammer. Cambridge, Mass.: Belknap Press of Harvard University Press, 1989.

Paulson, Ronald. *Representations of Revolution, 1789–1820*. New Haven, Conn.: Yale University Press, 1983.

Paulson, William. *Enlightenment, Romanticism, and the Blind in France*. Princeton, N.J.: Princeton University Press, 1987.

Petrey, Sandy. *Realism and Revolution: Balzac, Stendhal, Zola, and the Performances of History*. Ithaca, N.Y.: Cornell University Press, 1988.

Quinet, Edgar. "Le Panthéon." Pp. 316–21 in *Le Panthéon: Symbole des révolutions*. Paris: Picard, 1989.

Richet, Denis and François Furet. *La Révolution française*. Paris: Fayard, 1973.

Rigney, Ann. "Icon and Symbol: The Historical Figure Called Maximilien Robespierre." Pp. 106–22 in *Representing the French Revolution*, ed. James A. W. Heffernan. Hanover, N.H.: University Press of New England, 1992.

Robespierre, Maximilien. *Correspondance de Maximilien et Augustin Robespierre*. Ed. Georges Michon. Paris: Alcan, 1926.

———. *Plaidoyers pour le sieur de Vissery de Bois-Valé, appellant d'un jugement des échevins de Saint-Omer, qui avait ordonné la destruction d'un Par-à-tonnerre élevé sur sa maison*. Arras: Imprimerie de Guy Delasablionnière. 1784.

———. *Oeuvres de Maximilien Robespierre*. Ed. Marc Bouloiseau, Jean Dautry, Georges Lefebvre, and Albert Soboul. 10 vols. Paris: Presses Universitaires de France, 1926–67.

Romas, M. de. *Mémoire sur les moyens de se garantir de la foudre dans les maisons*. Bordeaux: Bergeret, 1776.

Rousseau, Jean-Jacques. *On the Social Contract*. Ed. Roger D. Masters, trans. Judith R. Masters. New York: St. Martin's Press, 1978.

———. *The First and Second Discourses*. Ed. Roger D. Masters, trans. Roger D. Masters and Judith R. Masters. New York: St. Martin's Press, 1964.

Rudé, George. *Robespierre*. Englewood Cliffs, N.J.: Prentice-Hall, 1967.

Sade, D. A. F. *The Complete Justine, Philosophy in the Bedroom and Other Writings*. Trans. Richard Seaver and Austryn Wainhouse. New York: Grove Press. 1965.

———. *Français, encore un effort*. Paris: J. J. Pauvert, 1965.

Saint-Amand, Pierre. "Terrorizing Marie-Antoinette." *Critical Inquiry* 20 (1994): 379–92.

Saint-Just, Louis-Antoine de. *Oeuvres complètes*. Ed. Michèle Duval. Paris: Gérard Lebovici, 1984.

Sartre, Jean-Paul. *The Words*. Trans. Bernard Fretchman. New York: George Braziller, 1964.

Scarfe, Francis. *André Chénier: His Life and Work*. Oxford: Clarendon Press. 1965.

Schama, Simon. *Citizens: A Chronicle of the French Revolution*. New York: A. Knopf, 1989.

Shelley, Mary Wollstonecraft. *Frankenstein or the Modern Prometheus, The 1818 Text*. Ed. James Rieger. Chicago: University of Chicago Press, 1982.

Soboul, Albert. Ed. *Actes du colloque Saint-Just*. Paris: Société des Etudes Robespierristes, 1968.

———. *Le Procès de Louis XVI*. Paris: Julliard, 1966.

———. *Saint-Just, ses idées politiques et sociales*. Paris: Editions Sociales, 1937.

Staël, Germaine de. *Considérations sur la Révolution française*. 3 vols. Paris: Delaunay, Bossange et Masson, 1818.

Starobinski, Jean. *1789, les emblèmes de la raison*. Paris: Flammarion, 1979.

Stendhal. *Oeuvres intimes*. Paris: Gallimard, 1982.

Taine, Hippolyte. *Les Origines de la France contemporaine*. 3 vols. Paris: Hachette, 1885.

Thibaut-Payen, Jacqueline. *Les Morts, l'église et l'état: Recherches d'histoire administrative sur la sépulture et les cimetières dans le ressort du parlement de Paris au XVIIe et XVIIIe siècles*. Paris: Fernand Lanore, 1977.

Thomas, Chantal. *La Reine scélérate: Marie-Antoinette dans les pamphlets*. Paris: Seuil, 1989.

Thureau-Dangin, Paul. *Royalistes et républicains*. Paris: Plon, 1888.

Vellay, Charles. "Robespierre et le procès dit du paratonnerre," *Annales Révolutionnaires* (January–March 1909): 25–37; (April–June 1909): 201–19.

Villa, Dana. "Beyond Good and Evil: Arendt, Nietzsche, and the Aestheticization of Political Action." *Political Theory* (May 1992): 274–308.

Vovelle, Michel. *La Mentalité révolutionnaire*. Paris: Messidor/Editions Sociales, 1985.

———. *Les Métamorphoses de la fête en Provence, 1750–1830*. Paris: Flammarion, 1976.

Walter, Gérard. *La Conjuration du neuf Thermidor*. Paris: Gallimard, 1974.

———. *Robespierre*. 2 vols. Paris: Gallimard, 1961.

White, Hayden. *Metahistory: The Historical Imagination in Nineteenth-Century Europe*. Baltimore: Johns Hopkins University Press, 1973.

Wright, Esmond. *Franklin of Philadelphia*. Cambridge, Mass.: Belknap Press of Harvard University Press, 1986.

Ziner, Craig. "Staging Stanislawa Przybyszewska's *The Danton's Case*." Pp. 163–79 in *Fictions of the French Revolution*, ed. Bernadette Fort. Evanston, Ill.: Northwestern University Press, 1991.

Index